"It's hard to imagine a more lucid and enlightening introduction to the work of Ruth Burrows, one of the most compelling spiritual authors of our time. What becomes clear, reading these pages by Michelle Jones, is the unique Gospel strength and startling freshness of the Burrows vision."

—*Paul Murray, O.P.*
Professor of Spirituality
The Angelicum, Rome

"Fresh, frank, and fruitful beyond measure is the wisdom of Ruth Burrows about what it means to be a Gospel mystic.

Michelle Jones has plumbed the depths of that wisdom and offers readers a clear and insightful exploration of Burrows's guidance for the Christian willing to stake everything on the crucified Jesus.

Jones's book shows why Burrows is one of the most important Carmelite authors in our time. A caution: the wisdom of Ruth Burrows may change your life."

—*Keith J. Egan, T. O. Carm.*
Adjunct Professor of Theology, University of Notre Dame
Aquinas Chair in Catholic Theology Emeritus, Saint Mary's College

"In this much-needed work, Michelle Jones provides . . . the most comprehensive, readable introduction to Ruth Burrows that is presently available.

This book is an important contribution to the field of spirituality and will, no doubt deservedly, become the textbook for studies on Ruth Burrows and her spirituality. It will also help clarify the concept of mysticism that should, in turn, help make more accessible to us the deep wells of the Christian mystical tradition.

We are in debt to Michelle Jones for this work. It not only presents Ruth Burrows to a wider audience, an audience she has long deserved, but also is an important contribution to the academy vis-à-vis the study of spirituality."

—*Ron Rolheiser, O.M.I.*
President, the Oblate School of Theology
San Antonio, Texas

"At a time when many are seeking not words about God but the experience of God, Michelle Jones writes of mysticism in precisely those terms. The church now has to become more mystical in order to be more missionary, and this book, drawing in fresh ways upon the Carmelite tradition, helps us understand what that might mean. It is both old and new, reaching for heaven yet down-to-earth."

—*Archbishop Mark Coleridge*
President of the Australian Catholic Bishops Conference
and Archbishop of Brisbane

The Gospel Mysticism
of Ruth Burrows
Going To God
with Empty Hands

Doreen Healy.
21st September 2020.

Sister Rachel Gregory, O.C.D. (Ruth Burrows)

The Gospel Mysticism
of Ruth Burrows
Going To God with Empty Hands

Michelle Jones

ICS Publications
Institute of Carmelite Studies
Washington, D.C.

ICS Publications
2131 Lincoln Road NE
Washington, DC 20002–1199

www.icspublications.org

© Washington Province of Discalced Carmelites, Inc., 2018

Published with Ecclesiastical Approval

Frontispiece photo of Ruth Burrows (Sister Rachel Gregory, O.C.D.) by Sister Gillian Leslie, O.C.D., Quidenham Carmel, UK; used with permission

Back cover author photo also by Sister Gillian Leslie, O.C.D.

Cover design and book design and typesetting by Rose Design
Produced and printed in the United States of America

Library of Congress Cataloging-in-Publication Data

Names: Jones, Michelle, 1976– author.
Title: The gospel mysticism of Ruth Burrows : going to God with empty hands / Michelle Jones.
Description: first [edition]. | Washington, D.C. : ICS Publications, 2018. | Includes bibliographical references.
Identifiers: LCCN 2018006928 | ISBN 9781939272515
Subjects: LCSH: Burrows, Ruth. | Mysticism.
Classification: LCC BV5095.B87 J66 2018 | DDC 248.2/2—dc23
LC record available at https://lccn.loc.gov/2018006928

ISBN 978-1-939272-51-5

10 9 8 7 6 5 4 3 2 1

Contents

Chapter 5

The Third Stage of the Spiritual Life according
to Ruth Burrows: Transformed into
the "Yes" of Jesus Crucified

A Word of Thanks

My deep and sincere thanks to Sister Rachel Gregory, O.C.D., of the Quidenham Carmelite Monastery (who writes under the pen name of Ruth Burrows) for so generously spending many hours with me sharing her spiritual insights, and for her ongoing encouragement. I am also very grateful to the entire community of Quidenham Carmel for so lovingly providing me with a spiritual home.

Additionally, I thank Professor Paul Murray, O.P., whose inspiration was the genesis of this work and who guided it throughout with wise and generous counsel. Further, I am indebted to Father Stephen Sundborg, S.J., for graciously making available to me both his thesis and unpublished works by Ruth Burrows. Carmel Forrest provided me with expert editorial support; I am sincerely thankful to her. I heartily thank too Patricia Lynn Morrison, editorial director of ICS Publications, for her enthusiasm for this work and her thorough attentiveness. Finally, thanks to my friend Father Charles Waddell for helping me to live the spirituality of Ruth Burrows.

ABOUT THE COVER ART

Albert Herbert, *Moses on the Mountain of God*, 1991

"Albert Herbert [is] probably the greatest of contemporary religious artists. . . . When Herbert paints *Moses on the Mountain of God* he involves us in the experience of setting out, frail and lonely, upon the painful and arduous business of a step by weary step ascent towards an unseen God. Moses is stripped, intent upon his end. St. John of the Cross, talking about the mystical mountain, wrote that there is nothing, nothing, nothing on the way, and on the mountain—nothing. Moses perseveres because he believes, because God matters immensely to him and he needs no proof of God's goodness. He goes on behalf of all the big-egoed people who stand at the bottom and watch from afar. He ascends for everyone, and his lonely cloudy encounter will be for us all. Herbert conveys the whole dramaless drama of the spiritual ascent in his small and exquisite painting."[1] ✓

1. Wendy Beckett, *The Gaze of Love: Meditations on Art* (London: Harper-Collins Publishers, 1993), 13, 16.

FOREWORD

Several years ago, Rick Warren, senior pastor of Saddleback Church, wrote a book titled *The Purpose Driven Life*. It sold fifty million copies. The book challenges us to live lives that are driven by the deep purpose that is imprinted into our very DNA as persons. Ruth Burrows, a British Carmelite and one of the renowned spiritual writers of our time, drawing out from the deep wells of Christian mystical tradition, puts a different slant to this. She challenges us to live a *mystically driven life*. How do we do that since, for most of us, the word *mysticism* connotes something that's exotic, extraordinary, or the prerogative of only a few spiritually elite?

Mysticism is not something we consider as common and accessible, an experience available to ordinary persons such as ourselves. When we think of mysticism and mystics what immediately comes to mind are persons such as Julian of Norwich, John of the Cross, Meister Eckhart, Hildegard of Bingen, Teresa of Ávila, Thérèse of Lisieux, and other spiritual masters before whom we feel somewhat intimidated.

I used to teach a class on mysticism and would always begin the first class by going around the room and asking each student why he or she was interested in taking this class. Their answers varied, from curiosity about the subject to being told by their spiritual director to take the class to genuine interest in the subject. One of the more interesting answers came from a woman who simply stated, *"I am interested in this subject because I'm a practicing mystic!"* From the reaction of the class she might as well have stated that she was a practicing fortune-teller.

Can we be practicing mystics? Yes, and Ruth Burrows tells us how. She begins by demystifying the concept of mysticism. Mysticism does not ordinarily refer to extraordinary spiritual experience, namely, to spiritual visions, altered states of consciousness, bodily levitations, appearances of angels, or any other type of extraordinary religious phenomena. These phenomena can happen and have happened in very extraordinary cases, but they do not define mysticism. Mysticism, as Ruth Burrows tells us, is being touched by God at a level that is deeper than what we can understand, articulate, imagine, or even affectively feel.

This isn't an easy concept to understand, and consequently mystical knowledge is generally called dark or inchoate knowledge, that is, a knowing that we grasp but cannot think or picture imaginatively, a knowing that is more like an intuitive sense in the soul than a conscious notion in the mind.

But how can we know something that we cannot think or imagine? Bernard Lonergan, the much-esteemed theologian and philosopher, offers a potential explanation: he suggests that the human soul does not come into the world as a *tabula rasa*, a clean sheet of paper onto which anything can be written. Rather, for him, we are born with the brand of the first principles indelibly stamped into our souls. What does he mean by this? Classical theology and philosophy names four things that they call the Transcendental Properties of Being, namely, *oneness, truth, goodness*, and *beauty*. For Lonergan, God brands these four things into the core of the human soul. We come into this world branded with these four things. Hence we come into the world already knowing, however dimly, perfect oneness, perfect truth, perfect goodness, and perfect beauty because they already lie inside us like an inerasable brand. We know these in our very DNA, but we do not normally, consciously think them.

Some spiritual writers give this a mythical expression: they suggest that the human soul comes from God and that the last thing God does before putting a soul into the body is to kiss the soul. The soul then goes through life always dimly remembering that kiss. The renowned spiritual writer Henri Nouwen calls this "dark memory" and explains it this way: Inside each of us, beyond what we can name, we have a dark memory of having once been touched and caressed by hands far gentler than our own. That caress has left a permanent ark, the imprint of a love so tender and good that its memory becomes a prism through which we see everything else. This brand lies beyond conscious memory but forms the core of our heart and soul.

A metaphor might be helpful here: We commonly speak of things as "ringing true" or "ringing false." But only bells ring. Is there a bell inside us that somehow rings in a certain way when things are true and in another way when they are false? In essence, yes! We nurse an unconscious memory of once having known oneness, love, goodness, and beauty perfectly. Hence things will ring true or false, depending upon whether or not they are measuring up to the love, goodness, and beauty that already reside in a perfect form at the core of our souls.

In essence, in each of us, at the very depth of our being, at that place where all that is most precious within us takes its root, there is the inchoate sense of having once been touched, caressed, loved, and valued in a way that is beyond anything we have ever consciously experienced. Mysticism is being in touch, however dimly, with this memory, with this brand on our soul, with this inchoate, dark, but most-real-of-all knowledge.

Ruth Burrows in her autobiography, *Before the Living God*, shares how, on a retreat as an seventeen-year-old, at a time in her life when she was not at all serious about God or faith, sitting in a chapel one day, she had a moment of deep clarity in which she touched this center inside herself. It wasn't magic, a moment of altered consciousness, a levitation, or a visit from an angel. It was rather simply a moment of clarity, graced clarity, about who she really was. It changed her life. Her becoming a Carmelite nun and entering a life of prayer and religious search stemmed very much from that moment of clarity, of knowing, in a dark but irrepressible way, who and what she really was. That is mystical experience, not something extraordinary, but knowing ourselves in graced clarity.

When, in making decisions and living out our lives, we draw upon that inchoate, dark center of memory inside us, we live mystically driven lives. Then we are living out of our truest, deepest center. Isn't this what we all ultimately desire to do? And there are few more trustworthy guides to mentor us on this journey than Ruth Burrows. She can turn us into practicing mystics.

Michelle Jones, in this much-needed work, provides, I believe, the most comprehensive, readable introduction to Ruth Burrows that is presently available. This book is an important contribution to the field of spirituality and will, no doubt deservedly, become the textbook for studies on Ruth Burrows and her spirituality. It will also help clarify the concept of mysticism that should, in turn, help make more accessible to us the deep wells of Christian mystical tradition. We are in debt to Michelle Jones for this work. It not only presents Ruth Burrows to a wider readership, an audience she has long deserved, but also is an important contribution to the academy vis-à-vis the study of spirituality.

Ron Rolheiser, O.M.I.
San Antonio, Texas

INTRODUCTION

"A long life of spiritual reading has convinced me," relates hermit and art critic Sister Wendy Beckett, "that there are very few writers who understand the Mystery of God and the absoluteness with which Jesus has shared with us all he is. Julian of Norwich understands . . . and so does St. Teresa of Ávila and St. Thérèse of Lisieux. To these names we can add another, Ruth Burrows."[1] Sister Wendy is referring here to one of the most stunning and influential spiritual writers of the contemporary era. She is a woman in whom the former Archbishop of Canterbury Rowan Williams, for one, has "found a mentor in the understanding of prayer with a very rare degree indeed of honesty and realism."[2] Ruth Burrows's compelling contribution to the Christian spiritual tradition is the focus of this book.

Ruth Burrows has been a Discalced Carmelite nun for over seventy-five years and belongs to the community at Quidenham in Norfolk, England. In 1975, she published her autobiography and first book, *Before the Living God*, which she wrote at the prompting of a friend and mentor. This work was followed by twelve further books and numerous articles on the Christian life in general and Carmelite spirituality in particular. Several of Burrows's books have been reprinted many

---

1. Wendy Beckett, foreword, in *Living in Mystery*, by Ruth Burrows (London: Sheed and Ward, 1996), vii.

2. Rowan Williams, introduction, in *Before the Living God*, by Ruth Burrows (1975; repr., London: Continuum, 2008; Mahwah, N.J.: HiddenSpring, 2008), ix.

times, with her works widely regarded as spiritual classics. Furthermore, a number of translations of Burrows's work have appeared, both early in her writing life and in recent times.

Burrows commands such sustained interest because she writes with the authority and conviction of one living in union with the crucified, glorified Jesus. As Sister Wendy puts it, "To read Ruth Burrows . . . is to take into your mind and heart the insight of somebody who is close to God, and has the rare ability to share that closeness with others."[3] So Burrows's body of writings issues from her own spiritual transformation; she illuminates us with the living wisdom that has first illuminated her own spiritual path.

To speak of illumination in relation to Ruth Burrows's spiritual journey is to speak of light enshrouded by darkness. By temperament, Burrows knows only the raw fragility of the human condition. She has been vividly aware since her earliest childhood of the terrifying reality of humanity's inescapable contingency and the fundamental chasm between God and humankind. Given that she finds within herself only emptiness—she knows no comforting, secure emotional supports upon which to establish a relationship with God—Burrows has long known that intimacy with God can only mean immersion in Jesus' intimate communion with the Father. In other words, being engulfed in the darkness of unmitigated vulnerability has compelled Burrows to abandon herself entirely to Jesus' trusting surrender to the love of God. Thus Ruth Burrows's singularly stark inner life has led her to be an exemplar of the central Gospel message that Jesus alone mediates the communion between God and humanity.

---

3. Wendy Beckett, foreword, in *Essence of Prayer*, by Ruth Burrows (London: Burns and Oates, 2006; Mahwah, N.J.: HiddenSpring, 2006), vii.

The utter commitment to the Gospel that shapes Burrows's life is the touchstone of all she writes about the spiritual life. This is strikingly evident in her treatment of the spiritual doctrines of Teresa of Ávila and John of the Cross. Rowan Williams describes Burrows as "one of the most challenging and deep exponents in our time of the Carmelite tradition—and indeed of the fundamental Gospel perspective."[4] In fact, for Burrows, the Carmelite tradition is itself essentially an articulation of the fundamental Gospel perspective. In discussing the work of Teresa and John, Burrows is interested first and last in extracting the pure Gospel essence from their mystical thought. Thus approaching the Carmelite greats with eyes only for the Gospel, Burrows treats their writings with perhaps unprecedented candor. She is unabashedly critical of Teresa and John (it is more often the former) in instances where she perceives that, through personal or sociocultural limitations, they present a doctrine other than that proclaimed by Jesus.

This book explores Ruth Burrows's contribution to the Christian spiritual tradition by analyzing her conception of the mystical life. Even though Burrows does not always use "mystical" language throughout her works, what she says in a "nonmystical" way can be readily integrated into her schema of the mystical life, encompassing as it does the full scope of the Christian journey. Burrows presents an understanding of the mystical life that has been forged in the furnace of her own relationship with the living God. It is a Gospel mysticism—a concept of mysticism that carries the absolute commitment to the Gospel, to the person and message of Jesus, which marks her interior life. For Burrows, the mystical life is about allowing Jesus to express within us his absolute, self-emptying "yes"

---

4. Williams, introduction, x.

to the inundation of the Father's love. And what such participation in Jesus' own intimate communion with the Father
requires of us, Burrows teaches, is that we trustingly accept
and embrace the raw poverty of our humanity as pure capacity
for the love of God. Immersed in the crucified and risen Jesus,
we go to God with empty hands.

Burrows's own work is the primary source of this study. In
addition to her published writings, I draw on various unpublished material in instances where it offers useful clarification or
elaboration of Burrows's life and thought. This material includes
correspondence, a series of interviews I conducted with Burrows, and unpublished writings. One unpublished work to
which I refer requires particular mention here. The original version of Burrows's autobiography had to be reduced in length
due to financial constraints at the time of publication.[5] Her
"manuscript" is a document that contains the passages that were
excluded from the published version of the work.[6]

Five chapters and a conclusion follow this introduction. In
chapter 1 we contemplate Burrows's own relationship with the
living God and see how her personal experience is the source of
her spiritual insights. What comes into focus here is Burrows's
unmitigated exposure to the sheer fragility of the human condition and the way in which she is led to respond to such intense
sensitivity by entrusting her nothingness to God as receptivity
to his love. To live in such empty-handed surrender is what it
means, Burrows discovers, to live through, with, and in Jesus.

---

5. Ruth Burrows, interview by author, Quidenham, UK, September 30,
2009. Burrows also commented during this interview that she regards the published version of her autobiography as an improvement upon the original as it
distills the message she was seeking to convey.

6. Because the page numbers are not consistent throughout this document
they are not included in references to the text.

The remaining chapters examine systematically the spiritual insights Burrows has discovered from her own life; as mentioned earlier, Burrows's understanding of the mystical life provides the framework for our exploration of her thought. Chapter 2 establishes Burrows's anthropology (her understanding of the human person) and theology (her understanding of God) as the foundations for her treatment of the mystical life. It becomes evident that it is only in the crucified and risen Jesus that humanity—created as capacity for the divine life—and divinity—an ecstasy of love—enter into perfect communion. We thus discover that for each person the spiritual pilgrimage is about a progressive transformation into the very life of Jesus. Burrows shows that this transformation is a threefold process and is the work of God's mystical grace within us.

Chapters 3, 4, and 5 deal with Burrows's presentation of the three stages of the spiritual life, that is, the three stages of our transformation into the crucified and risen Jesus. Chapter 3, which addresses the first stage, is about preparing to be drawn into the life of Jesus. It looks at how, by Burrows's account, beginners are characterized by their captivity to the ego and details her advice for anticipating that direct, or mystical, grace from God that breaks the stronghold of the ego and actuates our potential for the divine life.

The fourth chapter explores Burrows's conception of the second stage of the spiritual journey; this stage encompasses the beginning and development of the mystical phase of the Christian life. In this chapter we see that, for Burrows, the inflowing of God's mystical grace is essentially the life of the Crucified replacing the life of the ego. Additionally, we consider Burrows's teaching on the fundamental imperceptibility and effects of this grace, and her thought on cooperating with

God's mystical intervention by refusing to evade the reality of our neediness before him.

Chapter 5 examines the third stage of the spiritual journey and what, in Burrows's view, it means for a human person to be perfectly transformed into Jesus; it is about the culmination of the mystical life. Here we are presented with complete freedom from egocentricity and complete receptivity to the divine life and, at the same time, the full realization of human personhood. The lived experience of the spiritual summit is seen to be something essentially individual, even though common elements of this experience can be identified. And those at the third stage are shown to be possessed by a living knowledge of God and wholly united to Jesus' mission of establishing the kingdom of God on earth. Finally, the conclusion summarizes the principal ideas examined throughout the book and suggests a further application of Burrows's lived Gospel mysticism.

Ruth Burrows before the Living God

*The Source
of Her Spiritual Insights*

R uth Burrows's life before the living God is the wellspring of her spiritual insights. Her presentation of the mystical life as a participation in the life of the crucified Jesus, a participation that requires us to trustingly embrace our innate poverty as pure capacity for the God of love, is first articulated by her lived experience. Therefore, a detailed account of the person and life of Ruth Burrows is in order. What will emerge is that Burrows makes sense of her particular life experience by understanding it as an articulation of a universally significant word. That is, Burrows has come to understand her lived experience as an embodiment of the Gospel truth that Jesus is the only way to the Father. Finally, we will see that all Burrows's writings—even her apparently theoretical works, such as her commentaries on the spiritual doctrines of St. Teresa of Ávila and St. John of the Cross—are shaped by her own living knowledge of the Christian life.

RUTH BURROWS'S EXPERIENCE OF THE HUMAN CONDITION

Ruth Burrows was born in 1923.[1] The third of seven children, she was "brought up in a good Catholic home and the practices common to such—prayers together, faithful church attendance."[2] Burrows attended Catholic schools throughout her primary and secondary education where she received thorough formation in both the doctrinal and devotional aspects of the faith. After completing her secondary schooling, she declined an offer of a place at Oxford and entered Carmel in 1941.

Throughout her long life in Carmel, Burrows has served many terms as prioress and as novice mistress. As prioress, she "played a very vital role" in reforming her Carmelite community according to the directives issued by the Second Vatican Council.[3] In fact, Burrows has been described as a woman who "has done more than any other one person for the Teresian nuns in England during the post-Vatican II period."[4] As noted previously, in 1975 Burrows published her autobiography, *Before the Living God*. This work was followed by twelve further books and numerous articles on living the Christian life and the Carmelite spiritual tradition. "Ruth Burrows" is in fact the pen name our subject assumed for her autobiography and continued using for her subsequent publications.

The real significance of Burrows's life lies in its interior aspect. In a word, Burrows is temperamentally disposed to experience in a particularly stark way the reality of the human condition, in all its aching poverty, vulnerability, and dependency. She indicates this when she claims, "If one measures experience merely by such things as the number of countries one has visited, jobs one has held down and so on, then my experience is nil. But if it is measured by penetration into life, into human nature, then mine is great."[5] Burrows's singular inner life, this unmitigated exposure to the truth of the human condition, will become evident as we survey her autobiographical writings.

Burrows begins her autobiography by revealing, "I was born into this world with a tortured sensitivity."[6] Or, as she puts it in another work, she was "born with her eyes open" and is thus able to see "behind life's façade to its ugliness and grief."[7] Burrows goes on to elaborate: "Fundamental to me is a natural fragility. My whole make-up inevitably, I think, must experience void, peril, aloneness. . . . It is [God's] will that I should grope painfully along, experiencing to the depths what it is to be human. . . . I was to experience the bare bones of human poverty."[8]

It is perhaps already evident from Burrows's self-description that her innate vulnerability to the utter helplessness of the human condition implies a living awareness of the fundamental gulf between God and humanity, between Creator and created. "Often I have complained in my heart that God seemed absent from my life," she admits in *Before the Living God.* "It seemed to me that I had to live life all alone, eating it in its raw bitterness. He was not there to give me understanding and comfort. Even now I can sympathise with myself over this. A hidden God he has been to me."[9] Many years later she reaffirms that a felt absence of God belongs to her lived experience: "I have [had] nothing . . . ever . . . ever, never, on the level of what I could within myself feel, let's say, of God's love for me, God's presence to me. Never, I can honestly say that, never have I."[10]

In the light of this outline of her temperament, we can appreciate the portrayal of her overall lived experience that Burrows presents in her autobiography. She speaks to us from the other side of the breakthrough into meaningfulness that she eventually made and that we will explore in due course. Burrows relates,

> It is impossible to understand my life unless it is seen all the time against the background of black depression. This was my atmosphere. It was only a matter of degrees. It was like a blight and I could not understand it. . . . The heart of this depression seems to have been fear, fear not of this or that precisely, but an ultimate fear, fear of my relation to God. Unless one has security in the Absolute; unless there is ground to being and ground to my own being then any assurances, any "security," is mockery. To enjoy anything is mockery. A condemned man faced with a good meal! How acutely I felt all this. Life seemed to be poisoned.[11]

Referring again later to the effect of the "sheer fragility of [her] being," Burrows says, "Here was existential fear, the fear of existence itself. Here was threatened, meaningless existence. . . . My suffering lay at the very roots of existence which no mortal hand could reach. And God was utterly absent."[12]

Burrows details that her temperament made for a difficult childhood. She finds the lived reality of her early days to be well captured by the observation of another. "I had sent a snapshot of myself as a child of seven or eight to Elsa, my friend and counsellor," Burrows explains. "Elsa responded: 'This is a child made for tears, a child naked to reality, suffering, bewildered, quivering, a pathetic smile to propitiate the mystery round her. A small, closed world of fear and pain.'"[13] Burrows emphasizes throughout her autobiography that there was nothing in her childhood to mitigate her innate exposure to the ultimate fragility of being human. "Alas," she laments, "no one in my really loving home grasped the inner loneliness of the difficult child that was me."[14]

Furthermore, not even the slightest degree of consoling religious emotion was there to clothe the young Burrows's nakedness before reality. She recounts, "I can recall no religious impression whatever. Others have told me that God was very real to them in their childhood. I cannot say the same. I knew my catechism and shone at answering all questions on Confession, the Mass and Holy Communion, but so far as I know it was not in my heart."[15] In fact, with the death of her sister when Burrows was nine years old, Burrows came to perceive God as a detached observer of life's terrifying contingency. Her inner monologue ran, "Nothing is safe any more. Anything terrible can happen, it has happened once and can happen again and there is no one can stop it. God won't stop it."[16] Even further, she tells us, "Between the ages of thirteen and fourteen, I began to wonder about God. Did he really exist?"[17]

It is important to acknowledge here that while Burrows insists that, as a child, "No religious impressions got through to me,"[18] she also speaks of "the strong romantic elements in my nature."[19] "I was looking beyond and above," she narrates, "waiting for the secret door to open, waiting for the Beloved to appear and transform my life."[20] So, from her youth, the yawning chasm of her inner life asserted its need for fulfillment. Burrows found no correspondence between her yearning for a relationship of unbounded intimacy and the things of religion. She found "images of our Lord wholly insipid";[21] for her, "the world of religion was as drab as the real world."[22] Looking back at this basic disconnection between her inner restlessness and her received images of God, Burrows observes, "If my religious teachers had known how to exploit this inner world of mine, it may well be that my heart would have been won consciously for our Lord."[23]

The ultimate orientation of Burrows's fragile, threatened, aching existence was irrevocably set by a moment of grace she experienced in her seventeenth year; she calls it the moment of her conversion. "At the deepest level of my self," Burrows says of this grace, "I *saw* that God existed. He filled life. He offered intimacy to man. It was possible for us to be intimate with God!"[24] In the light of this revelation, she knew that "life could have no other meaning. I must give myself up to seeking this intimacy with God. The self-evident way was to be a nun, a nun in the most absolute way possible, an enclosed, contemplative nun."[25] Burrows is emphatic that this grace of conversion did not impact upon the sensible level of her being. She explains that "it was not experienced in an overwhelming way, rather it was veiled in obscurity and also by a web of natural movements."[26] Struggling to say more about the absolute hiddenness of her life-changing experience, Burrows relates, "Now, any way in which I could describe it . . . or say: 'I felt it here'—no. . . . That is what I can never get across, how 'nothing' it was. And yet it turned my world upside down. . . . Right down there, there was something, that I could never bring up, I could never tell anybody about it, [I] haven't got words, [it is] non-conceptual."[27]

The ineffable grace of her conversion set Burrows irreversibly Godward, yet it did not alter her quivering vulnerability to the innate contingency of the human condition. Burrows indicates that it was the same suffering self that was forever reoriented when she writes,

> This grace . . . set me on the mountain, at its base, but so firmly, so surely that it has been . . . impossible to withdraw. It would have been necessary to unmake my fabric, so to speak, for that to happen. But from then on and apart from that, my path lay in darkness, deep darkness. . . . Yet I think I can say truly that, thanks to this initial grace, not for one hour have I given up the climb. I have known utter dejection and near-despair. I have known intolerable bitterness and yet never have I ceased to turn within to him who, so obscurely, so hiddenly, drew me to himself.[28]

The religious doubts that plagued Burrows in her early teenage years were again present both immediately before and soon after the moment of her conversion. She relates that, given she experienced herself as irrevocably oriented to a God she was not sure existed, all she could do was reason, "If there is a God . . . then what I am doing is the best thing I can do. Yes, it will be terribly hard but I shall never turn back. . . . I shall go on whatever happens and even the longest life comes to an end. . . . And if there is no God, well, life is worth nothing anyway."[29]

The way of life Burrows adopted within the austere simplicity of the Carmelite monastery offered her no shelter from her frail, imperiled self. In fact, referring to the "hungry void and emptiness which is my being,"[30] she says that "the sheer exposure of Carmel, the absence of distraction, sharpened its edges intolerably."[31] In *Before the Living God*, Burrows recounts that for many years she remained without anyone to whom she could reveal the truth of her inner life.[32] And God remained totally absent: "All was utterly blank. For me God was not."[33]

In her early years in Carmel, Burrows perceived her interior life as radically at odds with her spiritual milieu. "My inner state frightened me,"[34] she relates. "I concluded that there must be something wrong with my spiritual life."[35] Burrows details that most of the books she found in her monastery's then impoverished library were concerned with the various phenomena commonly associated with progress in the spiritual life.[36] Describing in *Guidelines for Mystical Prayer* the impact this literature had upon her, Burrows writes, "For years I worried so. From all I read it seemed taken for granted that unless one received mystical graces then one was a second-class citizen with a second-class ticket. I was quite sure I'd received no mystical graces; I was dry as a bone and always had been. It wasn't that I coveted the experience I read about; on the contrary it put me off, but that sort of experience seemed a hallmark of God's favour and confirmed that one was pleasing to him."[37] We can see from this passage that Burrows's struggle with the predominant literature of her Carmel was twofold. First, it caused her to believe that her own dark, barren inner life was thoroughly deficient; "I was afraid of books on the spiritual life for they made me feel so hopeless,"[38] she recounts elsewhere. And second, even though they were regarded as marks of divine favor, Burrows was repelled by the "experiences" discussed in the books available to her. For her, presenting the Christian life in terms of what one can expect to feel at different stages "made the way to God seem 'professional' and unreal"—far from the simple way of prayer set forth by Jesus.[39]

There is a further dimension to Burrows's early sense of hopelessness in prayer. "For many years," she narrates, "I was to struggle with a subtle problem which now I can describe as that between God and the paraphernalia of God. . . . There seemed no relation between God and all that had been presented to me in teaching at school or what was being offered to me in religious life."[40] We have already noted Burrows's early sense of disconnection between her desire for an infinitely loving relationship and her received images of the divine. Essentially her problem was that any means to union with God recommended to her failed to fulfill her all-consuming yearning for intimacy with him. She explains, "My whole being seems poised to leap towards another person. Ideas, things, cannot really touch me. They occupy and amuse me a little but fail to touch *me*. . . . No ideas of God could touch me. I wanted him, the living God, wanted him to be bound to my inmost self, to be one with him—I knew not how—but there must be no 'separation,' no 'space' between. Lovely thoughts, those acts of faith and love, remained 'outside' me, mysteriously deepening the sense of loss, absence."[41] The nature of Burrows's spiritual dilemma becomes clearer as she recounts how, in particular, she related with Jesus:

> Jesus, too, was outside me. In my catechism I had learned
> that he was in heaven and in the Blessed Sacrament—not

everywhere, not "in" me. Therefore, to imagine I was with him, as St. Teresa advised, to think of myself beside him in the garden, on the mountainside at night in prayer, one of my favourite reflections, was just imagination and untrue and I could not feed on untruth. Because there was a strong tradition supporting this way of praying and it was advocated by those who knew, St. Teresa and others, I practised it but it remained "outside-prayer" and I longed for "inside-prayer."[42]

This feeling of being kept on the outside by the very means supposed to develop intimacy with the divine greatly contributed to Burrows's sense of God's utter absence from her. "This is for others, not for me," her felt reality proclaimed. "Others can drink of this fountain but it is barred to me. He is the God of others, he loves them, they please him, are dear to him, but I am outcast, cut off from him. He cares nothing for me."[43]

It was not just her sense of being a failure at prayer that worried Burrows and caused her to consider herself something of an imposter within the monastery. As she recounts, even after some years in Carmel, "I seemed to have just the same bad propensities as when I entered. I was ambitious. I wanted to be number one always. My thoughts were often critical and unkind. Such things were incompatible with progress in the spiritual life, I thought."[44] To be sure, Burrows made great efforts to grow in charity. In her autobiography we see her, expressly for the sake of charity, exerting from adolescence a constant and increasing effort to conceal her tortured interior life, to avoid displays of agonized emotions and moodiness. At one point, for example, she comments, "I was still a prey to depression. And yet I know I fought more and more to control my temperament. It was part of the responsibility I felt for

the community. . . . I tried always to be cheerful no matter how 'down' I felt."[45] Moreover, discussing how she acted
upon her "realisation of the supreme importance of charity,"
Burrows says, "I realised charity must be in the heart and so
tried to think kindly and lovingly. I have made it a principle
always to put others first; to think what would be best for others, to prefer their convenience to my own."[46] Evidently, however, despite her generous labors, Burrows experienced herself
as incapable of meeting the demands of charity presented by
her life as a Carmelite nun.

For all the distressing desolation she found in Carmel,
Burrows tells us that, impelled by the grace of her conversion,
from the beginning she turned to her absent God "to identify
consciously with his plan in spite of helplessness and unutterable shrinking."[47] This resolute exposure to God within
endless aching emptiness is evident, for example, when Burrows recounts, "'Only you, my Jesus,' is what my desolate,
frozen heart has whispered a thousand thousand times to him
from my earliest days until now, but there was no answering
response of love, no touch to reassure me that he was there,
that he cared. I felt he cared nothing, that he had brought me
into the desert to die of hunger and cold. I was utterly for-
lorn."[48] Or again, Burrows describes in her autobiography her
reaction to a visit from her brother and his wife on the eve-
ning of their wedding. She details, "I was deeply moved to see
him so changed, to see their radiant happiness. I thought of
them going off together, to the intimacy of their first night.
No sooner had they left the parlour than I burst into a fit of
weeping. My own lot seemed utterly bitter. Nothing, nothing,
nothing, bleak, cheerless, lonely. And yet I found myself turning in the darkness to him, telling him I would go on to the
end of my days feeling loveless if it pleased him."[49] Clearly,

Carmel has meant for Burrows descending deep into the abyss of human nothingness and, from within that darkness, deliberately facing the living God.

THE DEVELOPMENT OF A SPIRITUALITY OF TRUST

Eventually, Burrows reached a breakthrough regarding her inner state. It was a gradual awakening rather than a sudden change. In essence, Burrows came to understand her fragile, lonely, barren existence as precisely the ground of her union with God, rather than as an obstacle to that union. The key, she realized, was to entrust her suffering emptiness to God as pure capacity for the divine life. Such trust is not simply a grim, determined act of the will but rather the fruit of God's grace mysteriously enabling human volition. What is more, Burrows came to see that this trust, this graced surrender to God from the heart of nothingness, is nothing other than a participation in the kenotic Jesus' trusting "yes" to the Father's love.

In his doctoral thesis on Burrows's life, the Jesuit Stephen Sundborg observes, "The grace to trust is essentially a further development of the grace to accept but . . . is a much more interior thing."[50] Throughout *Before the Living God*, Burrows identifies several instances in her early Carmelite life in which she experienced the grace to accept external challenges that, were she left unaided, would have overwhelmed her. In these situations—which concerned accepting, for example, antiquated monastic practices and the appointment of an ill-qualified novice mistress—Burrows experienced God's grace empowering an impotent receptivity within her. As she details, "In the midst of . . . turmoil, when everything in me was raging 'can't, can't,' some fine point sought for God's hand. I seemed able, not to overcome the conflict, not to emerge from the storm but, in the very midst of the storm, engulfed in the 'can't' as it were, to move forward to God, leaving it to him to enable me to do what I experienced as impossible."[51] Sundborg's point is that the grace to trust is an extension of this process, "but now the object of acceptance is not something external but rather one's interior state, the poverty of one's self in relation to God";[52] now Burrows finds that it is the very emptiness of her humanity that is transformed from a barrier into a place of divine encounter.

So just how did Burrows come to entrust to God the essential nothingness of humanity and so make of this nothingness sheer capacity for Love? Burrows identifies the starting point as a thoroughgoing self-knowledge, together with the ability to own the truth of her being. In her words,

> It seems to me that God has given me the grace to seek the truth and to stand in the truth, and essentially this means the truth about myself. I may be very blind and thus speaking in blindness but, as far as I can see, a steady light always shone in my heart which revealed me to myself, whatever impression might be given outwardly. I think, too, I accepted this light and opened myself to it. . . . Early in my spiritual life I was given a deep self-knowledge. This was to be the foundation on which God wished to build. It forced me into the arms of his mercy.[53]

Thus Burrows tells us that, despite its frightening pain, she has long refused to evade the reality of being a human creature—inherently contingent, vulnerable, and needy. And it is only thus rooted in the truth of her being that she can launch out to the living God in trust.

Burrows relates that she first regarded the surrender of her very poverty to God as simply a necessary temporary measure. She writes,

> This general state of helplessness, the anxieties and fears that beset me, found an answer in humility and trust. . . . In my distress, at every revelation of my sinfulness and weakness I would fall back into this humility and trust and find peace. However, I saw this only as a provisional state, a sort of substitute until God gave me the real thing, so to speak. It was either this or despair. It was not a way I chose. I was driven to it as a last resort. Given the choice, no doubt I would have preferred a more interesting and satisfying spiritual life.[54]

We can detect this notion of trust being merely a last resort in Burrows's depiction of the way in which she approached her fraught inner life around the time of her solemn profession: "Oh there was no way out. No way except complete trust, dropping below this immense misery into the mercy of God. Gradually, in the fine point of my being, I was beginning to do this."[55] So, initially, Burrows "was far from grounded in trust, that trust which casts itself into the arms of God."[56] Yet, even if by default, she "was beginning to find meaning in [emptiness], to find God hidden in the depths of . . . poverty."[57]

Gradually, Burrows shifted from considering trusting acceptance of her poor humanity as something inferior and provisional to seeing it as the only authentic spiritual way and thus the path to be actively pursued. "This is where Thérèse came in and illumined my way for me,"[58] Burrows explains. She is referring to St. Thérèse of Lisieux and her audacious embrace and exposition of Jesus' exhortation to be as a child before God. "I think it was at the Christmas of 1950, or thereabouts," Burrows notes, "that my parents gave me a copy of the letters of St. Thérèse in an English translation."[59] In Thérèse, she finally found a "sister-soul and guide."[60] Burrows specifies that she was particularly influenced by two of Thérèse's letters to her eldest sister, Marie. In the first, Thérèse responds to Marie's request for an exposition of her spiritual doctrine, and in the second, she addresses the consternation this exposition evoked within Marie.

In her initial account of her thought, Thérèse depicts herself as "a weak little bird" that "wills to fly toward the bright Sun . . . the Divine Furnace of the Holy Trinity" in order to convey her attitude of sheer trust in God in the face of sheer limitation.[61] She details that flying is not even within the bird's power, yet, resolutely untroubled by its supreme weakness, it audaciously chooses to stay gazing upon the sun, undeterred by wind or rain, or dark clouds that may obscure the sun entirely. Thérèse admits that at times the bird's heart is beset by storm clouds and darkness seems the only credible thing. "This," she proclaims, "is the moment of perfect joy for the poor little weak creature . . . remaining there just the same and gazing at the Invisible Light."[62]

> Burrows shifted from considering trusting acceptance of her poor humanity as something inferior and provisional to seeing it as the only authentic spiritual way . . .

Developing her image, Thérèse maintains it is inevitable that, at times, "being unable to soar like the eagles, the poor little bird is taken up with the trifles of earth."[63] However, after engaging with such distractions, it does not indulge in introspective remorse, bewailing its wretchedness, but "turns toward its beloved Sun . . . thinking in the boldness of its full trust that it will acquire in even greater fullness the love of him who came to call not the just but sinners."[64] Indeed, as Thérèse breaks into prayer, we learn her greatest hope is that Jesus, "the Adorable Eagle, will come to fetch me, Your little bird; and ascending with it to the Furnace of Love, You will plunge it for all eternity into the burning Abyss of this Love."[65] Thérèse concludes this first letter by exclaiming to Jesus, "I feel that if You found a soul weaker and littler than mine, which is impossible, You would be pleased to grant it still greater favors, provided it abandoned itself with total confidence to Your Infinite Mercy."[66]

In addition to the parable of the little bird, Thérèse expresses in her first letter "extraordinary desires for martyrdom."[67] Not sharing these desires, Marie responds by articulating her concern that she could thus not possibly espouse Thérèse's spiritual way. Marie's dismay, claims Burrows, "brought forth from Thérèse her deepest thought."[68] In her next letter Thérèse insists to her sister, "My desires of martyrdom *are nothing*; they are not what give me the unlimited confidence that I feel in my heart. . . . Ah! I really feel that it is not this at all that pleases God in my little soul; what pleases Him is *that He sees me loving my littleness* and my *poverty, the blind hope that I have in His mercy.*"[69] Accordingly, she goes on to declare, "Ah! let us remain . . . *very far* from all that sparkles, let us love our littleness, let us love to feel nothing, then we shall be poor in spirit. . . . Oh! how I would like to be able to make you understand what I feel! . . . It is confidence and nothing but confidence that must lead us to Love."[70]

Of course, it is Burrows's response to Thérèse's words that is our real interest here. She says that in reading about the bird yearning for the ultimate yet experiencing only frailty, "I was reading about my own self."[71] Furthermore, she recounts, "By the grace of God I was able to take Thérèse literally. I knew that what she said was pure truth. What is more, I was that soul so much weaker than herself and I turned with trust to God as she said."[72] Parenthetically, in later years, Burrows would reiterate her conviction of the "pure truth" of Thérèse's doctrine by asserting, "It is this spiritual way that to me is so authentic, so real, so wise, so Gospel, that I would never doubt Thérèse, never."[73] Hence, to Thérèse's plea that Marie understand her, Burrows responds, "Oh Thérèse, I have understood. All my being understands. Poverty of spirit. . . . This is God's grace in me."[74] Clearly, then, Burrows found in Thérèse resounding affirmation of her hitherto hesitant spirituality of exposing her nothingness to God in trust. She experienced Thérèse counseling her, "This is right, if you just go on trusting, *go on trusting*, go on what Jesus said, take him at his word."[75]

While Thérèse definitively oriented Burrows toward the path of trust, she still had to labor to truly make this way her own. The chief source of resistance was her continual experience of fragility, the absence of God and existential fear. "In spite of this underlying state of confidence, I was still a prey to all sorts of troubles, fears, doubts," Burrows explains. "Thérèse of Lisieux died in her twenty-fifth year. I was going on to middle life and to areas of existence she never knew."[76] Or again, after detailing the encouragement she received from Thérèse's letters, she comments, "But [I] never got any assurance beyond that faith one. . . . [I] never had it within, that God was really interested in me, or that . . . I was pleasing to him, I felt awful."[77] All this is to say that while Burrows was now convinced that union with God consists in surrendering to him in profound trust the painful reality of being a dependent creature, this conviction and the reality of her suffering needed to be integrated. Many years later she would write, "Faith alone can overcome the world and the threat the world imposes. It does not follow that we lose the feeling of anxiety and fear—we would be the poorer for that—but these now play a role that is creative not destructive. Fear can cripple, paralyse, prompt us to shirk and evade life. Faith enables us to live with reality, braving its challenge."[78] Burrows was in the process of allowing her vivid existential angst to be transformed through trust into something creative, into capacity for God.

In order to facilitate this process of transformation, this task of making her frightening fragility pure openness to God, Burrows composed a written account of her inner state. "In a state of extreme inner suffering," she explains, "I sought relief in writing out my feelings."[79] In this account—which became the prototype of her autobiography—she considers the basic realities of her lived experience and the presence of God within that experience. Let us briefly look at Burrows's early self-assessment now and witness her laboring to find meaning in her suffering experience through trust.

Burrows begins her account of her inner state by establishing her fundamental spiritual dilemma. She says that in her childhood she experienced "a yearning for something unidentified—certainly not identified with God as presented to me."[80] With her conversion, this yearning became an explicit quest for intimacy with God; Burrows refers to the "profound, incessant restlessness" of her depths and identifies it as a desire for "oneness with a personal God."[81] However, and this is the dilemma, in Carmel she has continued to experience a disparity between her deepest hunger and the way to

God set before her. Burrows states that "practices from which other people derive satisfaction, making them aware that they are living with God" and "accounts of experiences of mystical union by Saints" only disgust her.[82]

We witness Burrows integrating the dynamic of trust with her lived experience in the way in which she responds to her dilemma. She writes, "There is a fundamental difficulty in my approach to God which I find impossible to express. It makes prayer impossible, and yet . . . may it not be that it is something very authentic, something that is really me and therefore should not be considered a drawback or a hindrance. Should it be accepted?"[83] Thus we see Burrows beginning to express openness to the possibility that, despite all indications to the contrary, her longing for intimacy with the living God is not something unrealizable. Continuing her self-analysis, she develops this approach to her interior state:

> Though I can in no way conceive of God, can in no way conceive of my identification with Christ, may I not trust the authenticity of this inmost yearning which seems to me to be the driving force of my being, and trusting it—believing it to be implanted by my Creator—accept the very absence, the very difficulty, the suffering, impotence, the hunger and void, as my way, my spiritual life, my prayer? And believe too that the desire, presumed authentic, points infallibly to its fulfilment; that Person for whom I am yearning; who, though his features are unknown, whose response unperceived, does exist. It is he who is the lodestone secretly attracting me.[84]

Through composing this account of her life, Burrows clearly comes to accept more deeply that the dark, hungry nothingness of her existence is a condition to be entrusted to

God. She allows herself to receive her inner void as an echo of God's primordial desire for union with her, thus accepting that her ongoing anguish can only become meaningful through trusting surrender.

The Burrows who writes *Before the Living God* is firmly established in the way of trust within raw neediness. In fact, as we will see, she composes her autobiography precisely because she is convinced that the nature of her response to the human condition is universally significant. Burrows's commitment to accepting her essential vulnerability as capacity for God is evident in her preferential regard for this state. She comments, "We want to be spiritually beautiful, to have an interesting, beautiful spiritual life. In his mercy he deprived me of all from the beginning. He has kept me in a state of poverty and helplessness. Now he has given me the grace to want this, to choose it."[85] Obviously Burrows is alive to the paradox that her nonglorious condition of spiritual barrenness is to be desired as, entrusted to God, it is a receptacle for divine glory. Indeed, she goes so far as to declare, "For my part, I know I must welcome every experience of weakness, every opportunity I get for learning how helpless I am."[86]

Burrows's committed stance of empty-handed trust before God is also evident in the imagery she uses to describe her inner reality. She relates, for example, that she once claimed, "There is a citadel within me that never yields."[87] Considering this self-assessment she concludes, "This is correct. It is not I who hold the citadel, but the living God."[88] Her fragility has become a stronghold because, through trusting surrender, God has taken possession of her inmost being. Furthermore, Burrows recounts speaking with a priest about that initial grace of conversion that set her firmly at the base of the mountain of the spiritual life. She says that when he asked if she was still climbing the mountain,

> I made the surprising reply, "In a way, I have already got there." . . . What I said sprang from my heart without reflection. I was to make a similar statement later and again recently. Each time I meant the same thing but with, I hope, deeper reality. What did I mean? I was referring to that profound surrender in trust; the surrender of poverty to God. I realised then, as I realise even more now, that this gave me to God and God to me. This was the essence of union, of sanctity. Not for a moment did I think I was perfect. Perfection has nothing to do with it. Given this profound hand-over, nothing can keep one from God. I expect to be imperfect to the end of my life and yet I am certain that God will accomplish in me all that he wills. . . . This was the rock on which my life was based. Usually it was submerged by the furious waves and I could not perceive it.[89]

Committed to descending into her nothingness with trust, Burrows knows in faith that she is culminating the ascent toward which her life was oriented so long ago.

The Discovery of the Christocentric Nature of Trust

We can turn now to Burrows's discovery that the grace to surrender her lived nothingness to God in trust is fundamentally Jesus living within her his unique openness to the Father's love, that is to say, her discovery that Jesus not only exhorts but also mediates, trusting self-abandonment to the living

God. Burrows actually came to understand the thoroughly Christocentric nature of the way of trust within poverty after definitively embracing this way. What we are looking at here, then, is her coming to realize that it is in Jesus that she is in communion with God, and her consequent deliberate identification of her lived experience with his. Or, to borrow Sundborg's words, we are looking at how her way of trust "becomes personalized, is given a specifically Christian name and face."[90]

Until many years after entering Carmel, Burrows's relationship with Jesus was represented by her statement, "I had not yet found Jesus and God in him."[91] She faced two problems concerning Jesus. The first dilemma was her inability to conceive of the real human Jesus and her consequent inability to relate her own human experience to his; it was due to a certain "unreality," or lack of humanness, in the images of Jesus set before her. We have heard Burrows lament that as a child she found images of Jesus "wholly insipid." And she says that for many years in Carmel, "When I wanted to think of the man Christ, I was faced with a difficulty. The pictures which had been presented to me over my life were off-putting and yet I could not free myself from these images when I wanted to think of him."[92] So, in experiencing nothing but the fragility of the human condition, Burrows could not think of herself as being in solidarity with Jesus in his humanity. His human experience was inexorably "other."

Burrows's second problem regarding her relationship with Jesus was more fundamental than her first. It concerned just how Jesus in his humanity could be "in" her, how it was possible to be in intimate union with the man Jesus. As we have seen, Burrows longed to relate with Jesus in an "inside" way, yet this desire seemed simply unrealizable; she had been taught "that he was in heaven and in the Blessed

Sacrament—not everywhere, not 'in' me." Thus it seemed to her that following Teresa's counsel and meditating on the sacred humanity of Jesus was a matter of fancy, not real relationship. If Jesus resided "outside" her, simply thinking about him could not possibly cultivate true intimacy.

Although Burrows for many years experienced herself as "outside" Jesus—she had not yet "found" him—she nevertheless strove to address her difficulties in understanding him and relating with him. We know that initially Burrows found little in her monastery's library to support her spiritual development. However, she details, "Abbot [Columba] Marmion's *Christ the Life of the Soul* was on the shelves and this appealed to me. It was objective. It did not talk about degrees in the spiritual life, it talked about Christ and our union with him. I found some comfort and support in this book."[93] Furthermore, she refers to the help she derived from "an occasional glimpse of what [Jesus] might have looked like as a boy or man and this was more likely to be in a real photograph of an Arab boy or swarthy Indian." She continues, "I found it helpful to look at pictures: a mother with a baby . . . my thoughts would wander over it . . . the helplessness, the relationship between them, breast-feeding . . . his need of her . . . and then 'this is God.'"[94] So Burrows sought to counter that sense of remoteness from the real humanity of Jesus caused by unreal, inaccessible images of him by contemplating images of actual people. This use of photographs also indicates Burrows's

> She came to understand the thoroughly Christocentric nature of the way of trust within poverty after definitively embracing this way.

search for contemporaneity with the human Jesus, beyond her interest in his actual, historical humanity.[95]

It was the Gospels, though, that most helped Burrows draw close to Jesus, if, for many years, from the "outside." As she recounts, "I was blessed in that, almost from the beginning of my serious discipleship, the New Testament opened up to me and the Jesus I found there, what he said, what he did, the way he was, became the rock on which I built my house."[96] She found John's Gospel especially compelling. "I read with awe," she recounts, "the mysterious prologue and then the beautiful scenes of the apostles' call. 'Master, where do you live?' I pondered long and lovingly on the texts and my keen mind and imagination were at work."[97] Burrows reveals here that she approached the Gospel of John according to her desire to relate to the real human Jesus. As Sundborg observes, "John's prologue . . . touches her problem of understanding the sacred humanity of Jesus . . . [and] the apostles' question, 'Master, where do you live?,' is her own question about how and where Jesus exists now to the end that she can relate to him in as real a way as did the apostles."[98]

It was similarly this "absorption in the mystery of the incarnation" that drew Burrows to, and was deepened by, the Gospel of Luke.[99] She tells us, "I loved too the infancy narratives of Luke. I found the birth, infancy and childhood of Christ easy to dwell on. I think this was due to the fact that here one faced the mystery of the incarnation starkly. 'The Word was made flesh'—in this mute, almost formless baby. There was no need to form a picture."[100] The early chapters of Luke exposed Burrows to the raw reality of Jesus' humanness; thus, unencumbered by "insipid," "off-putting" imagery, she could come closer to associating her vulnerable, helpless humanity with the lived experience of Jesus.

Burrows's struggles concerning Jesus—the elusiveness of his real human experience and the apparent impossibility of being in true union with his humanity—were theological issues, and while other means helped to some extent, they were finally resolved by theological sources. This was no matter of finding abstract solutions to abstract problems. Burrows remarks in *Guidelines for Mystical Prayer*, "For me, a theoretical problem is a practical one too."[101] Indeed, we have seen that her twofold Christological difficulty obstructed her from finding Jesus and God in him; she experienced herself as "outside" Jesus, yet she yearned for an "inside" relationship with him. As will become evident, the theological insights Burrows discovered permeated the fabric of her inner life and came to define her stance of utter trust within utter poverty.[102]

The first theological discovery Burrows made addressed the matter of how it is possible to be in real, intimate union with Jesus within oneself. She describes her finding in this way:

An objective, theological help to prayer came with my finding a passage in *The Lord* by [Romano] Guardini. I was thrilled when I read these words: "For the glorified Christ no limitations exist—also none of person. He can inhabit the believer, not only so that he constantly thinks of Christ or loves Him, but actually, as the human soul inhabits the body. Body and soul, Christ can inhabit the believer, for God's Son is not only soul, Spirit, but holy, glorious Reality, mystical Corpus. As such He is the renewer of life."

This was the first time I had met this thought. Hitherto I had learned that "Christ dwelt by faith in your heart" meant he dwelt in us merely through our thinking of him and loving him. He dwelt in us as Word but not as man. How puzzling! The Word is man for ever.

Again, "The Spirit of God opens all things, permitting being to flow into being, life into life, me into you without violence or loss of individuality." This was the sort of thing I was looking for. I could now commune with Jesus "within me."[103]

The doctrine of inhabitation revealed to Burrows the stunning possibility of an "inside" relationship with Jesus, the very type of relationship for which she had been searching. It is possible, she discovered, for Jesus, Word and man, to "inhabit" her; she can be in a living communion with the real Jesus within the reality of herself.

Burrows's inability to conceive of Jesus' real human experience, and her consequent struggle to identify her humanity with his, was resolved by her subsequent theological discoveries. She read *Christ of Faith* by Karl Adam, a text that "suggest[s] our Lord's human experience."[104] Detailing the insights she derived from this source, Burrows writes, "Our Lord knew the sense of absence from God. His was an utterly true humanity. I shall never forget the impact of his paragraph on the incarnation and kenosis, the Word's stepping over the boundary into creation, leaving behind him all his prerogatives, coming into the world utterly defenceless, at our mercy."[105] Adam, Burrows declares, brought her "definitive light. . . . All my being cried out, 'This is truth.' How moved I was! Here was a theologian supporting my longings."[106] This objective, theological treatment of the incarnation affirmed for Burrows that Jesus' experience of being human was not something unreal, inaccessible, or "other"; his was a bare humanity, emptied of the prerogatives of divinity. This is the truth toward which she had been moving through reflecting on the Gospels and images that evoked Jesus' humanness yet did not have the sanction to claim with certainty. Now Burrows realized that she could fulfill her longing and identify her own lived experience with Jesus', her solitary, dependent, threatened existence with Jesus' knowing "the sense of absence from God," his being "utterly defenceless, at our mercy."

This presentation of the stark human experience of the incarnate Lord was confirmed for Burrows by another theological source. As she details,

> A little later I read [F. X.] Durrwell's *Resurrection* and found the same rich teaching there. He speaks of the "weakness of this impoverished life of Jesus," the basic abasement of the sacred humanity in the days of his flesh. "Truly He shared our existence according to the flesh. Not in appearance only was He a slave: His subjection was rooted in nature. His earthly existence did not express His deepest reality . . . the secret glory of His holiness was locked in the depths of His being. . . . Not only in His body, but all the faculties, even intellectual, by which He was in contact with the world and through which He carried out our redemption, were so incompletely possessed by the divine life that He was able to experience in them the need of being comforted by God."[107]

Once again, Jesus' human experience was depicted as an experience with which Burrows could identify fully. Like her, Jesus knew the frightening contingency, vulnerability, and neediness of being human. "I was able to feed on this doctrine," Burrows relates. "It was to nourish my understanding of poverty."[108]

So Burrows resolved her two principal obstacles to being in living communion with Jesus through discovering, first, that it is possible for Jesus to inhabit her unique human existence and second, that in the incarnation Jesus assumed a real human nature. The next step was for her to integrate this knowledge into her lived experience. Burrows refers to giving herself wholly up to Jesus "in" her and to finding Jesus and God in him.[109] Just what was involved in her surrender of herself to the life of the indwelling Jesus?

Burrows arrived at the understanding that being in true communion with Jesus means accepting and living out her humanity in the same way that Jesus accepted and lived out his humanity. In other words, if Jesus is to be incarnate within her particular human existence, then she must approach being human in the same way that Jesus approached being human. Burrows presents this position when she writes,

> How foolish to wish to feel sublime when Jesus accepted such poverty and gave himself to his Father in it. Always he was the beloved of the Father. In this life we share his lowly state. In heaven we shall share his glory. This lowly state is really a sharing in his glory. It seems to me, in praying the invocation of the offertory of the Mass, that we may share the divinity of him who deigned to share our humanity, we are really praying to share to the full his humanity, for the grace to accept to be fully human, to taste the salt dregs of humanness as he did and to offer to the Father the pure selfless heart of his Son crying to him from our earth.[110]

Clearly, Burrows here conveys the idea that Jesus lived out his perfect receptivity to the Father's love by embracing unto death the sheer poverty of the human condition, and if this Jesus is to live within us, we must also consent to be fully human, to be a fragile emptiness before the living God. As the passage implies, we can only make such a consent through the enablement of God's grace.

So, integrating her Christological discoveries into her lived experience, Burrows concluded that living with the life of Jesus consists in making the graced consent to be a living vulnerability totally surrendered to the Father's love. However, Burrows had already resolved to remain in empty-handed trust before the living God before she grasped that to be thus disposed is to live with, in, and through Jesus. As Sundborg observes, "In her discovery that it is through acceptance of her humanity as a capacity for God that she can be united with Jesus, Ruth is realizing clearly what she has long perceived and practiced as the way to God through trust but has not been able to relate explicitly to Jesus."[111] It follows that Burrows's growth in insight about Jesus did not require her to commit herself to God in any new or deeper way. Rather, it was a matter of her shifting her understanding of the basis of her trust and accepting that Jesus is the mediator and exemplar of her way to the Father. To cite Sundborg again, "Her discovery and surrender to Jesus changes her trust in God by making it the trust of Jesus in the Father. The trust is still utter but it is no longer blind or without support because it is a participation in the trust of Jesus who alone knows and reveals the Father."[112]

> If Jesus is to be incarnate within her particular human existence, then she must approach being human in the same way that Jesus approached being human.

Burrows's conviction that Jesus mediates her naked trust in the Father's love underlies *Before the Living God*. In her introduction to the book, for example, Burrows declares, "Already, it seems to me, I have grasped the mystery of my life. One long searching look into my past and I see, there in the depths, the face of Christ gazing back at me."[113] So Burrows conceives of her entire life as a participation in the singular life of Jesus. It is as if her life is a seamless garment woven in the thread of Christ. Her stark vulnerability to the essential fragility of the human condition is endured within Jesus' complete embrace of the frightening reality of what it means to be human; her bitter, ongoing sense of God's absence is a sharing in Jesus' living knowledge of the fundamental chasm between God and humanity; and her surrender in trust of her threatened, solitary existence to God is an expression of Jesus' perfect exposure of humanity's emptiness to the inundation of the Father's love.

The idea that her spirituality of trust is a participation in Jesus' relationship with the living God is articulated even more explicitly by Burrows at the conclusion of her autobiography: "St. Thérèse was to say that the suffering face of Jesus was the heart of her spirituality. A fact rarely alluded to. I can say the same. I have come to realise that the mystery of my own life lies here. From the first he has hidden his face from me, his face of glory. He has revealed his suffering, humbled face, the man of sorrows who came to sit with us in our loneliness, in our absence from God, in our desolation and wretchedness, in our hunger and thirst. He drank the salt dregs of humanness and has asked me to share it with him."[114] Burrows makes it clear here that her suffering life bears the living imprint of the cross. Jesus' assent to the Father's love reached its culmination in his utter descent into humanity's destitution on the cross; thus Burrows can claim that inasmuch as she cooperates with grace and trustingly accepts the bitter vulnerability of being human, she shares in the life of the Crucified. She looks in trust to the living God, resolutely rooted in her poverty, through the suffering face of Jesus. It is in the light of this depiction of her life as lived within the life of Jesus crucified that we can understand the epigraph Burrows places at the beginning of *Before the Living God*: "Without beauty, without majesty, we looked on him—and turned away our eyes."[115]

There is one final passage to consider regarding Burrows's presentation of Jesus as the mediator of her trust in God. It concerns the effect that knowing she is "in" Jesus has upon her existential anxiety. Burrows addresses this matter when she relates,

> I put all my faith in Jesus, in what he said about God. Without being able to satisfy my intellect, which always yearned for clear expositions, I dimly realised that he had sunk into the abyss, had shared the anguish of death. He had gone through it and then cried out: "It is all right. It is God, it is heaven." Only he had the right to say to us frail creatures "fear not," because only he could guarantee our existence, our relation to the infinite. And this word, "fear not," was strewn through the pages of the Gospel. Truly our God knows the heart of man and knows that fear is his natural atmosphere. He has revealed to me the dreadfulness of human existence, the cliff-hanging aspect. In this way he has purified my faith and trust.[116]

We noted earlier that Burrows's commitment to the way of empty-handed trust did not mitigate her painful awareness of life's contingency and her concomitant fear of existence. Here she details that the Jesus in whom she trusts in God ensures that fear does not have the final word over her existence. His resurrection guarantees that entrusting to God the terrifying poverty of the human condition truly is the way to union with God. We have heard Burrows claim, "Unless one has security in the Absolute . . . then any assurances, any 'security,' is mockery." Only the One who has spanned the chasm between God and humankind by sinking with total trust into the abyss of humanity's nothingness can assure Burrows that the cause of her fear truly is capacity for Love.

RUTH BURROWS'S WRITINGS AS AN EXPRESSION OF HER LIVING KNOWLEDGE OF THE SPIRITUAL LIFE

We have now surveyed the contours of Burrows's inner life and established that she understands her life to be fundamentally a graced participation in Jesus' perfect trusting surrender to the Father's outpoured love from the depths of human fragility. At this point, we can turn to consider what Burrows offers through her written works. To do this, we must first identify the true value of her autobiography, *Before the Living God*. Burrows herself supplies the insight we need here. Burrows prefaces her account of her life with a letter to her friend Mother Elsa of Jesus. She begins, "Here I am at last complying with your continual urging to write the story of my life."[117] Burrows reminds Elsa, "You thought . . . that my experience would help others; that the very complexity of my nature, its tortuous searchings and above all, the gift—a dubious gift I am tempted to say—of self-analysis, have led me to an understanding and insight that could benefit others."[118] "Had you not urged me to it, Elsa," she goes on to admit, "I would never have presumed that an account of my life might be a help to others but since you have done so I am prepared to consider why it might be useful."[119] Burrows proceeds to specify two interrelated reasons why she thinks the story of her life would be of value to others.

Burrows indicates to Elsa that she considers her lived experience useful principally because it clearly demonstrates what it truly means to be human; she goes on to emphasize this universal relevance of her personal experience several times as she tells her story. For Burrows, hers "is but the common experience, but the common experience understood."[120] Referring to her spirituality of trust, she writes,

> It may appear a poor sort of way, even a cowardly one, but it is my way and his choice for me. More than that, I know that, ultimately, in its essence, it is the only way. Sooner or later everyone must be brought by him to this deep poverty, and everything depends on acceptance of it. Personalities, temperaments differ and God leads all according to their own character. Roads may appear different but ultimately they converge. Sooner or later we must take the narrow path and leave behind all our spiritual riches. We have to go to God with empty hands. We have to let him be wholly and totally God. How hard this is. We want to feel good, want to feel we have something to offer him of our own.[121]

The point Burrows is making is that the meaning she has found in her life is the meaning written into the blueprint of humanity. As fundamentally contingent beings created by a God of outpoured love, humans are intrinsically oriented to stand in trusting vulnerability before the living God. This is the very disposition that Jesus—perfectly yielded to God's ecstasy of love—proclaims, models, and, most importantly, mediates.

It is evident from what Burrows says above that it is her naked trust, not her specific inner makeup, that lies at the heart of being human. She believes, however, that her particular temperament means that she manifests the common call of humanity in an especially clear manner. Burrows expresses this idea in the following analogy:

It is easier for some natures to trust God than for others. They have a basic security and, in spite of difficulties, life is experienced as good. But for others of a less robust and solid structure it is much more difficult. If a pewter mug and an egg shell china cup were conscious, their experiences would be very different. The latter would live with a sense of peril. So the fragile nature has no natural foundation for trust and when it truly trusts in God its trust is pure. The more solid nature cannot know how authentic is its trust in God until its inner security is taken away and it is reduced to a similar state of deprivation and fragility.[122]

Burrows obviously has an eggshell china nature: humanity's innate helplessness is frighteningly immediate to her. And this makes it possible for her to be a singularly vivid witness of the trust in God toward which humankind is intrinsically directed. Given her unmitigated fragility, Burrows can only face God with unmitigated trust, and it is only with such radical self-abandonment that any human being can truly commune with the divine, no matter what sense of security he or she may naturally know.

Burrows perceives a secondary usefulness to her life story in the reality that personal expressions of universal truths tend to be more authoritative and effective in conveying those truths. As she explains to Elsa,

If I were to say that what I want to show people is that what really matters is utter trust in God; that this trust cannot be there until we have lost all self-trust and are rooted in poverty; that we must be willing to go to God with empty hands, and that the whole meaning of our existence and the one consuming desire of the heart of God is that we should let ourselves be loved, many spiritual persons would smile at my *naïveté*. They are likely to murmur: "But we know all that; we can read that in any spiritual book. Does she think she is telling us something new?" All I can say is that, although I too have known this in theory, it is only now that it is integrated into my life. . . . I feel that it is in the story of my life, of my own search and journey, that what I want to say will be revealed and may strike home in a way that a purely theoretical exposition of these truths will never do.[123]

Burrows draws on her personal experience to support her thinking here. She cites the influence that St. Thérèse's autobiography has had on her: she says that Thérèse's lived expression of the Gospel "has been, from the early years of my suffering, difficult spiritual life, one of God's ways of bringing me light and peace."[124] Moreover, Burrows notes that she has already witnessed her own lived experience being beneficial: in counseling others, she relates, "I have found that drawing on my own experience has helped them."[125]

So the value of *Before the Living God*, as Burrows herself perceives, lies in its being a living articulation of the basic Gospel message. And this is, in fact, precisely what Burrows offers through the rest of her writings. All of Burrows's writings are derived from her lived experience. In Burrows's own words, what she offers is "a *lived* theology."[126] Thus, Burrows's observation concerning Teresa of Ávila—"Not only have we her autobiography and letters, but her treatises are autobiographical"[127]—can be applied to Burrows herself. She, like Teresa, never writes in a purely objective, theoretical manner but always filters her presentation of the spiritual life through the lens of her own Christian journey. Sundborg also notes this essentially autobiographical character of Burrows's writings and comments, "She is influenced particularly by Teresa of Ávila, John of the Cross, and Thérèse of Lisieux; but rather than make an exposition of their spirituality, she makes use of their doctrine to illumine and confirm her own immediate experience. Similarly, she has a more than adequate grasp of psychology, contemporary theology, and Scripture studies. However, what she writes is not based directly on these but rather employs these as instruments to elaborate her insights gained from what she has lived."[128]

In addition to being derived from her lived experience, all Burrows's writings are principally concerned with elaborating that universally applicable pattern she has found woven into the fabric of her life: the dynamic of sharing in the kenotic Jesus' perfect receptivity to the Father's love by surrendering our fundamental human fragility to God in trust. Burrows points directly to this orienting core of her work when she asserts, "What my books are saying is pure Jesus—nothing else, but a Jesus poor, threadbare, a Jesus who is nothing but himself and wants to be accepted thus. And this Jesus can unite himself to us only if we consent to become like him—without beauty, glory, grandeur."[129] In the same vein, she speaks of a consistent theology informing her writings and remarks, "From first to last it is Jesus: something of what it means to have been given Jesus 'for us and for our salvation.'"[130] And, approaching her core message from the other angle, so to speak, Burrows writes, "There is a ruling insight that covers and controls my life and . . . runs through everything I have written: God offers himself in total love to each one of us. Our part is to open our hearts to receive this gift."[131]

The consuming focus of Burrows's writings is also revealed by the way in which she aligns her basic message with St. Thérèse's doctrine of trust. She first draws this parallel when, in introducing her autobiography, she concedes Elsa's idea that to lay open the story of her life

> God offers himself in total love to each one of us. Our part is to open our hearts to receive this gift.

will be to offer "an exposition of St. Thérèse's doctrine, but in the idiom of our times."[132] Further, looking back at what she has communicated through her writings, Burrows says,

> You could possibly say that it's basically the doctrine of what Thérèse saw but it's me . . . a northerner who doesn't use that imagery of flowers and dewdrops, and . . . is much more rational . . . [and who has had a] very different upbringing. . . . And I've had to live it out in middle age, in office of great responsibility . . . [and] then into really old age. . . . I feel that, in a way, it's her doctrine, lived out in a very different personality, right into old age.
>
> But . . . both are Gospel. You see, to me, Thérèse grasped hold of the heart of the Gospel. It's all gift, it's given . . . we don't earn it—it is absolute trust through thick and thin, giving oneself—it's an acceptance of being human, which we don't find easy. . . . We are children. . . . To me, I think, the basic image Jesus is after [in exhorting childlikeness] is not this "sweetness" and all that, but helplessness and dependency.[133]

Burrows's writings spring from the well of her living knowledge of the spiritual life, and accordingly, they are fundamentally an exposition of the Christocentric spirituality of trust that defines her life.

It is important to make particular mention here of the autobiographical device Burrows uses to convey her lived spiritual insights in *Guidelines for Mystical Prayer*. Burrows begins the work with the declaration, "This book has been born from the womb of life."[134] She goes on to discuss how it emerged from her coming to understand "mysticism" in a radically new way. As we saw earlier, Burrows previously associated the term with the range of phenomena supposedly bestowed in the life of prayer as signs that one is near to God and enjoys his favor. Within this perspective, she relates, the mystical life "seemed to me to be unrelated to Jesus, to be . . . something cultivated, a fascinating possibility, something that gave promise of a wonderful experience."[135]

Burrows maintains that the shift in her understanding was wrought by her interactions with two women—"Claire" and "Petra." Claire came into Burrows's life heralded as a mystic because "her way of prayer was extraordinary."[136] Burrows details that she was initially reluctant to attribute any special significance to a life of prayer in which "things happen," but this reluctance was overcome upon coming to know Claire. "'There is nothing pseudo here,' I thought," Burrows narrates. "Every note rings true. Here is profound humility and total surrender to God. Only God matters to this woman. She is immersed in God. Jesus lives in her."[137]

What is of greatest significance is that, in Burrows's words, "Claire . . . drew my attention to Petra."[138] Petra is, in fact, not a third person but Burrows herself (and Claire is "Elsa" from *Before the Living God*).[139] Burrows recounts, "I had known [Petra] for many years and certainly she was a faithful nun but there was nothing to single her out. . . . She did nothing more than what others were doing. Claire told me quite emphatically that Petra was a mystic. I asked her why she said that. What did she see in Petra? 'Petra never says "no" to God, is always looking to him to see what he wants and, chief of all, accepts to be totally poor, to have no holiness of her own.'"[140]

This effected the transformation in Burrows's conception of mysticism. Specifying just what it was she came to perceive, she writes, "If this ordinary woman, who like me had never known spiritual experiences, who was always in darkness and aridity, was a true mystic just as Claire was, then mysticism had nothing to do with 'experiences.' What was mysticism? Surely Jesus living in one, self drained away."[141] Burrows expresses this same realization in a different way when she announces, "At long last all has fallen into place for me and been reduced to a beautiful simplicity that my deepest heart has always known: that Jesus is everything, and that theology, the mystical life, and practical living form but one whole: Jesus first and last, Christ crucified, the wisdom and the power of God."[142] Burrows says that in making this crucial discovery, "I realised I had learnt something of immense importance that I must share with others."[143] Hence, she wrote *Guidelines for Mystical Prayer.*

So, although she is concealed under the guise of "Petra," *Guidelines* is actually a discussion of the mystical life composed in the light of Burrows's own graced participation in Christ's kenosis. The book is born out of the womb of her living union with Jesus crucified; in fact, discussion of the lived experience of Petra frequently serves a didactic function throughout the text. In *Guidelines for Mystical Prayer*, then, Burrows establishes the dynamic that she will pursue throughout all her writings: she hides herself, at least partly, while elaborating her living knowledge of the Gospel.

Summary

Ruth Burrows's contribution to the Christian spiritual tradition is at once wholly particular and wholly universal. Her response to her singularly stark exposure to the contingency of the human condition has yielded insights that are relevant to all people. Finding herself a living nothingness irrevocably oriented to intimacy with God by the grace of her conversion, Burrows was gradually led to surrender her very poverty to him in trust as sheer receptivity to Love; this surrender was no mere act of grim self-will but a response to God's enabling grace. Burrows came to understand that resolutely to stand with naked trust before the living God is precisely what it means to live with the life of the crucified Jesus; her "yes" to Love uttered within the raw neediness of her humanity is a participation in the kenotic Jesus' perfect "yes" to the Father. The particularity of her lived experience, then, is nothing other than an incarnation of Jesus' proclamation that he is the only way to union with the Father. This Gospel truth proclaimed by the text of her vulnerable, trusting existence is what Burrows conveys to others throughout her various writings on the spiritual life.

Notes

1. In her autobiography, Burrows altered the chronology of her life and mixed up names and personalities in order to protect her identity and that of the people she mentions in the text. Accordingly, she was born earlier than she indicates in *Before the Living God*. Nevertheless, she is accurate in detailing how old she was when particular events occurred. Ruth Burrows, interview by author, Quidenham, UK, September 30, 2009.

2. Ruth Burrows, *Before the Living God* (1975; repr., London: Burns and Oates, 2008; Mahwah, N.J.: HiddenSpring, 2008), 54.

3. Burrows, interview, September 30, 2009.

4. Elizabeth Ruth Obbard, review of *Carmel: Interpreting a Great Tradition*, by Ruth Burrows, *Bulletin, Our Lady of the Assumption: British Province of Carmelites* 31, no. 8 (Winter 2001): 11.

5. Ruth Burrows, unpublished manuscript, c. 1973 (?), typed pages.

6. Burrows, *Before the Living God*, 5.

7. Ruth Burrows, *Guidelines for Mystical Prayer*, foreword by B. C. Butler (1976; repr., London: Continuum, 2007; Denville, N.J.: Dimension, 1980), 109. Burrows is ostensibly referring here to a nun named Petra. As we will see, however, Petra is none other than Burrows herself.

8. Burrows, *Before the Living God*, 55.

9. Ibid., 31.

10. Burrows, interview, September 30, 2009.

11. Burrows, *Before the Living God*, 80–81.

12. Ibid., 110.

13. Ruth Burrows, *Living in Mystery*, introduction by Wendy Beckett (London: Sheed and Ward, 1996), 11. This incident was originally related in Burrows, unpublished manuscript.

14. Burrows, *Before the Living God*, 26.

15. Ibid., 10.

16. Ibid., 17.

17. Ibid., 27.

18. Ibid., 32.

19. Ibid., 31.

20. Ibid.

21. Ibid., 32.

22. Ibid.

23. Ibid.

24. Ibid., 34.

25. Ibid.

26. Ibid.

27. Burrows, interview, September 30, 2009.
28. Burrows, *Before the Living God*, 35.
29. Ibid., 37.
30. Burrows, unpublished manuscript.
31. Burrows, *Before the Living God*, 79.
32. See, for example, ibid., 52.
33. Ibid., 54.
34. Ibid., 52.
35. Ibid., 80–81.
36. See ibid., 52; and Ruth Burrows, *Interior Castle Explored: St. Teresa's Teaching on the Life of Deep Union with God* (1981; repr., London: Continuum, 2007; Mahwah, N.J.: HiddenSpring, 2007), 37.
37. Burrows, *Guidelines for Mystical Prayer*, 2.
38. Burrows, *Before the Living God*, 52.
39. Ibid., 85.
40. Ibid., 54–55.
41. Ibid., 79. Emphasis original.
42. Ibid., 80.
43. Ibid., 79.
44. Burrows, unpublished manuscript.
45. Ibid.
46. Burrows, *Before the Living God*, 74.
47. Burrows, unpublished manuscript.
48. Burrows, *Before the Living God*, 56.
49. Ibid., 82.
50. Stephen Sundborg, "Sexual-Affective Integration in Celibacy: A Psycho-Spiritual Study of the Experience of Ruth Burrows in the Light of the Psychology of Rollo May" (STD diss., Pontifical Gregorian University, 1984), 436.
51. Burrows, *Before the Living God*, 66–67.
52. Sundborg, "Sexual-Affective Integration," 437.
53. Burrows, *Before the Living God*, 73.
54. Burrows, unpublished manuscript.

55. Burrows, *Before the Living God*, 81.

56. Ibid., 73.

57. Ibid., 72.

58. Burrows, unpublished manuscript.

59. Burrows, *Before the Living God*, 99.

60. Ibid., 84.

61. St. Thérèse of Lisieux, *Story of a Soul*, trans. John Clarke, 3rd ed. (Washington, D.C.: ICS Publications, 1996), 198 (emphasis removed).

62. Ibid. (emphasis removed).

63. Ibid.

64. Ibid., 198–99 (emphasis removed).

65. Ibid., 200.

66. Ibid.

67. Sister Marie of the Sacred Heart, letter to Thérèse, September 17(?), 1896, in St. Thérèse of Lisieux, *General Correspondence*, vol. 2: *1890–1897*, trans. John Clarke (Washington, D.C.: ICS Publications, 1988), 997.

68. Burrows, unpublished manuscript.

69. Thérèse of Lisieux, letter 197 to Sister Marie of the Sacred Heart, September 17, 1896, in Thérèse, *General Correspondence*, 2:999.

70. Ibid., 2:999–1000.

71. Burrows, unpublished manuscript.

72. Ibid.

73. Ruth Burrows, interview by author, Quidenham, UK, October 4, 2009.

74. Burrows, unpublished manuscript.

75. Burrows, interview, September 30, 2009.

76. Burrows, unpublished manuscript.

77. Burrows, interview, September 30, 2009.

78. Ruth Burrows, "Carmel: A Stark Encounter with the Human Condition," in *Essence of Prayer* (London: Burns and Oates, 2006; Mahwah, N.J.: HiddenSpring, 2006), 185.

79. Burrows, unpublished manuscript.

80. Ibid.

81. Burrows, unpublished manuscript.

82. Ibid.

83. Ibid.

84. Ibid.

85. Burrows, *Before the Living God*, 115.

86. Ibid., 102.

87. Ibid., 81.

88. Ibid.

89. Ibid., 112.

90. Sundborg, "Sexual-Affective Integration," 529.

91. Burrows, *Before the Living God*, 55.

92. Ibid., 78.

93. Ibid., 52.

94. Ibid., 78.

95. See Sundborg, "Sexual-Affective Integration," 519.

96. Ruth Burrows, *Love Unknown: The Archbishop of Canterbury's Lent Book 2012*, foreword by Rowan Williams (London: Continuum Books, 2011), 7.

97. Burrows, *Before the Living God*, 77.

98. Sundborg, "Sexual-Affective Integration," 518.

99. Burrows, *Before the Living God*, 78.

100. Ibid.

101. Burrows, *Guidelines for Mystical Prayer*, 1.

102. Sundborg makes a noteworthy observation here: "Unfortunately these theological discoveries were eliminated from her published autobiography by the editor as perhaps diverting attention from her actual experience. But, because of Ruth's basic drive for understanding, they are as much 'experiential' as other aspects of her life." Sundborg, "Sexual-Affective Integration," 523n59.

103. Burrows, unpublished manuscript.

104. Ibid.

105. Ibid.

106. Ibid.

107. Ibid.

108. Ibid. The extent to which Burrows assimilated this teaching on the true human experience of Jesus is evident in a conference she presented to her community at around the time of making this theological discovery. She taught, "It seems to me we easily fail to grasp the realism of the incarnation. We tend to think of our Lord walking the earth as God. Behaving as man, it is true, but all the time thinking, knowing, judging, feeling, loving as God. This is not so. So untouched, so complete, so like ours was the sacred humanity that without a special illumination from the Blessed Trinity dwelling within him as within us, he would not have been aware of the fact that he was God, the Word. The Word did not communicate his attributes to the sacred humanity. He communicated only autonomy. This Man, utterly real man, is yet God. It is as if the Word, when he would step over the boundary of eternity into time left on the other side his divine attributes, entering the world invested only with human nature." Burrows, unpublished manuscript.

109. See Burrows, *Before the Living God*, 55, 80.

110. Burrows, unpublished manuscript. It is important to point out, if only parenthetically at this stage, that for Burrows, participating in Jesus' lowly human experience in no way excludes participating in his resurrection. Rather, as this passage indicates, Burrows believes that to share utterly in Christ's humanity is precisely to share in his glory; Godfulness is the reverse side of selflessness. This central aspect of Burrows's spirituality surely stems from her devotion to the Gospel of John. John portrays the crucifixion of Jesus as his "hour," his "glory."

111. Sundborg, "Sexual-Affective Integration," 535.

112. Ibid., 539.

113. Burrows, *Before the Living God*, 1.

114. Ibid., 115.

115. Is 53:2, as cited in Burrows, *Before the Living God*, v.

116. Ibid., 113–14.

117. Ibid., 1.

118. Ibid.

119. Ibid.

120. Ibid., 118.

121. Ibid., 115.

122. Burrows, *Before the Living God*, 101.

123. Ibid., 2–3.

124. Ibid., 3.

125. Ibid., 2.

126. Ruth Burrows, letter to author, March 9, 2009 (emphasis added).

127. Burrows, *Guidelines for Mystical Prayer*, 97.

128. Sundborg, "Sexual-Affective Integration," 240.

129. Ruth Burrows, letter to Stephen Sundborg, July 18, 1979. Cited in Sundborg, "Sexual-Affective Integration," 534–35.

130. Burrows, letter, March 9, 2009.

131. Burrows, *Love Unknown*, 38.

132. Burrows, *Before the Living God*, 4.

133. Burrows, interview, September 30, 2009.

134. Burrows, *Guidelines for Mystical Prayer*, 1.

135. Ibid., 2.

136. Ibid.

137. Ibid., 3.

138. Ibid.

139. Sundborg explains that "Ruth uses this device of speaking about Petra as if she were another person because after the publishing of *Living God* her own identity did not remain for long a secret." Sundborg, "Sexual-Affective Integration," 241n14.

140. Burrows, *Guidelines for Mystical Prayer*, 3.

141. Ibid.

142. Ibid., 1.

143. Ibid., 3.

CHAPTER 2

The Anthropology and Theology of Ruth Burrows

*Foundations
of Her Mystical Doctrine*

I n the previous chapter we established that through her
graced response to her inner desolation Ruth Burrows has
become an embodiment of the Gospel proclamation that Jesus
is the only way to communion with God. Realizing that her
way—allowing Jesus to live out in her raw poverty his perfect
surrender in trust to the Father's love—is essentially everyone's
way, Burrows expresses this spirituality of trust throughout all
of her writings. In order to make a critical examination of Burrows's lived spiritual doctrine, we will now detach her teaching
from her personal experience and explore her presentation of
the mystical life.

In *Guidelines for Mystical Prayer* Burrows herself indicates
the way forward with this task. There, she asserts that "both
our understanding of God and our understanding of man
will affect the way in which we think of and try to express the
mystical."[1] So, an exploration of Burrows's mystical doctrine
needs to begin with an examination of her theology and her
anthropology. This chapter will lay these foundations of her
thought. From looking at Burrows's conception of human
nature, then her conception of divine nature, it will emerge
that she understands both humanity and divinity to be perfectly expressed, and in perfect communion, in the kenotic
Jesus. We will conclude by briefly considering the three-stage
view of the Christian life that arises from Burrows's anthropology and theology.

RUTH BURROWS'S UNDERSTANDING OF HUMANITY

We can arrive at Burrows's thought on human nature by way
of her depiction of the general experience of human life.

Humanity as Capacity for the Divine Life

According to Burrows, "Basic to human experience is the
awareness of limitation, even of helplessness, and of how little
control we have over our life: the events that overtake us, the
circumstances that surround us and even over that intimate
part of us, our body. And what about our psychic, emotional
life? How inexorably even this reflects our inheritance, our
conditioning. We have been worked on before ever we were
born, with no awareness, no consent of our own. Age brings
not lesser, but deeper awareness of dependency and insecurity. . . . Fear is our most pervasive emotion, deriving from
the experience of contingency."[2] Burrows continues by stating,
"Our restlessness, our insatiable longings, our discontent and
experience of helplessness are to be traced to our divine destiny."[3] This claim takes us to the threshold of her understanding of what it means to be human.

Burrows sounds the keynote of her anthropology when she
declares that "each of us by the very fact of being human is
made for union with God. . . . We have within ourselves,
or rather we *are* ourselves, a potentiality for this union."[4] For
Burrows, to be human is to be fundamentally oriented toward
relationship with God; it is impossible to speak of human existence without at the same time speaking of God. "Our nature,"
she insists, "is to be all aspiration, a leaping upwards towards
fulness of life in God; it is to be a purity able to reflect the
beauty of God, an emptiness to receive plenitude."[5] Depicting
this divine destiny in more biblical terms, Burrows remarks,
"One of the profoundest ways of expressing our human vocation . . . is that we are called, each one of us, to be a son of
God."[6] Burrows is clear that the vocation to self-transcendence
and union with God forms the very origin of human existence.

As she explains in *Interior Castle Explored*, "Man is the being to whom God cries, 'Come to me.' . . . The call 'Come to me' is not an afterthought as though God first made man and then decided to call him to intimacy with himself. This divine call is what constitutes man."[7]

The inexorable vulnerability that belongs to the human condition is, as Burrows sees it, the reverse side of our being created as a capacity that only God can fill. She presents this other side of humanity's essential receptivity to the divine life when she affirms, "To be human means that we are a dependent being by very essence. Not only are we absolutely dependent on other persons and things for our bodily survival but we have to look beyond ourselves for our meaning. We have no fulfilment within ourselves and, what is more, we know that we are answerable not merely to ourselves but to another outside ourselves. . . . We are frighteningly, pitifully dependent."[8] Expressing this idea in a different way, Burrows points out that we may be called to the glory of divine sonship, but to be a son of God is to be dependent on God, from moment to moment receiving life from him.[9]

Becoming Human

If, according to Burrows's anthropology, to be human is to be essentially inclined toward God, a quivering potential for intimate communion with him, it follows that, for her, a principle of growth, of dynamism, is written into human existence. "It is one thing to be just a member of the human species," she says, "and another to become fully human, growing into a true man or a true woman."[10] Thus Burrows makes her own what she calls the "great, important insight of our times . . . of man becoming."[11] Elaborating on what is contained in this pivotal anthropological insight, Burrows writes,

> Man, to use the classical expression, is a capacity for God. Unlike every other form of life that we know of, he does not come into the world ready made. The baby animal is animal, whole and entire. It grows, reaches maturity and fulfilment within the bounds of its own being and the world around it. The human creature, this being made up of the same stuff as the world and thrown up by its evolution, is not ready made. It comes into the world incomplete, with no possibility of completion within itself or within the bounds of the material world. It is a capacity, a possibility; a capacity that may never be filled, a possibility that may never be realised, for, in this instance, the creature has a choice. Man is a capacity for God, he comes into existence insofar as he consents to be what he is, a "for-Godness." The human being is not a man until the possibility which he is, is totally realised, the capacity which he is, expanded to its limits.[12]

Burrows uses various organic images to illustrate this idea that we grow into our humanity to the extent that we surrender to the summons to be filled with the fullness of God. For example, she allegorizes, "If the growing point of a seed were to remain folded up within the acorn it would come to nothing. It has to uncurl, push itself out, up and away." And she concludes, "We can only become by leaving ourselves."[13]

Burrows's view of what is actually involved in this process of becoming human by fulfilling our capacity for the divine life will be examined presently. But for now, let us briefly consider how Burrows relates her basic understanding of human existence to her received theological framework.

Characteristically, Burrows anchors her anthropological insights in the New Testament. She tells us,

> The idea that we are not there yet, that we have to become—shall we say, I have to become *me* and my *me* has to become God—finds firm basis in scripture in its talk of being born anew, a new creation, something wholly new and other coming into existence. The concept of the distinction between spirit and flesh is particularly important for our theme. For both Paul and John, "flesh" seems to indicate simply "what is not God." Thus the human being in itself is "flesh." "Spirit" stands for the God-realm. . . . All that can be said of man who is "flesh" is that he is open to spirit, he has the capacity to be touched by and transformed into spirit, becoming one spirit with the Lord who is Spirit. His whole destiny lies in being born again into spirit. . . . It is only when flesh has become spirit totally that we have man.[14]

Burrows is adamant that in grounding her dynamic anthropology in the biblical spirit-flesh dichotomy she is not espousing a dualistic view of human existence: to speak of becoming human in terms of leaving flesh and becoming increasingly alive with God's spirit life is not to exclude the body from the process. "We are never allowing an opposition between soul and body," she insists. "When we use spirit, or soul . . . we mean the whole person insofar as they have been touched by God and are being transformed into spirit."[15] Indeed, so integral is the body to Burrows's vision of becoming human that she claims "a Christian joyfully accepts his bodiliness, knowing that he can go to God only through his body and that God comes to him through his body."[16]

When Burrows comes to the Carmelite spiritual tradition, she reads the concepts of human nature that she finds there through the lens of her dynamic anthropology. She observes that there seems to be significant difference between Teresa of Ávila's understanding of being human and her own. To begin with, she acknowledges that "we find ourselves somewhat embarrassed by [the] dualistic notion of soul and body" evident within Teresa's writings.[17] However, Burrows quickly assures that Teresa's dualism "need not worry us. Conditioned as she was by the thinking of her times, as we are by ours," Burrows reasons, "she could not have expressed herself otherwise."[18] For Burrows, more important divergence is manifest in Teresa's depiction of the soul as a castle in whose innermost room God dwells and in her consequent conception of spiritual growth "as a journey inwards, a penetration of this interior castle."[19] She points out that according to Teresa's image, "The castle is *already there*, our souls are, so to speak, *ready made*, we have only to get to know them by entering in."[20] Of course, such

> Burrows reads the concepts of human nature that she finds in the Carmelite spiritual tradition through the lens of her dynamic anthropology.

imagery is contradictory to Burrows's dynamic anthropology, and so she protests: "There is a problem but [Teresa] avoids it by not seeing it! . . . To say that we are not yet in our castle, at least not in any but the outer-most court, is really saying the mansions *are not there yet*, they come into existence."[21]

Burrows goes on to explain that while she finds Teresa's castle imagery problematic, there is actually essential agreement in their respective understandings of the human vocation. She says that "Teresa grasped *practically* but did not express clearly in her use of a static image,"[22] the idea that we gradually realize our humanity as we progressively fulfill our potential to be penetrated by God's life. Indeed, Burrows notes that this anthropological insight is not wholly lacking in Teresa's castle image. "What we have to do," she encourages, "is see what Teresa is really saying about the soul. She is saying that it is *for God*; it is a capacity for God. . . . This soul, this castle of immeasurable beauty and capacity is ourselves."[23] For Burrows, more revealing of Teresa's grasp of the dynamic, unfolding nature of human existence is her use of the image of the silkworm's transformation into a butterfly in the fifth mansion of the *Interior Castle*. Through this image Teresa conveys her understanding that on the journey of being human "generous effort in the first stages brings about a growth which allows something new to happen, a new stage in the evolution of the human being begins."[24]

It is important to note that Burrows does not dismiss Teresa's use of the castle image as simply an unfortunate, misguided choice. While she admits that the image of the human soul as a "ready made" palace is limited in its ability to express her core idea that we become human, Burrows nevertheless finds in the image a representation of what ultimate human fulfillment is like. Furthermore, Burrows claims that it is Teresa's own fully realized humanity that we glimpse through the interior castle image:

> There is an anecdote of how Teresa came by her image of the castle. She confided to a friend in an unguarded hour, that it [had] been given to her through a vision when she was longing for some insight "into the beauty of a soul in grace." Now, by her own testimony she was already

dwelling in the seventh mansion when she wrote her book, *The Interior Castle.* . . . Teresa's insight into the workings of God in the soul were always personal. May we not conclude that her vision was not of soul in general but of her own soul, her own transformed being? By this time she had reached full spiritual growth. What, in her as in us all, has at the outset been mere potentiality, has now become reality under the constant action of God and her own surrender to this action. . . . She gives us an idea of what God will do in a surrendered heart.[25]

So Burrows points to great value in Teresa's castle. Here we witness one who has truly become human, one who has truly realized her capacity for intimacy with God, and this serves as a sign of hope and encouragement for us on our own journey of becoming.

Burrows finds John of the Cross's view of humanity more immediately congenial to her own approach. In her book on John's spiritual teaching she states that "John is enamoured of human transcendence." In fact, "John's pathway up the mount," she says, "could rightly be entitled, 'On becoming human.'"[26] Burrows recognizes, though, that John's use of scholastic philosophy in his analysis of human existence could obscure the fundamental kinship between their anthropologies. She observes, "This philosophy with its endless divisions and subdivisions is alien to our way of thinking. We seek to unify. How easily we get the impression of departmentalism in John and of a programme to be pursued systematically."[27] So while Burrows envisions becoming human as a dynamic, unified process that unfolds to the extent that one exposes themselves to God, John's approach to this process, Burrows contends, can appear contrived and mechanistic.

Burrows sets out to show that this impression of John is "totally false,"[28] and in doing so emphasizes the common ground in their respective understandings of humanity. She penetrates to the essential teaching that John has framed with his scholastic categories and reveals that, like her, John actually views becoming human to be one progressive transformation that proceeds according to our surrender to God. Burrows comments, for instance, that we can be true to John's message and yet "sit light to the division of the night into two distinct parts, sense and spirit. They denote one growth, not two separate operations in two departments of our being."[29] And as to what occurs within this dark night, she begins by explaining that for John "God is always there intent on bringing us to the union with himself for which he made us. His presence to us in love has a two-fold simultaneous effect—that of purifying and transforming. God does not purify us through some agent other than himself and then when we are purified come to us and transform us."[30] Accordingly, while the dark night image "clearly suggests the aspect of purification as it is experienced by us . . . we must never forget that transformation (or we could equally well say 'becoming') is in exact proportion to purification."[31]

The Process of Becoming Human

We have established how Burrows situates her anthropology within her principal theological sources. So, as she marshals these, and other, less central, writings, to convey her insights, just what does Burrows say about how the process of becoming human "works"? This crucial question takes us to the very heart of Burrows's mystical doctrine.

Burrows expresses the fundamental task involved in the process of becoming human as a battle for faith, or trust, to triumph over the ego. It is worth noting here that in Burrows's usage, "faith" and "trust" are equivalent. As Elizabeth Ruth Obbard observes, "A word which comes up continually in all [Burrows's] writing is *faith* and its more usual counterpart, *trust*. . . . Faith is worked out in daily life by a growing trust in God."[32] Within her dynamic concept of "man becoming," Burrows sees faith, or trust, as "the march of our feet towards our journey's end; it is the beat of our wings of transcendence. . . . It is going forth from our finite world into the infinite being of God."[33] To introduce another image, to have faith is confidently to go to the God of love with empty hands. To act in faith, therefore, is to allow the emergence of our true self, our true human identity; "faith is perfect obedience, perfect response to the call of love, loyalty to our transcendence."[34] In a word, faith is consenting to become what we are: pure capacity for God.

The ego, on the other hand, is our "innate drive to control, possess, to find fulfilment within ourselves, of ourselves."[35] Quite contrary to the trajectory of faith, "the ego curls inwards and, like a carnivorous flower, draws everything else within it, destroying both them and itself";[36] its orientation is a betrayal of our fundamental call to transcendence, our call to be pure receptivity to the divine life. Accordingly, Burrows asserts that the "ego-centered movement is a perversion, it is disobedience in the fullest sense. It is sin."[37] Clearly, Burrows understands sin to consist not so much in specific, individual acts as in this ego-driven "refusal to respond to God's summons to become, to receive the only real life which he wishes to give. It is choosing to stay 'flesh.'"[38]

Becoming human, then, is a matter of launching outward in faith to be more and more possessed by God. And "faith can only develop," as Burrows says in the language of St. John of the Cross, "in so far as we impose 'night' on . . . that [innate] ego-desire to be for oneself, to have for oneself, to control, to possess, to be self-centered."[39] So how do we effect this "nighting" of the ego that is growth in faith? Burrows notes that here John of the Cross, for instance, "advises a frontal attack. He wants us to go clean against our desire for satisfaction, pleasure, consolation and *seek* the opposites."[40] She, however, is not convinced of the soundness of such an approach. "Far be it from me to say such a course is unwise," she deferentially insists, "but at least I would warn of dangers and suggest that, for most of us, it is not the best way."[41] She goes on to caution, "Such an approach tends to focus on ourselves, there is something contrived and self-conscious in it."[42] Burrows proposes that "the healthiest, most effective way" to escape the snare of the ego and so grow in faith "is to renew our fundamental intention of giving God everything, then fulfil our duties, serve our neighbour with all love regardless of whether it is pleasant or unpleasant to do so. Never fail to do a good work . . . because of lack of pleasure or sweetness; be ready to do those that are distasteful. . . . Even in spiritual exercises we must be indifferent and persevere whether they are pleasurable and satisfying or not."[43] Thus Burrows presents a method for developing the movement of faith that is thoroughly and simply integrated into the grain of everyday life. "This fundamental choice is actualized in the thousand and one concrete details that fill our hours and days."[44]

It is clear that Burrows's understanding of faith's daily exodus from selfishness to God-fullness, this process by which we become our true selves, encompasses our relationships with others as well as our relationship with God. In fact, Burrows perceives that loving relations with others mediate the development of our communion with God; "we love God in loving others," she affirms.[45] Expanding upon this idea, Burrows remarks, "We have an absolute need of others if we are to grow to full personhood but we need others in order to squander ourselves upon them."[46] We reach full personhood only when we are utterly penetrated by the divine life, so Burrows is implying here that the self-squander demanded by loving others opens out our surrender to God. As for how to actualize the diminishment of the ego and the increase of faith in one's immediate relationship with God, Burrows urges a flight from being guided by subjective emotional states in the interior life. "The only wise thing," she counsels, "is to abandon ourselves trustfully into God's hands. Until we pull ourselves out of our own spiritual lives, we only confuse and hinder. We need to cease our concern with our subjective reactions and stop our attempt to assess how we stand spiritually."[47]

> We have an absolute need of others if we are to grow to full personhood but we need others in order to squander ourselves upon them.

According to Burrows, the daily unfurling of egocentricity into trusting abandonment to God that lies at the heart of becoming human is realized through a collaboration between human effort and God's grace. She tells us, "The heart must be totally purified of egotism if we are to receive God fully. . . . Although we have to do all we can to deny our egotism wherever we meet it, its overthrow can only be a divine work."[48] Burrows adds an important nuance to this outline of the human-divine interplay in the work of faith when she explains, "We must go to our limits, helped by his ordinary grace. Only when we have come to the end of what we can do

is he able to step in with a direct, unmediated communication."[49] Evidently, there is for Burrows no such thing as "pure"
human effort in the battle for faith to triumph over the ego:
what we bring to the process of becoming human is already
undergirded by what she calls "ordinary grace." She describes
this grace as God's "ordinary presence and assistance to men
without which they could not exist, let alone act and grow."[50]

Even with the aid of ordinary grace, however, human effort
can only take us so far in the process of transforming the innate
inward drive of the ego into surrender in trust to God. As is
evident above, Burrows teaches that we must reach this natural
limit and then God will directly intervene with his "'over-and-
above' help" to truly transform our natural self-seeking into
trusting self-abandonment.[51] This immediate action of God
beyond the scope of what is humanly possible, which in fact
effects our full becoming as humans, is what Burrows names
"mystical grace." As she expounds in *Guidelines for Mystical
Prayer*, "God, in his love, offers himself to us as our fulfilment
and perfect happiness. He chooses to draw us into his own
radiant life. He calls us to transcend our natural limitations.
This call, his gracious working in us beyond our natural limits
and operations, and the transcendent goal to be reached, are
precisely what we call the mystical."[52] An important corollary
to note here is that since Burrows understands God's mystical
intervention to be intrinsically bound up with the call to be
human, she holds that the mystical life is intended for all; it is
"not the privileged way of the few."[53]

The idea that we are dependent upon the mystical action
of God to reach our true human fulfillment introduces a critical further dimension of Burrows's anthropology. We have
seen that, for Burrows, God's mystical intervention is his
direct, unmediated touch. In other words, it is God breaking

in upon the human being as "pure" God, God communicating his very self to humanity. Now it follows that if the infinite God is thus to give himself directly to a finite human being, God must himself forge the pathway of communication. As Burrows puts it, "This encounter with God himself, must, of its nature, bypass, or transcend our material faculties."[54] That God's mystical action is necessarily communicated in a supernatural mode contains an implication that is our real interest here. We will follow Burrows as she delineates her thought: "To say that, when God touches being with his own being, when he would give himself to us as God, he must necessarily by-pass the ordinary routes into the self and create one for himself which only he can use, is at the same time saying that this visitation, this contact is, of itself, inaccessible to ordinary perception. By the very nature of things it must be secret, hidden."[55] This pivotal idea that God's mystical action is inevitably hidden from human apprehension Burrows finds writ large in Scripture and in the work of John of the Cross.

The fact that the mystical action that ultimately effects our human becoming is necessarily hidden from ordinary human perception has a defining impact upon Burrows's anthropology. She sums up the essence of her thought here when she observes, "What is of most significance, what is most truly ourselves, escapes our detection, at a level not normally available to our conscious mind."[56] To be human, then, is to know one's true self only in unknowing; we are called into life as a potentiality for union with God, and the fulfillment of this potentiality is beyond not only human capability but also human comprehension. Burrows generally expresses this aspect of her anthropology in terms of mystery. She declares, for example, "We are beings oriented to mystery, we are made for it. Human fulfilment lies not in a vast treasure-house of knowledge of which we are master, not in a laying bare the secret of reality, not in dissolving mystery but in the full immediate experience of it."[57] Fundamentally related to the God who is infinite mystery, we necessarily have mystery written into our being; even more, "we ourselves are mystery and our proper ambience is mystery."[58]

Jesus Crucified as the Mediator of Human Fulfillment

Burrows's teaching on the only possible matrix within which to realize the process of becoming human now comes into view. According to Burrows, we can only realize our human vocation in Jesus crucified; only by entering into the utter self-emptying of Jesus can we fulfill the call to be utterly filled with the fullness of God. Clearly, then, Burrows considers the journey to human fulfillment that we have been tracing as something thoroughly Christocentric.

Throughout her writings Burrows affirms, "In Jesus we learn what man is, what God intends him to be."[59] For her, Jesus is the unique exemplar of what it means to be human; "he is *the* man."[60] Developing this thought, Burrows explains that Jesus is "the archetype of human transcendence. . . . He never deflected from the 'upward call,' never compromised with what would have detained him within the limits of 'the world.' He never stood for himself, never claimed self-sufficiency and independence. He saw himself always as an emptiness for receiving his Father."[61] Jesus was, in other words, the perfect Son of God. So in Jesus, and Jesus alone, that invitation to intimacy with God that constitutes human existence is accepted without reserve; he makes an absolute leap away from ego and into God, and so actualizes once and for all the capacity for union with God that defines humanity. In Burrows's words, "Human being only becomes what it is when it is handed over, given up and lost in the incomprehensible mystery of God. In Jesus this open-ended, self-abandoning, self-transcendent being has attained its goal, that towards which by its very essence it strives."[62]

Burrows details that Jesus' perfect realization of what it is to be human was something unfolding, dynamic. She observes that "Jesus . . . unlike the rest of us, [was] never less than he ought to be. Nevertheless, like all human beings he was subject to the law of human development. He had to become more fully who he really was."[63] Throughout each moment of his life, then, Jesus progressively activated his utter faithfulness to transcendence. "Day by day in the working out of his human existence in his dealings with persons and things, in trouble and disappointments, in searching for his Father's will" he was in an ever-deepening ecstatic movement towards the Father.[64] Burrows emphasizes that Jesus' "perfect surrender to his Father, enacted all his life, reach[ed] its climax in his death."[65] It was on the cross, she says, that "Jesus 'was made perfect,' achieved the term of transcendence."[66] Thus Jesus crucified is the supreme representation of what it means to be human; here self-emptying is at its greatest extent, openness to the inflow of God's love is complete.

It is vital here to make explicit what is already implicit: whenever Burrows discusses the crucifixion of Jesus, she also has his resurrection in mind. For her, these two realities are not sequential but simultaneous; they interpenetrate. We see this exemplified when, referring to Jesus' suffering and death, she writes, "He is caught up in the whirlwind of agony unabated. This is his hour of glory, his hour of purest love, when everything is outpoured, when his 'Amen' reaches its climax. This total self-emptying has an automatic counterpart, so to speak—he is fulfilled by the Father in his resurrection, glorification, ascension. It is consummated."[67] She expresses the same idea in a slightly different way with the claim, "In the same movement in which the Son delivers himself, dedicates himself, sacrifices himself, the Father receives, transfigures and glorifies him."[68] Evidently, in Burrows's view, Jesus' self-emptying death is but the reverse side of his being utterly penetrated by the divine life.

So, as Burrows sees it, all humans are fundamentally oriented to realize their selfhood through union with God, yet it is only in the crucified, risen Jesus that this human destiny is actually fulfilled. It follows that Jesus must function as a mediator if men and women are to become fully human; we can only become sons of God in the unique Son of God. Burrows introduces this idea when she comments that, whether they are aware of it or not, "every human person, just because a human person is a blood brother or sister of Jesus, is caught up into his life and destiny."[69] Created as a potential that is beyond our capability to actualize, we are inherently directed towards the One in whom our possibility is reality. Thus, while the ego-driven false self protests otherwise, the truth is that of ourselves "we do not know what human fulfilment is. We can neither conceive of it nor the path to it except in Jesus and him crucified."[70]

The struggle for faith to triumph over the ego that lies at the heart of becoming human, then, is intrinsically related to the life of the kenotic Christ; it is impossible to thrust away from selfishness and into intimacy with God apart from him. Expounding this doctrine that Jesus mediates the realization of our human vocation, Burrows remarks, "Jesus experienced himself as having no life of his own, no power, no wisdom. All these he derived from his Father. On our side, we derive all from Jesus. As the Father is his life, so Jesus is ours and thus the Father is ours. One with Jesus we live with him in the Father, from the Father. We must not think for a moment that transformation into Jesus robs a person of individuality, that from henceforth they have no emotions, no preferences, no interests. Transformation into Jesus means we become fully human."[71] If we are to become human we must become Jesus, and him crucified; there is no other way.

Burrows maintains that the two phases in the process of becoming human—the stage of human effort undergirded by ordinary grace and the mystical stage—are fundamentally an ever-deepening association with the life of Jesus crucified. Expressing her thought through her presentation of the teaching of John of the Cross, Burrows explains, "At the beginning of our spiritual journey John bids us take Jesus as our model, bids us have an avid appetite to imitate him in everything, constantly meditate on him. When we have grown spiritually we are invited to a deeper intimacy, a deeper sharing. John points us to Jesus in the great act of redemption, stripped of all, emptied out, brought to nothing. If we are to receive all God wants to give us we too must enter into this mystery of self-emptying."[72] So initially, desire to imitate the crucified Jesus motivates us to do what we can to release the true self from the tyranny of

> We must not think that transformation into Jesus robs a person of individuality, that from henceforth they have no emotions, no preferences, no interests. Transformation into Jesus means we become fully human.

the ego. What is necessary here, of course, is that "the appe-tite for self-gratification . . . be replaced with an appetite for Christ, for living our human lives as he lived his."[73] Modeling our lives on the life of Jesus, we exert every effort to imitate his refusal to seek fulfillment within the boundaries of the created world and his unswerving confident surrender to God's love.

For Burrows, while generous efforts to imitate the life of the kenotic Jesus are indispensable they are ultimately insuffi-cient. We saw earlier that God's mystical intervention is needed to effect that complete undoing of the ego that is the complete activation of our capacity for union with God. This is because, according to Burrows, the substance of God's mystical activ-ity is to immerse us directly into the life of the Crucified. "To attain to God," she writes, "we must die with Jesus: not of our-selves, or by ourselves, but 'in him.' I must enter into his death. This death is a death to my self-centeredness and self-posses-sion. . . . I cannot achieve it myself; it is wrought by God and is the effect of God's mystical contact."[74] Burrows goes on to explain that, in fact, "what we call the mystical, a direct, unme-diated contact with God, *is* Jesus. He is his living touch. We have this direct contact only in him. . . . His life is secretly, escaping our consciousness, substituting itself for ours. We are becoming Jesus. . . . Jesus *is* surrender, and what he shows us, what he enables us to do, is to surrender also. We have no other objective in this life; it is the fulfilment of our nature to effect this surrender."[75] The essence of the mystical life, then, is Jesus drawing us into his communion with God by living out his self-surrender in us. Thus we must become mystics, alive with the life of Jesus, if we are to become fully human.

The picture of Ruth Burrows's anthropology is now com-plete. It has become obvious that the figure of the crucified Christ stands at the center of her understanding of what it means to be human. Called into being as a capacity for the fullness of God, we gradually become human as faith progressively detaches the suction cups of the ego's insistence on finding this-worldly fulfillment and disposes us to remain upturned as pure receptivity for God. Burrows insists that only in Jesus is the human vocation realized perfectly; only Jesus was utterly faithful to humanity's essential orientation to self-transcendence, remaining always opened out in surrender to the Father. Jesus' perfect enactment of the human calling, his unwavering trusting abandonment to the Father, reached its culmination on the cross. In order to become what we are meant to be, then, we must abide in the life of Jesus crucified; our faith must derive from that of the Crucified if we are to become unalloyed emptiness for God's plenitude.

Ruth Burrows's Understanding of God

As we proceed now to explore Burrows's understanding of God, it will become evident that her anthropology is essentially an echo of her theology: human nature is what it is because of who God is. We will see that the pivot is Jesus crucified: at once he reveals both the fullness of humanity and the fullness of God.

The Essential Unknowability of God

The starting point of Burrows's theology is that the nature of God is completely unknowable to the unaided human intellect. Burrows opens her book *Living in Mystery* with the declaration,

> Holy Mystery. That has become my chosen way of speaking of ultimate reality. To say "God" is already to introduce

revelation. "God" is a relational term and that it can be used of the holy Mystery, that the holy Mystery offers to be our God, we know only through revelation. The world, of itself, does not reveal God. Even so, our God remains total Mystery, inaccessible to the created intellect, indefinable. . . . "Mystery," I suggest, leaves our subject outside all categories, beyond the range of words and concepts, stretching to infinitude. At least, it seems to me, the best we can do is to refuse definition or description.[76]

For Burrows, this notion of the fundamental incomprehensibility of the divine essence is grounded in Scripture. "In the scriptures," she observes, "God is 'holy' and this term was used in an effort to express his transcendence, his inmost being, his own world utterly separate from the world of men. It means God's own, unutterable existence."[77]

Revelation to the People of Israel

God's being is inaccessible to the created intellect, therefore, as Burrows notes, "if we are to know God it can only be because he chooses to reveal himself."[78] Following the traditional line of Catholic theology, Burrows maintains that God first revealed himself to the people of the Hebrew Scriptures. "This people," she writes, "had courage to believe in what we call revelation: that the incalculable, the unutterable Mystery had in some way 'spoken' to them, had not left them defenceless and in total ignorance. Holy Mystery had revealed itself to be their own God who made demands indeed, but who cared."[79] While holding this position, however, Burrows also points to a certain opaqueness in the revelation that we have through the Old Testament. She explains that "God was struggling, as it were, to break through," yet there was no human heart malleable enough completely to bear God's self-offer;[80] or, to change the image, "there was no one of sufficient transparency to receive him."[81] For Burrows, then, the Old Testament offers a valuable, but ultimately inadequate, window upon the inner life of God.

Jesus Crucified as the Definitive Revelation of the Divine Nature

Not lingering with the incomplete vision of God rendered by the Old Testament, Burrows centers her theology on the truth that Jesus Christ is the definitive revelation of God. In other words, in order to say what there is to say about the unutterable God, Burrows looks to Jesus, for in him "God's own self is given to us, nothing less. In Jesus' person we encounter the holy Mystery directly."[82] Burrows approaches Jesus' perfect manifestation of the divine reality by way of his complete actualization of the human vocation. Thus, according to Burrows, it is precisely by being perfectly self-transcendent, always dispossessed of self and poised toward the infinite, that the man Jesus is the incarnation of God himself. "Jesus is a receptivity so absolute that he is true God of true God."[83] To put it a different way, "For Jesus, God's name, his true being, is precisely Father."[84] And it is in being Son—utterly empty, utterly dependent, the definitive embodiment of what it means to be human—that Jesus perfectly reflects the Fatherhood of God.

If the very essence of the divine penetrates Jesus' perfect realization of the human vocation, and if this perfect realization of the human vocation reaches its culmination on the cross, then it follows that, for Burrows, it is ultimately in the Crucified that we see what it means for God to be God. What we learn from Christ crucified, Burrows observes, is "that the very essence of the Father is to be self-giving love, a love that keeps nothing back, that is totally ecstatic. We see what we could never have dreamed of, omnipotence that operates only in weakness and self-sacrifice."[85]

Elaborating on this stunning mystery of the cross as the doorway upon the divine, Burrows declares,

> If we want to know God, Reality, Bedrock and Ground, Absolute Origin, ineffable Mystery . . . we must look at Jesus crucified. Holding up the cross, bidding us gaze into that bleeding, humiliated face, the Holy Spirit's focus is not first and foremost on suffering, or even on sin and its consequences, but on a love that is absolute, "out of this world," "other," "what no eye has seen, nor ear heard, nor the human heart conceived." We must gaze and gaze with fullest attention and then affirm: this is God; this is what God is really like. Through this vision we have the certainty of what is beyond our comprehension, that God is love and nothing but love, and that he is love to and for us. . . . What we see in Jesus is a Self-gift on God's part that is the fullest content of love. God gives not gifts but God's own Self.[86]

Burrows holds that the ecstasy of love revealed on the cross is the lens through which the other divine characteristics are to be contemplated. "Power, holiness, justice," she writes, "whatever other attributes we impute to . . . God are nothing but expressions of God's nature as Love. It is Love that is almighty, unutterable holiness, supremely just, and so forth. . . . And this Love has the special quality of compassion, tender understanding and loving acceptance of us in all our sinfulness."[87]

Summary: The Three Stages of the Spiritual Life

It has become clear that the final word of Burrows's anthropology and of her theology is the cross. As Burrows concludes, "Jesus crucified [is] at once the expression of human transcendence and the self-expending love of God."[88] We see in the Crucified that the very reason humanity is called to be self-abandoning, all aspiration toward the divine, is because God is an ecstasy of love. "It is the Father's excess of love for us that, in filling the heart of Jesus, drives Jesus to his self-emptying."[89] And it is into this kenosis that we must be drawn if we are to become human and if we are to allow God to be God.

In the following chapters, Burrows's thought on being immersed into the "yes" to love of Jesus crucified will be examined. For Burrows, to speak of being drawn into the kenotic Christ is to speak of the workings of God's mystical grace—so what follows is an exploration of Burrows's conception of the progress of the mystical life. In various ways throughout her works, Burrows adopts the tradition of dividing the spiritual journey into three stages. She asserts that this "is no fanciful fabrication but arises from the very nature of things, God being what he is and we being what we are."[90]

In the beginning, says Burrows, "We have not yet 'come' to Jesus."[91] Confidently self-possessed we live, so to speak, on the outskirts of the Crucified; the first stage, then, is about preparing to be immersed directly into the life of Jesus. Burrows describes the second stage of the spiritual life as "the soul's encounter with the suffering Son of Man, a sharing in his death."[92] This stage of gradual transformation into the crucified Christ is generally long and rigorous, Burrows observes, involving as it does a complete undoing of the ego.[93] And at the third stage of the spiritual life, one is finally "totally possessed by Jesus, identified with him in his surrender to his Father."[94] Here one is alive with the risen life of Christ, knowing in an incomparable way that "his death . . . is only the reverse of life,"[95] that to be utterly dispossessed of self is to be utterly possessed by God. Of the one dwelling at the summit of the spiritual journey Burrows writes, "This happy creature is at last fully Christian, fully human."[96]

Notes

1. Ruth Burrows, *Guidelines for Mystical Prayer*, foreword by B. C. Butler (1976; repr., London: Continuum, 2007; Denville, N.J.: Dimension, 1980), 9.

2. Ruth Burrows, "Carmel: A Stark Encounter with the Human Condition," in *Essence of Prayer* (London: Burns and Oates, 2006; Mahwah, N.J.: HiddenSpring, 2006), 183.

3. Ibid., 185.

4. Ruth Burrows, *Ascent to Love: The Spiritual Teaching of St. John of the Cross* (London: Darton, Longman and Todd; Denville, N.J.: Dimension, 1992, 1987), 19.

5. Ibid., 42.

6. Ruth Burrows, *Our Father: Meditations on the Lord's Prayer* (London: Darton, Longman and Todd, 1986; Denville, N.J.: Dimension, 1986), 25. Burrows clarifies here that the word "son," in the sense she is using it, "transcends gender."

7. Ruth Burrows, *Interior Castle Explored: St. Teresa's Teaching on the Life of Deep Union with God* (1981; repr., London: Continuum, 2007; Mahwah, N.J.: HiddenSpring, 2007), 10.

8. Ruth Burrows, *To Believe in Jesus* (1978; repr., London: Continuum, 2010; Mahwah, N.J.: HiddenSpring, 2010), 39.

9. See Burrows, *Our Father*, 28.

10. Burrows, *To Believe in Jesus*, 39. This dynamic character of Burrows's anthropology means there is a certain elasticity in her terminology. Hence terms such as "man," "human," "human being," "humanity," "self," and "person" can refer both to the capacity for union with God and to that capacity as fulfilled or activated. Accordingly, it is best to focus not so much on the precise words that Burrows uses in her discussion of humanity but rather on her guiding principle that we are to become what we are in potential.

11. Burrows, *Guidelines for Mystical Prayer*, 9. Karl Rahner was a chief exponent of this dynamic understanding of human nature, and Burrows acknowledges her indebtedness to him at several points throughout her writings. In *Living in Mystery*, for example, she writes, "Karl Rahner's essay, 'The Concept of Mystery in Catholic Theology,' continues to inspire me. There I found, long years ago, conceptual expression for what I hold to be my deepest convictions." Ruth Burrows, *Living in Mystery*, introduction by Wendy Beckett (London: Sheed and Ward, 1996), 5.

12. Burrows, *Interior Castle Explored*, 7.

13. Ibid., 31.

14. Ibid., 8.

15. Ibid.

16. Burrows, *To Believe in Jesus*, 69.

17. Burrows, *Interior Castle Explored*, 6.

18. Ibid.

19. Burrows, *Interior Castle Explored*, 6.

20. Ibid., 7.

21. Ibid.

22. Ibid.

23. Ibid., 6.

24. Ibid., 79.

25. Ibid., 10–11.

26. Burrows, *Ascent to Love*, 7.

27. Ibid., 10.

28. Ibid.

29. Burrows, *Ascent to Love*, 50.

30. Ibid., 49.

31. Ibid., 49–50.

32. Elizabeth Ruth Obbard, introduction, in *The Watchful Heart: Daily Readings with Ruth Burrows* (London: Darton, Longman and Todd, 1988), xii.

33. Burrows, *Ascent to Love*, 104.

34. Ibid., 23.

35. Ibid., 21.

36. Ibid.

37. Ibid.

38. Burrows, *Interior Castle Explored*, 13. See also Ruth Burrows, *Before the Living God* (1975; repr., London: Burns and Oates, 2008; Mahwah, N.J.: HiddenSpring, 2008), 11.

39. Burrows, *Ascent to Love*, 23.

40. Ibid., 33.

41. Ibid.

42. Ibid.

43. Ibid.

44. Ibid., 104.

45. Burrows, *Guidelines for Mystical Prayer*, 23.

46. Ibid., 77.

47. Ruth Burrows, "Faith, Trust, Surrender to God: This Is Prayer," in *Essence of Prayer*, 29.

48. Burrows, *Ascent to Love*, 107–8.

49. Ruth Burrows, "Prayer That Is Jesus," in *Essence of Prayer*, 38.

50. Burrows, *To Believe in Jesus*, 22.

51. Ibid., 32.

52. Burrows, *Guidelines for Mystical Prayer*, 9.

53. Ibid., 10.

54. Burrows, *Interior Castle Explored*, 38.

55. Burrows, *Guidelines for Mystical Prayer*, 45–46.

56. Burrows, *Living in Mystery*, 3.

57. Burrows, *Ascent to Love*, 72.

58. Ibid., 20.

59. Ibid., 7.

60. Ibid., 82.

61. Ibid., 7.

62. Ibid., 117.

63. Burrows, *Living in Mystery*, 83.

64. Burrows, *Ascent to Love*, 82.

65. Burrows, *To Believe in Jesus*, 80.

66. Burrows, *Ascent to Love*, 7.

67. Ruth Burrows, *Through Him, With Him, In Him: Meditations on the Liturgical Seasons* (London: Sheed and Ward, 1987; Denville, N.J.: Dimension, 1987), 88.

68. Ibid., 98.

69. Burrows, *Living in Mystery*, 33. See also Burrows, *Through Him*, 14.

70. Burrows, *Ascent to Love*, 47.

71. Burrows, *Interior Castle Explored*, 115.

72. Burrows, *Ascent to Love*, 96.

73. Ibid., 23.

74. Burrows, "Prayer That Is Jesus," 38.

75. Burrows, *Interior Castle Explored*, 108.

76. Burrows, *Living in Mystery*, 7. It must be noted that while Burrows claims here that "the world, of itself, does not reveal God," she admits in another work, "we have St. Paul telling the Romans of the God they can know from the observation of visible things." Burrows, *To Believe in Jesus*, 16. This apparent contradiction is due to Burrows's varying use of the word "God." In the passage from *Living in Mystery* "God" points to the inner life of the divine, whereas in the passage from *To Believe in Jesus* the word is used in a more broad sense. In both works, Burrows insists that the essence of God is unknowable to the created human faculties. Indeed, the passage from *To Believe in Jesus* is followed by the assertion that, to the human intellect, "he is essentially the 'unknown God.' . . . Beyond the fact that he is maker of heaven and earth we know nothing about him." Ibid.

77. Burrows, *To Believe in Jesus*, 90.

78. Burrows, *Our Father*, 30.

79. Burrows, *Living in Mystery*, 8–9.

80. Ruth Burrows, interview by author, Quidenham, UK, October 4, 2009.

81. Burrows, *Ascent to Love*, 97.

82. Burrows, *Living in Mystery*, 32.

83. Burrows, *Ascent to Love*, 117.

84. Burrows, *Our Father*, 26.

85. Burrows, *Ascent to Love*, 82–83.

86. Ruth Burrows, "If You Knew the Gift of God . . . ," in *Essence of Prayer*, 46.

87. Mark Allen and Ruth Burrows, *Letters on Prayer: An Exchange on Prayer and Faith* (London: Sheed and Ward, 1999), 42–43.

88. Burrows, *Ascent to Love*, 83.

89. Burrows, "If You Knew," 47.

90. Burrows, *To Believe in Jesus*, 30.

91. Ibid.

92. Burrows, *Interior Castle Explored*, 55.

93. See Burrows, *To Believe in Jesus*, 31.

94. Burrows, *Guidelines for Mystical Prayer*, 118.

95. Burrows, *Interior Castle Explored*, 108–9.

96. Burrows, *Guidelines for Mystical Prayer*, 118.

CHAPTER 3

The First Stage of the Spiritual Life according to Ruth Burrows

Preparing to Be Drawn into the "Yes" of Jesus Crucified

According to Ruth Burrows's thought, the first stage of the spiritual life is "pre-mystical." It is about beginning to become human. As we saw in the previous chapter, for Burrows "God's call to us to receive love and be drawn into sacred intimacy is what defines our humanness."[1] We become human to the extent that we thrust away from complacency and respond to the divine invitation to relationship. This process of becoming human can only be realized within Jesus crucified, the singular exemplar and mediator of human existence. The first stage of the spiritual life represents the fragile beginnings of our assent to God's self-bestowal; it is the nascent actualization of our essential "for-Godness." Burrows insists that what distinguishes those at this initial stage is that they are not yet participating directly in the life of Jesus and sharing in his unique communion with God. Given that the human person is created for intimacy with God, this stage is obviously not an end in itself. "God doesn't want us to stay here," says Burrows. "He didn't create, didn't redeem us for this."[2] Rather, its proper function is as a preparatory ground for the advent of God's mystical grace, the dawning of our transformation into the kenotic Christ.

In this chapter we will first explore Burrows's view of how the human capacity for God begins to be activated and what she says about the mystery of coming to faith in Jesus. Following this we will discuss Burrows's portrayal of the characteristics of Christian beginners and the advice she offers beginners for preparing to be drawn into the life of Jesus crucified.

ACTIVATING THE FIRST STAGE OF THE SPIRITUAL LIFE

For Ruth Burrows, to be created human is to be in potential at the first stage of the spiritual life. If God's invitation to relationship is the origin of human existence, if we are "born into natural life with a potential for receiving God himself,"[3] then to be human at all is to be oriented toward the spiritual life. However, this capacity to enter into communion with God is not activated automatically. Burrows explains, "We cannot not be within [the] divine enfolding and self-offering of God. . . . But this relationship can remain undeveloped. A baby in its mother's womb is in relationship with her but is unaware of it and does not respond to the mother's intense love and desire to give herself to her child. The relationship with God on the human side can remain as minimal as that of the baby. Love must be freely given, freely received and freely returned."[4]

Burrows expresses this same idea in a different way in *Guidelines for Mystical Prayer*. There, referring to the first island,[5] she declares, "Everyone . . . is born into it, comes to birth in the caverns under its surface."[6] What Burrows is indicating here is that while we are born within the orbit of God's transformative action, we come into being curled in upon ourselves in instinctive self-seeking; the surface of the island is not inaccessible to us, yet we are born ensnared within its caverns' "sweet, fascinating, deadly charm . . . that of independence, 'godhead,' the primal, ever-recurring temptation."[7] The stronghold of self-orientation needs to be shaken if we are to activate our potential to enter into God's own life.

With the slightest fraying of the tether of self-centeredness, the first stage of the spiritual life proper begins; we truly begin to become human. According to Burrows, most human beings are at this early stage of realizing their potential for communion with God. Surveying the surface of the first island she remarks, "What a vast land is this first island and how densely populated! It can be presumed that the great majority of men and women dwell on it. Its inhabitants range from those with the crudest of moralities, following their feebly-lit, maybe erroneous conscience, to those who like the young man in the Gospel, can sincerely say of the commandments of God, 'all these have I kept from my youth.'"[8] The main thrust of Burrows's doctrine is that fidelity to the divine call to self-transcendence is enacted through relationship with Jesus Christ. However, as this passage reveals, Burrows suggests within her writings that it is also possible to activate our essential "for-Godness" in ways that are not explicitly religious. This aspect of her spiritual doctrine accounts for Burrows's perception of the surface of the first island as densely inhabited.

Burrows's openness to the possibility of nonreligious actuation of our capacity for God derives from her understanding of the human person. We are created for relationship with God, so we are oriented to the absolute horizon prior to encountering any explicit formulation of that horizon. In the words of Karl Rahner—a theologian in whose writings Burrows has found her own convictions expressed—"Man always lives by the holy mystery, even where he is not conscious of it."[9] So with her view of the human person as primordially inclined toward the infinite, Burrows can claim that "human beings desire happiness and are endlessly seeking for it. They are longing for what is beautiful, good and, ultimately, for what is absolutely so. In the measure that we choose rightly, choose what is really true and good, we become ever more authentically human and our Maker and Lover is able to communicate with us in increasing fullness. We become imbued with eternal life, God's own life."[10] Clearly, Burrows is suggesting here that the movement beyond the self that enables our human becoming need not be deliberately religious; we need not know that we are choosing God in choosing what is true, good, and beautiful. She makes this position explicit when she rhetorically asks if we can "conceive of a human being who has not one spark of goodness in him, who is mere smoking flax." She continues, "It might be no more than kindness to a bird or animal but in so far as it is goodness, in so far as it is human, it is truly godly, truly 'heaven' and heaven belongs to heaven."[11] It is important to note that Burrows understands God to be intimately involved in this nonexplicit opting for the divine life. She holds that any advance out of the ego is "the effect of grace, of God's will to draw us into his own life," even if the object of that advance is not perceived as divine.[12]

Notwithstanding what we have just discussed, we know Burrows's primary position is that we actuate the first stage of the spiritual life through assenting to the person and message of Jesus Christ. Of course, it must not be assumed that by assenting to Jesus individuals automatically activate their capacity for communion with God; one can profess belief in Jesus and remain entirely cocooned within the self. As Burrows puts it, "We must allow for the possibility of sinners, believers or unbelievers, for those who have deliberately chosen to dwell in the caverns underground."[13] Be that as it may, in keeping with the spirit of Burrows's writings, the assumption in all that follows is that a decision to follow Jesus contains some degree of effort to move off the ego and into relationship with God.

> The movement beyond the self that enables our human becoming need not be deliberately religious; we need not know that we are choosing God in choosing what is true, good, and beautiful.

COMING TO FAITH IN JESUS CHRIST

So just how does one come to faith in Jesus Christ? How does one come to make that choice to accept Jesus of Nazareth as the revelation of God through which we become human? Not only is Burrows brief in her treatment of how we come to faith, but also what she does say on the topic is not entirely consistent. In *Ascent to Love* Burrows observes that "the relation between our human activity and the activity of God remains mysterious and delicate and is not easily expressed."[14] It is precisely this elusive relationship between the grace of God and the human will that Burrows variously handles as she considers the question of how one comes to believe in Jesus. Although she is consistent in her insistence that both grace and human volition are involved in the process of conversion, Burrows gives varying emphasis to each of these factors throughout her writings.

On the few occasions in her earlier works that she addresses the subject of coming to faith in Jesus, Burrows tends to stress the activity of the human will. She declares in *To Believe in Jesus*, for instance, "Faith is a gift but a gift that will undoubtedly be given if we take the necessary steps and choose to believe, choose to take God at his word and stake our lives on it."[15] In the same vein she later insists, "Sooner or later we have to make a decision. We have to choose to believe or reject belief. The great, fundamental question put to us, in which all else is contained, is precisely 'do you believe in the Son of Man?'"[16] This emphasis on the human part to be played in the process of conversion is echoed in *Ascent to Love*. "We are not asked to make a completely irrational act of belief," explains Burrows. "There are facts for the mind to consider and weigh so as to bring us to a decision whether or not we are justified in putting our faith in Jesus, in his insights, his knowledge of

God, his values. It is a human judgment and a human assent such as we make in ordinary relations. Of course the gravity of the matter and its consequences give it a unique character: its object lifts it far above all other acts of faith, but *as a human act* it is on the same level."[17] These passages obviously indicate that in the earlier phase of her writings Burrows conceived of coming to faith as principally an act of the human will. Without denying the necessity of grace, she conveys that it is enough to will conversion for conversion to be effected.

In her more recent writings, Burrows generally shifts to highlighting the impenetrable workings of God when she visits the topic of coming to faith in Jesus. "Faith itself is a mystery," she admits in *Living in Mystery*.

> Why is it that some people are able to believe and others not? . . . What of those, apparently sincere who, having examined the claims of Christianity, read the New Testament and still withhold belief? People can be exposed to the same influences, given the same teaching and perhaps only one or two of a group will give committed assent. The evangelist John brooded over this question. Though he rounds on some as deliberately refusing the light, choosing not to see because their self-interest is threatened, he realises that this is not always the case and he bows before the mystery. "No one can come to me unless the Father who sent me draws him." . . . Faith, then, is not merely a human decision but a divine gift, given to some, withheld from others.[18]

This conception of conversion is obviously some distance from the one we saw articulated in Burrows's earlier works. It is a position that she also presents to her correspondent in *Letters on Prayer*. "There is an unbridgeable gap," she states, "between seeing/hearing a creative, life-giving 'word' (that can come as event, an inner or outward experience) and its fruit-bearing. . . . Ultimately it is the Holy Spirit who bridges the unbridgeable gap between belief and unbelief."[19] Burrows's treatment of the corollary of emphasizing the role of grace in coming to faith is noteworthy. She reflects, "Can God have favourites? A god who gives gifts to some but arbitrarily denies them to others? This is not the Father of Jesus who, in Jesus, gives all there is to give. . . . In Jesus we are sure that all is always love and ordained to love: gifts given, gifts withheld."[20]

In the end, the tension between Burrows's emphases on human willing and the activity of God is most representative of her perspective on how we come to faith. For Burrows, the primary commitment to follow Jesus emerges from a collaboration between grace and nature about which neither she nor any other theologian is able to speak with any precision. Burrows is clear that, however it is effected, conversion may be a marked occurrence, or it may be something more gradual. Perhaps mindful of her own personal experience, Burrows is comfortable allowing "conversion" to denote "that 'moment'—not infrequently it is a memorable event—when a person, hitherto rather heedless of divine things, casual in relation to life's deepest meaning, is suddenly enlightened, shocked into realisation and, of course, is faced with the decision to live a 'Yes' or a 'No.'"[21] At the same time, Burrows is well aware that "many people can never point to [a] particular moment when they came to a clear realisation of the shoddiness of their lives and the paramount need to do something about it."[22] She insists, though, that a hidden, cumulative decision to assent to the revelation of God in Jesus of Nazareth need not be any less authentic than a more obvious, immediate one.

CHARACTERISTICS OF THE FIRST STAGE
OF THE CHRISTIAN LIFE

The first stage of a life explicitly committed to following Jesus covers, as it were, a considerable amount of spiritual territory. Nevertheless, Burrows is able to identify and discuss overall characteristics of the initial stage of the Christian journey.

Beginners as Fundamentally Self-Possessed

For Burrows, the distinguishing feature of beginners in the Christian life is that they are not yet sharing in the life of Christ crucified and participating in his singular intimacy with the Father. Burrows sums up their condition when she asserts that, although they have decided to follow Jesus, "They still approach God in Old Testament fashion. . . . They are bypassing Jesus, settling within the confines of created things, managing themselves, basically seeking themselves. This is not to enter into the mystery of the crucified Jesus."[23] To be sure, this is a rather severe appraisal of people who would, after all, call themselves Christian. Still, Burrows maintains that to truly be Christian (indeed, to truly be human) is to live immersed in the Crucified, and so she treats this lesser state accordingly.

If individuals have not entered into the life of Jesus cruci-fied, have not made their own his trusting, self-abandoning "yes" to the Father, it must be that they are living from the cre-ated self, the ego. Thus, another way to present Burrows's per-spective on what basically characterizes beginners is to say that, for her, they are fundamentally self-possessed. Even though there is some weakening of the innate dominance of the ego at the first phase of the spiritual journey, some emerging real-ization of our capacity for God, the self remains ultimately in command. As Burrows allegorizes about our Christian beginnings, "It is as if God endows us with wing structure. We have to work the muscles of these embryonic wings to make them develop but no matter how much we try, we cannot get off the ground, that is, away from self."[24]

Relating to God through Material Agency Alone

Given that the created self is the only center of operation that beginners can know, it follows that there is a basic materiality to the first stage of the Christian life. Burrows unpacks this point by explaining, "What we usually mean by will and understanding relates to our material being, commensurate with ourselves. . . . To begin with there is nothing more to us than this materiality. We are "flesh" in the scriptural sense. When we relate to God consciously, when we pray we do so with what we are: we try to know him and love him within the bounds of what we are, which is 'flesh.'"[25] If our relationship with God at the first stage of the spiritual life is defined by the capacity of our human faculties, this relationship, by Burrows's account, must be fundamentally limited: we cannot know and love God as he is in himself.[26] She holds that here the content of faith is "more or less notional and not part of the self. It is truth about God, God 'out there.'"[27] Burrows is keen to make clear that the intrinsically limited relationship between God and the Christian beginner, this "miserable, unworthy manner of knowing and loving him," is not due to any lack of generosity on God's part.[28] "On his side it is total gift," she stresses; "it is on our side that the check lies."[29] In the beginning our capacity for God is simply not sufficiently realized for us to receive God as God.

So, practically, what does it mean for beginners to commune with God according to the material agency of the will and the intellect? Burrows teaches that "where there is no spiritual 'depth' for God to touch directly, [and so] he can only communicate with the [material] reality that is there . . . God's appeals come through the body, through the senses, by means of good conversations, sermons, books, good thoughts and feelings, sickness, trials and other events of life."[30]

Thus at the nascent stage of becoming human, when our potential for receiving God is yet only commensurate with the capacity of our human faculties, God communicates to us indirectly, through the various means that are the proper data of the human faculties. Burrows parallels God's indirect self-communication to the beginner with his dealings with the people of the Old Testament. To the people of Israel, says Burrows, "he reveals himself in signs and figures; through the events of history he trains and forms his people until the time has come for his direct intervention."[31] Burrows maintains that the drama of salvation must be played out in every human heart: as the "signs and figures" of Israel's history gave way to the person of Jesus, so must the divine echoes in the life of the beginner prepare the way for the unmediated presence of God.[32]

The Spiritual Self-Confidence of Beginners

Burrows details that the self-orientation characteristic of beginners also means that a spirit of security and complacency pervades the first stage of the spiritual life. "The sense of well-being on this [first] island must be stressed," she declares in *Guidelines for Mystical Prayer*.[33] With the ego wholly in command and thus the extent of the beginner's relationship with God determined by the innate possibilities of the human faculties, the task of Christian living appears eminently achievable to the beginner. As Burrows puts it, "Just because we are limited to our own activity, just because God is giving himself only in a far-off sort of way under ideas and concepts which are the proper data of human activity, we are at peace. We can cope, are in control of the situation. Often enough, we will feel spiritually capable, will feel that we really do know and love God."[34]

Evidently, the self-assurance experienced by beginners leads them to believe that they are in fact living at the summit of the Christian life. "Those who live on the first island," observes Burrows, "feel it is the whole world, they do not know there is anything beyond."[35] There is thus a great paradox at the initial stage of the Christian life. Living outside of the Crucified, one is far from fulfilling the human vocation to be possessed by God, yet they feel spiritually secure, successful. Burrows teaches that if we are truly to become human, "if God is to take possession of us, we must be drawn out of this security, we must lose control, or rather hand over the control of our life to God."[36]

According to Burrows, the spiritual self-confidence of beginners, paradoxical as it is, finds its most pronounced expression in what may broadly be termed their approach to the moral life. In the beginning, she maintains, we are compelled by "an innate drive to seek our own perfection within the dimensions of what we understand and consciously experience."[37] Or, presenting this same insight in a different manner, Burrows comments that at the first stage of the Christian life, "we see ourselves as the agents of our own sanctification, God being there simply to help us."[38] How, in Burrows's view, does this confident thrust toward self-perfection develop? She details that, as fundamentally self-possessed beginners, we have the tendency to "reduce God to our own likeness, and this in great measure . . . because we have not taken the trouble to go to the source, to find out for ourselves in the scriptures, and above all in Jesus, what he is really like. We prefer to live with our preconceived notions or with what others communicate to us, and the result is a caricature of God."[39] Of course we do not admit that we are fashioning God in our own likeness; that would only

> If God is to take possession of us, we must be drawn out of security, we must lose control, or rather hand over the control of our life to God.

nullify our self-satisfaction. Yet, following the demands of our egocentricity, we secretly place ourselves at the center of the spiritual life.

Burrows explains that, dealing with a God of our own creation, we subtly feel assured of achieving perfection. Having created God in our own image, we are in control of establishing the boundaries of the spiritual life; accordingly, "we can . . . set a level of virtue for ourselves that lies within our own compass and so remain complacent."[40] However, precisely because we are charting the path of righteousness for ourselves, our apparent perfection is really rooted in selfishness. In beginners, Burrows notes, "virtue is often more apparent than real, the roots of sin remain strong and tenacious but the foliage, for the present, looks alright."[41] As we saw in the previous chapter, for Burrows the basis of all sin is choosing to remain in our primordial egocentricity.[42] Burrows perceives that the illusory nature of the beginner's "perfection" is shown for what it is when the primacy of the self is threatened. She draws our attention to "those seemingly trifling incidents, a slight that arouses my indignation; note how I stand on my dignity, claim my little rights."[43] Such defensiveness, says Burrows, clearly indicates that the tyranny of the ego is far from overthrown.

Probing further, Burrows reveals that in confidently, albeit unconsciously, approaching the Christian life as a set of self-made precepts to be mastered, the beginner is essentially attempting to strong-arm God into guaranteeing their spiritual security. "We like to feel sure that, if we have done our duty well, kept the law, lived to the best of our lights, everything must be alright. Justice is satisfied; not even God can ask more. God owes it to us to see that we get a just reward!"[44] Obviously, if God is created in our own fallen likeness, we cannot have a living knowledge "that all is pure gift, that I can't earn advancement, that I can't, by doing this, that, or the other, demand of God, 'now do your part!'"[45] So Burrows shows us that, in the quest for sanctification, the ego-directed beginners instinctively prefer to pull the strings of a puppet God rather than entrust themselves to the God whose nature is mystery to the created self.

There is a corollary to be noted here. Burrows observes that living by a God whose standards we set, we cannot risk not meeting those standards, "we can't afford to be ugly."[46] If God is not the unconditional lover revealed by Jesus but is, like us, swayed by human performance, there is no place for moral failure. "We bury it all deep down," Burrows remarks, "and manage to achieve a state of relative self-satisfaction."[47] In the end, then, what Burrows discloses is that at the first stage of the Christian life, "tremendous inner energies are at work to produce this 'perfection' which has in fact nothing to do with true growth."[48] Only when the ego is replaced by the life of Jesus crucified is sanctification truly possible.

RUTH BURROWS'S ADVICE FOR BEGINNERS

The objective of the advice that Ruth Burrows offers those at the first stage of the spiritual life is that they prepare themselves to be drawn into the mystical life, that is, that they prepare to be taken into the life of Jesus crucified. We have seen that, by Burrows's account, Christian beginners know a very early realization of that capacity for self-transcendence and communion with God that makes us human; they are able to relate to God in an indirect manner. Ultimately, though, Burrows considers beginners to be anchored in the ego; while they profess faith in Jesus, they are fundamentally living from the self rather than within the life of the crucified Christ. Burrows insists that "we cannot rid ourselves of this deeply rooted pride and self-possession by our own strength. Only the Holy Spirit of the Crucified and Risen One can effect it."[49] So it is only through an infusion of God's mystical grace, only through allowing Jesus to live his definitive "yes" to the Father within us, that we can truly be released from self and become fully human.

Burrows is concerned to show beginners how they can strive to conform themselves to the pattern of the crucified Christ. If she wants beginners to prepare to be drawn away from egocentricity and into the self-abandonment of the Crucified, the way to achieve this is surely through counseling them to imitate the kenotic Christ to the full extent of their human capabilities. While Burrows is clear that no amount of human effort can merit God's coming to us to break the innate stronghold of the ego, she asserts that it is necessary that we work generously to dispose ourselves to God's mystical intervention. Expanding upon this point, she writes, "God isn't standing by saying: 'Now let me see you trying. When I see you have really tried, I will step in and help.' No, this delay of God is in the nature of things. God is offering himself to me here and now but I cannot receive him. I must have reached a certain level of development before I can begin to do so. . . . God can only come in with his mystical 'over-and-above' help when man has reached his limits and can go no further."[50] Burrows's advice to beginners, then, is about how they can beat their wings of transcendence, knowing that such sustained effort is inherently incapable of lifting them away from self, yet a necessary anticipation of the gracious intervention of God. Before moving on, it is important that we recall here that, for Burrows, we never labor unaided in the Christian life; our human efforts at "unselfing" are always undergirded, she says, by God's "ordinary grace."[51]

So, as we survey her various writings, just what emerges as Burrows's advice to beginners? How does she propose that we strive to carve out the pattern of Jesus crucified upon our lives in preparation for his gratuitous coming to us to take us directly into his own perfect self-abandonment? In her article "Initial Prayer within the Carmelite Tradition," Burrows claims that "if we are to receive this priceless gift or Gift, we must make up our minds to a sustained moral effort and mental labour."[52] Moral effort and mental labor, or, respectively, asceticism and meditation, constitute the two interrelated foci of Burrows's counsel to beginners.

The Mental Labor of Meditation

In Burrows's vision, the labor of meditation both indicates the shape of, and provides the incentive for, the beginner's ascetical efforts.

Discovering the Way of the Crucified Christ

If the beginner is to make a serious attempt to take on the life of Jesus crucified, it is first necessary that he or she comes to know about this Jesus. "We must strive to acquire an intellectual knowledge of him," she declares, "of his attitudes, values and teaching. This intellectual knowledge is certainly not intimacy, certainly not a 'knowing Jesus,' but it is an indispensable ingredient for intimacy and real knowing."[53] We have noted that a chief characteristic of beginners is that their relationship with God is defined by the capacity of their human faculties; here Burrows is exhorting them to use the mind's capacity to the full.

Burrows fervently maintains that knowledge of Jesus must derive primarily from persistent meditation on the New Testament, especially the Gospels. "My advice to all," she pronounces, "is to study the New Testament, especially the Gospels, in order to get to know Jesus and so recognise him as the Way, Truth and Life."[54] As Burrows sees it, "We become so familiar with the Gospel parables and stories; we have listened to them time and time again, so that we think we know and understand them. But have we really 'heard' them? Have they resounded in our hearts with power?"[55] Thus Burrows counsels beginners—indeed, all believers—that earnest engagement with the New Testament is imperative to grasping what it means to live according to the crucified Christ; there we can perceive that mind of Christ we are called to make our own.

For Burrows, prayer is a privileged setting for acquiring knowledge of Jesus through meditation on the New Testament. She presents beginners with a method of prayerfully meditating upon the Scriptures intended to expose them to the person and message of Jesus. Burrows notes that this method of hers "is closely akin to what St. Teresa was suggesting to her novice" in chapter 26 of the *Way of Perfection*.[56] Expounding her method of prayer, Burrows writes,

> We don't have to go back two thousand years and imagine ourselves in Palestine. The same Jesus whom we meet in the Gospels, healing, forgiving, loving, is with each one of us at this moment, immediately available. Take his words, bring them right down into your heart, brood over them in his presence, and know that he is speaking them to *you*, in you. You have his undivided attention. . . . "If you knew the gift of God and who this is who is speaking to *you*, you would ask of him and he would give *you* living water." "Jesus, help me to know the gift, to value it above everything . . . help me to know you . . . give me that living water." "Lord, that I may see." "If you will you can make me clean." "Of course I will: be made clean" . . . and so on.[57]

Burrows emphasizes that "the enormous merit of this method is that it is founded on objective truth and not on subjective emotions, psychic projections or make-believe."[58] Hence, it is an effective means by which beginners can come to know the inner contours of the kenotic Christ and thus discern what it means to live in conformity with him.

In Burrows's view, meditation on the New Testament comprises not only prayer but also the use of contemporary biblical scholarship. She observes that "today we have unparalleled opportunity of knowing [Jesus], his mind, his values, of viewing God and the world with his vision. Modern scholars have opened up the scriptures for us as never before."[59] So Burrows urges beginners to study the work of these Scripture scholars if they are to acquire knowledge of Jesus in order to imitate him. "We must avail ourselves of their labours, must enter in and make them our own."[60] Such mental labor, remarks Burrows, is an invaluable antidote to our familiarity with "trite interpretations . . . which we . . . take as the truth."[61]

There is a final piece of advice to be detailed regarding Burrows's encouragement of beginners to get to know Jesus through the work of the mind, through meditation. While Burrows's prime focus is on meditating on the New Testament, she also exhorts praying with and studying the Missal, "a rich source of theology and prayer at hand for each of us."[62] "Study the four Eucharistic Prayers," she counsels, "the Prefaces throughout the yearly seasons and the great doxology 'Glory to God in the Highest.' Look carefully at the Collects, especially the one so easily overlooked, the 'Prayer over the Offerings.'"[63] For Burrows, such study inevitably facilitates a deepening of our understanding of the Mass. This sacrament is, says Burrows, "Jesus' perfect prayer, that of his very being as he surrendered in passionate love to his Father in his death on the cross."[64] Accordingly, such growing understanding of the Mass is obviously a key means whereby the beginner can perceive what is implied in living as Christ crucified. As we will see in the following chapter, Burrows will have more to say about our participation in the Mass in her teaching on the mystical life.

Being Motivated to Imitate the Crucified Christ

It would be misleading to treat Burrows's commendation of meditation to beginners as if it involved acquiring knowledge of the self-emptying Christ simply for the sake of discerning how the life of the Crucified may take shape in our lives. In Burrows's perspective, the labor of the mind, meditation, also serves to stimulate the will to actually choose to take on the life of Jesus. Burrows urges beginners to meditate so they may come to want to follow Jesus crucified more than they want to follow their innate impulse toward self-gratification. To make this point in Burrows's own words, "Everything . . . depend[s] on what I really want, what I prize, what I hold to be my true good. Meditation . . . keeps us looking at the values of Jesus so that we may choose to make these our own."[65] Or again, she explains, "In the early stage of prayer, before any mystical grace has intervened, the mind has an all-important role. At the bidding of the heart it must labour to furnish motives and strong convictions for loving and serving God."[66] It is worth noting that Burrows does "not equate the heart with feeling" but rather associates it with "the inmost self, appreciating, recognising the worth of values and responding"; "heart," in other words, refers to the faculty of the will.[67]

Burrows is convinced that beginners are not adequately counseled to meditate in order to be compelled to undertake a Christlike exodus from the ego. "Not sufficient importance is attached to the work the mind must do to set before the heart the motives for choosing what is not immediately and sensibly appealing."[68] Burrows contends that "there is a tendency to think that good desires and strong motives will be infused; that if we remain quietly before the Lord in prayer, they will be born in on us; that, when we are tempted and troubled we have only to go before the Lord and we will be changed."[69] Such an attitude overlooks, however, that at the first stage of the spiritual life, we have not realized our human vocation sufficiently to be in direct contact with God; any decision for God rests on the orientation of the human faculties, supported, as they are, by grace. In order to counter this misguided trend, Burrows stresses to the beginner,

> We must always have in hand the sword of the spirit which
> is the word of God with which to combat the temptations
> to give up the struggle, to fall back into worldliness, to sin

in one way or another. We have to be ready with the motives for resisting. By and large this seems badly neglected. We fall, we are sorry, but we don't take any special precaution against the future. What we should do, if we are in earnest, is to have our sword ready in hand for the attack—some thought, some word of remembrance of Jesus which, through deep pondering, has become powerful for us.[70]

So just what can the mind present to the heart to stimulate the beginner to adopt Jesus' pure receptivity to God's love? What sort of content gleaned from meditation can induce the will to escape the primordial allure of selfishness? Here, Burrows primarily focuses on Jesus' revelation of a God who is an ecstasy of infinite love; this is not surprising given that, for Burrows, meditation principally entails the mind laboring in the field of the Scriptures. Through praying with and studying the Gospels, the mind exposes the heart to this love and the heart is invited to be drawn by its desirability. Exploring this dynamic, Burrows writes that we "ponder over and over again the reality of God's freely given love, as Jesus shows it to us, try to base our lives on this love, hold firmly to the truth that we are in the Father's house, already loved with no need to prove ourselves."[71]

This is not the extent, though, of Burrows's view on what the mind can present to the heart to entice it away from egocentricity. "There are other powerful incentives," she maintains, "that perhaps have to precede the loving preoccupation with Jesus: consideration of the brevity of our life-span, its mysteriousness, what it is for, its gravity and the appalling danger of wasting it."[72] Clearly, whatever it takes, Burrows is determined that beginners use their minds to convince their wills to follow Jesus crucified; entirely dependent on their created faculties, there is no other way beginners can make progress in the spiritual life.

The Moral Effort of Asceticism

It is clear that Burrows teaches beginners that through meditation, or mental labor, they can both come to know the shape of the heart that beat in Christ crucified and derive the incentive to live according to that heart. Asceticism is the moral effort that we exert to actually translate into our own lives the pattern of the Crucified that we have discerned and desired through meditation. We saw in the previous chapter that Burrows commends a thoroughgoing asceticism that is yet gently and simply woven into the fabric of our everyday lives. Here we will explore in turn the two interrelated dimensions of her ascetical advice, this advice for daily loosening the grip of the ego and surrendering to God in imitation of Christ's kenosis: the personal and the communal. It is important to note at the outset Burrows's insistence that "we cannot bring *ourselves* to complete surrender, God must achieve this for us; nevertheless whether he does or not depends on the realism of our desire."[73] Or to say this in more homely terms, for Burrows, we can, and must, pull the heads off the weeds of our self-preoccupation; only the living presence of Jesus crucified within us, however, can completely uproot them.

Asceticism Practiced within One's Personal Life

A basic aspect of Burrows's advice regarding how beginners can work to integrate Jesus' abandonment to the Father into their personal lives concerns developing self-knowledge. Burrows contends that while "profound, searching self-knowledge is infused . . . it is our duty to do all we can to gain what light we can."[74] The distinctive feature of Burrows's perspective on acquiring self-knowledge is that we should appraise ourselves first of all by our interior dispositions rather than by specific acts we commit; "it's the heart, the inner attitude that matters,"[75] she affirms. She would have us cast a searching light around our inner world to detect where the will is not wholly oriented to God. "Each of us has to look into our dark world," she counsels, "recognise the forces that bind us, the blind instincts, the compulsions which, though they give the illusion of power, freedom, adulthood, ensnare us."[76]

With its emphasis on coming to know the orientation of the heart rather than on simply weighing up external deeds, Burrows sees her approach to self-knowledge as a powerful means to launch out from the ego and into Christlike self-abandonment to God. Her point here is that while external acts can be neatly categorized and judged, and thus lead one to believe they can control their place in the divine scheme,

> We can, and we must, pull the heads off the weeds of our self-preoccupation. But only the living presence of Jesus crucified within us can completely uproot them.

intentionality is not so easily evaluated. We can never be scrupulously certain, according to Burrows, of our inner disposition. It is best to allow Burrows to speak for herself here:

> We are all the time wanting to find ways of making ourselves safe, devising categories and measurements well within our compass which can give us an illusory sense of "being alright," we know where we are. Whereas God

has never given us such safeguards and securities. He calls
always . . . for our total trust in him alone. We are always
wanting to protect ourselves from him by these and other
means; he gives us no *thing* whatever in which to trust—
only himself. We are blessed if we really accept that we do
not know whether we are worthy of ourselves of praise or
blame, when we refuse to summon any legalism to our
defense but stand humbly and trustfully as sinners before
the Lord.[77]

Quite evidently, then, for Burrows, the ascetical practice of
self-knowledge is a vital means whereby beginners can work
to unhinge themselves from the ego's pretensions to spiritual
control and take on the crucified Jesus' stance of utter trust in
the goodness of the Father.

In further discussion of how beginners may practice Jesus'
fidelity to self-transcendence within the boundaries of their
personal life, Burrows counsels a degree of "self-imposed austerity."[78] She expounds this advice by first insisting that "pleasure and satisfaction accompany every proper human activity.
This is God's loving ordinance for us, both to ensure that we
fulfil our functions, activate our potentialities and grow, and
also to make our earthly life as happy as possible."[79] Nevertheless, Burrows notes, intrinsically good though it may be,
the pleasure attendant upon the rightful use of created things
can stymie the beginner's progress in the Christian life. "In our
selfishness," she explains, "we seek pleasure at the expense of
love and duty. . . . We have a passion for pleasure and satisfaction. . . . Unless we take careful stock of this, without
realising it we shall become enslaved and at the mercy of our
likes and dislikes."[80] So with the ego in command at the first
stage of the spiritual life as it is, the beginner can readily find

that a hunger for seeking pleasure from created things can keep them bound within the stronghold of the self.

Lest our egocentric drive for pleasure ensnare the wings of our self-transcendence, Burrows advises that we integrate some measures of self-discipline into our lives. "Mastery and control do not drop from the skies," she begins. "We have to discipline ourselves for the sake of love. There must be times when, to ensure our freedom, to ensure that we can say 'no' to ourselves, we must deny ourselves some perfectly legitimate pleasure. We have a right to it but for love's sake, to ensure that we can love, we deny ourselves."[81] Discussing from a slightly different angle this practice of voluntary renunciation for the sake of gaining mastery over the demands of the ego, Burrows emphasizes the "yes" to God that it expresses. She details that it is a "practical affirmation that God is my life and I will let nothing take the edge off the need for him. It is a way of living out our hunger and thirst and refusing to be satisfied. Only one way, it is true, but we are body and express our hearts through our bodies and it seems inconsistent to keep on telling God he is my all, I want nothing but him, and then living as if I had settled for this world with plenty of all I need around me."[82] Evidently, if we are to become human, if we are eventually to share in Jesus' ecstatic surrender to the Father, Burrows would have us labor from the beginning to gain the upper hand over the ego's attachment to pleasure.

Burrows presents beginners with some basic guidelines as to how they might set about implementing some degree of self-imposed austerity within their lives. She points out that "at the beginning of our life for God we have to be tougher on ourselves, especially if we have indulged ourselves and had everything pretty much as we want it."[83] Additionally, Burrows recommends that beginners have recourse to the wisdom of others as they discern just what pleasurable use of creation they should forego in their efforts to orient themselves Godward. "We will need wise counsel," she says, "for we are not good judges of our own motives. Our Lord wills us to seek light and guidance."[84]

The most important guideline that Burrows articulates here is that we must guard against the austerity we impose upon ourselves in order to check the desires of the ego becoming in itself a source of ego satisfaction. We must not seek "the security of feeling we have got it just right, that we are mortified, we are giving him everything," she maintains. "It must not be a comfortable self-image we seek but God."[85] With this precaution in mind, Burrows counsels, "It is far better to have established simple, prudent rules for what to eat, how long to sleep and so on, and keep to them. Better moderate, unspectacular discipline than outbursts of sensational penance which do little more than gratify our sense of having done something worthwhile. We are not likely to get much satisfaction from our small but constant acts . . . but if they are kept up for the love of our Lord, to express in tangible form that we want God to be our heart's love they are of great value and efficacy."[86]

Adding further detail to her advice on how the beginner might emulate Jesus' self-emptying within their personal life, Burrows applies her basic ideas on self-imposed austerity to the practice of prayer. "Watchfulness over the desire for pleasure and satisfaction must extend to spiritual things as well,"[87] she asserts. To appreciate this aspect of Burrows's counsel, we first need to widen the lens in order to take in her position on "spiritual" experiences or sensible consolation; we will discuss this topic in far greater detail in the following chapter. To be clear, what is at issue here is that range of phenomena that leads people to claim "that God can be experienced in some way, 'tasted,' 'seen,' 'felt.'"[88] The crux of Burrows's perspective on "spiritual" experiences is that they belong to the created realm. The principle informing her here is a simple one: "God, infinite mystery . . . lies outside the range of [the human person's] senses and rational mind";[89] therefore, "Anything that can be conceptualised or looked at is not God."[90]

In Burrows's view, sensible consolation can be both valuable and dangerous to those at the first stage of the spiritual life. It is of value because it may be one of the created means that God uses to draw the beginner further along the spiritual path. It "can be an incentive and help," she affirms. "God may positively make use of this apparatus when he sees it would help."[91] Developing this idea Burrows writes, "I never want to run down emotion in the spiritual life. Far from it. It can be enormously helpful. . . . If spiritual emotion leads us, as it should, to greater generosity, then it is a blessing."[92] But Burrows is unrelentingly adamant that we are clear "that the apparatus is the same in kind as that with which we understand a book, are uplifted and inspired by music, moved by another person. . . . In themselves they belong to the realm of sense which cannot know spirit directly."[93]

The danger that Burrows discerns in religious feelings is that, wrongly understood, they can keep us captive within the realm of flesh. It is in light of this concern that she enunciates her ascetical advice on prayer. Burrows observes that "it is instinctive for us to . . . [take] for granted that our conscious experience is to be trusted, that it is the way things really are, the way we are, the way God is—that this *is* our life."[94] Accordingly, sensible consolation can be sought out, consciously or unconsciously, as some mark that one is progressing in the spiritual life. "I fear many a sincere person is seeking an 'experience,'" Burrows remarks, "an exalted state of consciousness."[95] However, if "spiritual" experiences are essentially material, then ambition after them in the name of spiritual progress is obviously inevitably futile. "To seek and highly value 'experience' . . . is to choose a created reality instead of God, and ultimately self instead of God."[96]

Given that to seek out sensible consolation is basically to choose self over God, Burrows urges "that we never allow such satisfaction to become a motive force" in our practice of prayer.[97] Developing this advice she claims,

> We are not asked to reject the delight we might feel in our devotional activities, of course not, but we must not give this delight a significance it has not got. Because we get a greater sense of God's presence at a prayer meeting than at Mass or in silent prayer, it does not mean that God is in fact more for us in the prayer meeting and that we are justified in opting for that form of spiritual activity rather than those which give no satisfaction. . . . To take up this or that because it pleases, because it is interesting, and to drop it when the interest goes; to pray when we feel like it and not when we don't, is to make a farce of prayer and to use God for our self-indulgence.[98]

To counteract the ultimately egocentric tendency to orient one's spiritual praxis around the consolation different activities provide, Burrows calls for "perseverance in spiritual duties."[99] To maintain fidelity to prayer even when it does not offer any felt satisfaction is, for Burrows, a central way to weave Jesus' self-abandonment into the fabric of life.

The final dimension of Burrows's ascetical advice about how beginners can imitate Christ crucified in their personal life concerns establishing control over the emotions. Burrows

affirms from the outset that "there is no question of saying that we should pay no attention to our emotions; they
are signals telling us something about ourselves."[100] Furthermore, she makes it clear that, in encouraging emotional control, she is not promoting "freedom from emotion or such a
levelling of emotion that we are never ruffled, never elated,
never saddened, ceasing to respond vitally to things."[101]
Rather, Burrows's intention is to ensure that, in handling
our emotions, we work to ground ourselves in God and not
the ego.

Burrows observes that, either periodically or chronically,
we experience painful emotions that will not resolve of their
own accord. "Sometimes discovering the cause of a strong
emotion can change the emotion, dissipate anger, for instance,
but this is not always so," she notes.[102] Moreover, "Some
natures suffer very much from inner turmoils, bouts of depression and resentment which they cannot will away."[103] According to Burrows, anchored in the ego as we are at the first stage
of the spiritual life, efforts to alleviate such emotional suffering can be an exer-
cise in selfishness. "We
think we know what
we need for our well-
being and happiness and
demand this of life," she
contends. "We say we
must feel fulfilled, that
we have a right to this
or that because we need

To maintain fidelity to prayer even when it does not offer any felt satisfaction is a central way to weave Jesus' self-abandonment into the fabric of life.

it for our fulfilment." Consequently, says Burrows, we make
the pursuit of fulfillment "our sole aim . . . subordinating
other people and things to our own needs."[104]

Since she holds that it is only in thrusting away from the self that we are truly fulfilled, Burrows is convinced that the beginner's ego-guided attempts to orchestrate happiness are inevitably ineffective. Instead, Burrows counsels tracing the self-emptying way of Christ crucified upon our response to emotional suffering. Outlining her thinking here she writes, "It seems to me that sooner or later each of us has to learn to put up with painful emotions, pay little attention to them, get on with doing what we have to do, attending to our neighbours' welfare, putting all our trust in God. We who know Jesus can surely afford to feel insecure. . . . We can afford to feel fragile, fearful. Surely these painful emotions can be an opportunity for pure trust."[105]

Burrows continues in the same key in her article "Smile Though Your Heart Is Aching" when she asserts "that to pay attention to what we are doing and why we are doing it, being aware of our moods and emotional thoughts and consistently choosing to live by the voice of Truth is an unrivalled means of purification and sanctification. . . . Secret, known only to God, it is a constant, deeply personal choice of God over self."[106] Thus, if we are to make progress in the Christian life, Burrows would have us imitate the confident vulnerability of the Crucified by sustaining emotional fragility rather than obey vain devices contrived by the ego to assuage such suffering.[107]

Asceticism Practiced within One's Life with Others

Having explored Burrows's thought on the various ways of imitating the kenotic Christ that we initiate ourselves, we can turn to the scope for "unselfing" that she sees contained in our interactions with others. Parenthetically, in detailing her ascetical advice concerning communal life, Burrows has in mind all the various situations in which men and women interact with each other.[108] For Burrows, our relations with others afford myriad opportunities for integrating the pattern of Jesus crucified into our daily lives. She points out that these interactions abound in possibilities for the ego to exert its dominion. "Deep in us all is the will to power," she says, "the will to control the world, to control people in order to serve our own ends."[109] Accordingly, Burrows views community life as a privileged field in which beginners must labor to turn their innate selfishness into the selflessness of the Crucified. She asserts that "nothing so reduces the ego as the realities of living with others and not demanding that they change so as to suit ourselves."[110]

Outlining her position on what it means to dethrone the ego through our engagement with others, Burrows remarks, "If we would be utterly obedient to the 'upward call' then we must learn how to submit ourselves to others, to circumstances, to the community welfare. Our will, our choice, must be in a very real sense to be without choice, waiting on God, abandoned, prepared to let this or that go, to be redirected, have our plans upset and so forth. It does not imply complete passivity, lack of initiative; it does mean flexibility, detachment, flowing from the faith-filled vision that discerns 'it is the Lord'—the Lord revealed not directly but through other human beings and events."[111] Burrows adds nuance to this broad conception by considering the selflessness demanded by the dynamics of interpersonal relations. "We shall suffer from the temperaments and habits of others," she observes, "but they are workmen whose job it is to polish the stone before it can be fitted into the building. Some will chisel with words, others by what they do, others by what they think of us."[112] In view of this opportunity to be fashioned into Christ's image presented by our human interactions, Burrows exhorts a wholehearted acceptance of all that these relations involve. "All this is precious; want it, use it, do not shirk it."[113]

Burrows maintains that if beginners are to put into practice the advice she presents regarding relating with others, they must develop an attitude of self-unimportance. With her characteristic challenging insightfulness she observes, "A little honest reflection shows us that naturally we are our own horizon, the most important person in the universe. Our attention and energy are largely employed in looking after ourselves in one way or another. . . . We assume unquestionably that we have the right to be treated justly, allowed independence, be consulted, recognised, appreciated. We are very, very important to ourselves and we demand that others recognise this importance."[114] This innate orientation must be reversed, says Burrows, if we are to emulate the self-abasement of Jesus crucified. Echoing the counsel of John of the Cross, she insists, "If you want God, if you want to begin the ascent of the mountain, then you have to make a decision against self-importance. You have to remove yourself from the centre-stage, see yourself as a member of a family, a community which you must serve."[115]

As to how beginners might cultivate this disposition of self-unimportance, Burrows indicates the direction in which they should channel their interior life: "Think little of yourself and be happy that others do not consider you very important. Have a lowly opinion of yourself, not in the sense of unhealthy self-denigration but in that you do not consider yourself the pivot of the universe. Keep correcting in the silence of your heart the contrary natural attitude. Keep reminding yourself that others are more important than you are, that their well-being is more than the satisfaction of your ego."[116] Burrows emphasizes that such interior efforts to undo our native thoroughgoing self-importance need to be undergirded by faith in God's love. If we ground ourselves on the belief that "each of us is utterly important to God," she counsels, "we can afford to relax a bit and let him look after our little selves."[117]

Summary

In *To Believe in Jesus*, Ruth Burrows creatively portrays Nicodemus as the quintessential Christian beginner. This portrayal provides us with a useful framework for summarizing the main themes of this chapter. In the beginning, through a mysterious interaction of nature and grace, we assent to the person and message of Jesus and so begin to actuate that capacity for relationship with God that makes us human. "Like Nicodemus we draw near to Jesus in our night of ignorance. . . . We make an act of faith, an all-important, primal one, 'We know that you are a teacher come from God.'"[118] Also like Nicodemus, however, we do not know that we are actually profoundly ignorant of spiritual things. We do not realize that we are not yet participating in the life of Jesus crucified and so sharing in his immediate relationship with the Father. We do not realize that, although we are not entirely captive to our innate selfishness, we are essentially in the grip of the ego, that we are "still trapped in the sphere of the flesh, and flesh can never attain God."[119] Thus, just as "Nicodemus considers himself a virtuous, wise man," we approach the spiritual life with great self-confidence.[120] With the ego in command, we feel assured of achieving perfection for ourselves. All along, though, we are only able to relate to God to the extent of our created human faculties.

If we are to progress in the spiritual life, we need to heed the advice which Jesus gives Nicodemus. "Jesus . . . tries to make Nicodemus understand what must happen if he is to go further, if he is to enter the kingdom, that sphere where God, not man, is in supreme control. . . . The master of Israel must, like Paul, lay aside his own ideas and consent to become a little child. . . . Nicodemus has to die to his own life and be born again, otherwise he can never enter the kingdom."[121] Every effort must be made to surrender our innate control over life and to be, as Jesus, a little child before the Father. We need to generously dispose ourselves to be born anew within the kingdom, within the life of the Crucified. We need to prepare to be taken into the mystical phase of the spiritual life.

Notes

1. Ruth Burrows, *Living in Mystery*, introduction by Wendy Beckett (London: Sheed and Ward, 1996), 96.

2. Ruth Burrows, *Guidelines for Mystical Prayer*, foreword by B. C. Butler (1976; repr., London: Continuum, 2007; Denville, N.J.: Dimension, 1980), 15.

3. Ruth Burrows, "Doctor of the Dark Night," in *Essence of Prayer* (London: Burns and Oates, 2006; Mahwah, N.J.: HiddenSpring, 2006), 100.

4. Burrows, *Living in Mystery*, 96.

5. In *Guidelines for Mystical Prayer* Burrows tells us that she and her "coauthors," Claire and Petra, "take over the almost unanimous tradition that in the spiritual life there are basically three stages." She explains that they "differ from most authors, at least in emphasis, by insisting that these three stages are totally distinct from one another, each representing a wholly new relation to God or a wholly new intervention on the part of God." The image of three islands is used: "It helps," says Burrows, "to show the three stages and their relation

to and distinctness from each other. We have to imagine that we are looking down on to a vast sea in which are set three islands. They really are islands, that is they are cut off from one another, for there are no harbours, no boats, no traffic between them." Burrows, *Guidelines for Mystical Prayer*, 13, 14. As with all metaphors, the three island imagery has its limitations. (Are, for example, the islands truly "cut off from one another" if, as Burrows claims in the same context, "there is a narrow bridge spanning the sea between the first island and the second"? Admittedly, the bridge is of the supernatural order rather than a "natural" formation that one can simply make for and traverse.) Nevertheless, it is on the whole an effective tool for conveying her understanding of the spiritual life.

6. Burrows, *Guidelines for Mystical Prayer*, 27.

7. Ibid., 17.

8. Ibid., 15.

9. Karl Rahner, "The Concept of Mystery in Catholic Theology," in *Theological Investigations*, trans. Kevin Smyth, vol. 4 (London: Darton, Longman and Todd, 1974), 54. Cited in Burrows, *Living in Mystery*, 7.

10. Mark Allen and Ruth Burrows, *Letters on Prayer: An Exchange on Prayer and Faith* (London: Sheed and Ward, 1999), 62.

11. Ruth Burrows, *To Believe in Jesus* (1978; repr., London: Continuum, 2010; Mahwah, N.J.: HiddenSpring, 2010), 108–9.

12. Allen and Burrows, *Letters on Prayer*, 62.

13. Burrows, *Guidelines for Mystical Prayer*, 16.

14. Ruth Burrows, *Ascent to Love: The Spiritual Teaching of St. John of the Cross* (London: Darton, Longman and Todd; Denville, N.J.: Dimension, 1992, 1987), 93.

15. Burrows, *To Believe in Jesus*, 1.

16. Ibid., 6.

17. Burrows, *Ascent to Love*, 70.

18. Burrows, *Living in Mystery*, 31.

19. Allen and Burrows, *Letters on Prayer*, 56–57.

20. Burrows, *Living in Mystery*, 31.

21. Allen and Burrows, *Letters on Prayer*, 63.

22. Ruth Burrows, *Interior Castle Explored: St. Teresa's Teaching on the Life of Deep Union with God* (1981; repr., London: Continuum, 2007; Mahwah, N.J.: HiddenSpring, 2007), 20.

23. Burrows, *Ascent to Love*, 96–97.

24. Burrows, *To Believe in Jesus*, 91.

25. Burrows, *Interior Castle Explored*, 58.

26. See Burrows, *Guidelines for Mystical Prayer*, 17.

27. Ibid.

28. Burrows, *Ascent to Love*, 50.

29. Burrows, *Interior Castle Explored*, 11.

30. Ibid., 21. While Burrows specifies that this is the condition of those in the second of Teresa's mansions, it actually also applies to those in the first and third mansions. It is only with the fourth mansion that the unmediated encounter with God begins.

31. Ibid., 54.

32. See ibid.

33. Burrows, *Guidelines for Mystical Prayer*, 18.

34. Ibid.

35. Ibid., 14.

36. Ibid., 18.

37. Burrows, *Ascent to Love*, 46.

38. Burrows, *To Believe in Jesus*, 21.

39. Burrows, *Interior Castle Explored*, 28–29.

40. Burrows, *Living in Mystery*, 78.

41. Burrows, *Interior Castle Explored*, 30.

42. See Ruth Burrows, *Through Him, With Him, In Him: Meditations on the Liturgical Seasons* (London: Sheed and Ward, 1987; Denville, N.J.: Dimension, 1987), 61.

43. Burrows, *Interior Castle Explored*, 30.

44. Burrows, *Living in Mystery*, 78.

45. Burrows, *Interior Castle Explored*, 33.

46. Ibid., 29.

47. Ibid.

48. Ibid.

49. Ruth Burrows, "Amen: The Human Response to God," in *Essence of Prayer*, 78.

50. Burrows, *To Believe in Jesus*, 32.

51. Ruth Burrows, "Prayer That Is Jesus," in *Essence of Prayer*, 38.

52. Ruth Burrows, "Initial Prayer within the Carmelite Tradition," *Mount Carmel* 48, no. 3 (October–December 2000): 15.

53. Ruth Burrows, "Growth in Prayer," in *Essence of Prayer*, 17.

54. Ruth Burrows, "Prayer Is God's Work," interview by Amy Frykholm, *Christian Century*, April 4, 2012, 11. In a longer, unpublished version of this interview, Burrows laments, "It seems to me that Jesus Christ is not known. The Gospels are not *devoured* as they should be."

55. Burrows, "Initial Prayer," 16.

56. Ruth Burrows, "Carmelite Prayer," in *Essence of Prayer*, 177.

57. Burrows, "Initial Prayer," 17.

58. Ibid., 17–18.

59. Burrows, *Ascent to Love*, 25.

60. Ibid.

61. Burrows, "Carmelite Prayer," 176–77.

62. Ruth Burrows, "Reflections on Prayer," in *Essence of Prayer*, 9.

63. Ibid.

64. Ibid.

65. Burrows, *Ascent to Love*, 37.

66. Burrows, *Interior Castle Explored*, 68.

67. Allen and Burrows, *Letters on Prayer*, 55. See also Burrows, *Interior Castle Explored*, 62–63.

68. Burrows, *Interior Castle Explored*, 23.

69. Ibid.

70. Ibid., 24.

71. Burrows, *Living in Mystery*, 77.

72. Burrows, *Interior Castle Explored*, 23–24.

73. Burrows, *Ascent to Love*, 25.

74. Burrows, *To Believe in Jesus*, 56.

75. Burrows, *Interior Castle Explored*, 18.

76. Burrows, *Guidelines for Mystical Prayer*, 25.

77. Burrows, *Interior Castle Explored*, 15.
78. Burrows, *Guidelines for Mystical Prayer*, 22.
79. Burrows, *To Believe in Jesus*, 72.
80. Ibid.
81. Ibid.
82. Burrows, *Guidelines for Mystical Prayer*, 23.
83. Burrows, *To Believe in Jesus*, 73.
84. Burrows, *Ascent to Love*, 28.
85. Ibid., 29.
86. Burrows, *To Believe in Jesus*, 72.
87. Ibid., 73.
88. Burrows, *Guidelines for Mystical Prayer*, 45.
89. Burrows, *Ascent to Love*, 6.
90. Burrows, *Guidelines for Mystical Prayer*, 50.
91. Burrows, *Interior Castle Explored*, 48.
92. Allen and Burrows, *Letters on Prayer*, 102.
93. Burrows, *Interior Castle Explored*, 48.
94. Burrows, "Amen," 78.
95. Burrows, *Guidelines for Mystical Prayer*, 19.
96. Burrows, *To Believe in Jesus*, 28.
97. Ibid., 73.
98. Ibid., 73–74.
99. Ibid., 73.
100. Burrows, *Ascent to Love*, 34.
101. Ibid., 36.
102. Ibid., 34.
103. Ibid.
104. Ibid., 46–47.
105. Ibid., 34.
106. Ruth Burrows, "Smile Though Your Heart Is Aching," *The Tablet*, April 19, 2014, 10.
107. Without denying the obvious wisdom it contains, one can perhaps question whether Burrows's advice here is sufficiently nuanced. It is

surely possible to relieve emotional suffering in ways that are not self-serving, in ways that do not subordinate people and things to our own needs.

108. See Burrows, *Ascent to Love*, 40.
109. Burrows, *To Believe in Jesus*, 42.
110. Burrows, *Ascent to Love*, 40.
111. Ibid., 41–42.
112. Ibid., 35–36.
113. Ibid., 36.
114. Ibid., 37–38.
115. Ibid.
116. Ibid.
117. Ibid.
118. Burrows, *To Believe in Jesus*, 30.
119. Ibid.
120. Ibid.
121. Ibid., 30–31.

CHAPTER 4

The Second Stage of the Spiritual Life according to Ruth Burrows

*Becoming the "Yes"
of Jesus Crucified*

We have now arrived at the core of Ruth Burrows's thought on the spiritual life. For Burrows, the second stage of the spiritual journey marks the beginning and development of the mystical phase of the Christian life. It is the dawning realization of what was anticipated in the previous stage. Here God graciously intervenes and touches the human person directly. Such immediate contact with God implies that now Jesus crucified is effecting his own surrender to the Father within us; it is only within Jesus' definitive self-abandoning "yes" to the Father that we encounter God as God is in himself. In Burrows's view, being drawn into the life of Jesus crucified means dying to our primordial self-possession and self-centeredness. And this means a qualitative leap in the process of becoming human. No longer is the ego ultimately in control, limiting our relationship with God to indirect communications. With the overthrow of the ego, our human vocation to be unalloyed receptivity to God's self-giving love becomes a living reality.

This chapter has a three-part structure. We will begin by discussing Burrows's understanding of the essence of the second stage of the spiritual life. Next, we will examine what, according to Burrows, we experience of the second stage; her position on sensible phenomena in the mystical life and her account of the effects of God's mystical intervention will be chief components of this second section. Finally, we will consider Burrows's teaching on how we should respond to the inbreaking of God's mystical grace. Her basic insight here is that we must cooperate with the trajectory of God's grace by making a trusting descent from self-importance and so increasingly become an emptiness to receive the divine life.

THE ESSENCE OF THE SECOND STAGE
OF THE SPIRITUAL LIFE

Of the three phases, it is the second phase of the spiritual life that receives the greatest share of Burrows's attention throughout her writings. This is not surprising. Her spiritual doctrine is centered upon that transformation into the crucified, risen Jesus for which we were created, and it is here that the transformation begins to take effect. Furthermore, Burrows understands the second stage of the Christian journey to extend from the delicate beginnings of God's direct contact with the human person to the state immediately preceding the consummation of the divine-human relationship. Thus she holds that ordinarily it is the longest stage of the spiritual life.

Nonetheless, it is not too audacious to claim that a simple allegory in *To Believe in Jesus* conveys the kernel of Burrows's understanding of the nature of the second stage of the spiritual life. We saw Burrows comment in the last chapter, "It is as if God endows us with wing structure. We have to work the muscles of these embryonic wings to make them develop but no matter how much we try, we cannot get off the ground, that is, away from self."[1] She then goes on to explain, "When the wings, through exercise, are sufficiently grown, then comes a divine influence, a wind, that not only uplifts us but something of its strength penetrates the wings themselves so we can begin to fly, leaving self behind first from time to time, then for longer periods. Thus eventually we are in the painful condition of not being wholly in self and yet not belonging wholly to God."[2] This image points to the two interrelated constituents of Burrows's view of the essence of the second stage. First, in this phase God gratuitously initiates us into a wholly new mode of relationship that, while unattainable by human effort, is necessary for human fulfillment (the newness of "flight" is pure gift yet entirely proper to the human condition). And second, the newness of this stage consists precisely in being taken into the self-surrender of Jesus crucified (the divine influence "penetrates the wings themselves"). We will look at each of these interrelated characteristics in turn.

The Direct Touch of God

By Burrows's account, the second stage of the spiritual journey "is something entirely *new*. It is not a deepening of what has gone before, an increasing expertise, not a continuation, but a break."[3] We left the beginner generously striving to imitate the self-transcendence of Christ, though essentially held captive within the primordial snare of the ego. Burrows observes, "Because it is God's deep desire to give himself, since he is this very desire, and we exist solely to be the happy recipients of his love, it goes without saying that he will give himself whenever and wherever and in the measure that it is possible. Thus when we are really in earnest, steadily pursuing God's will, it will not be long before we are given his life-giving touch."[4] This touch, this wholly divine initiative anticipated by human effort, is precisely the immediate presence of God himself within the substance of the human person. Burrows speaks of God's direct, hidden contact with terms such as "mystical grace," "supernatural prayer," "infused contemplation," and "mystical contemplation."[5]

Burrows maintains that with the dawning of God's mystical action the dominion of the ego begins to crumble. "Each mystical encounter momentarily effects," she remarks, a "wrenching of the self away from its self."[6] In other words, the touch of God's immediate presence releases the true self, openness to the divine life, from the false self, that innate drive to seek fulfillment within the human horizon. When Burrows states that God's mystical grace at once "*purifies* and *transforms*," it is this simultaneous undoing of the ego and realization of our human vocation that she has in mind.[7]

Examining this dynamic more closely, Burrows comments that when God makes direct contact the person "is being given a divine knowledge of God and inevitably leaps up to embrace Love showing himself in uniting himself to me."[8] God's mystical intervention, then, breaks open the intellect and will such that they are no longer bound to created realities but enabled to receive the very life of God. As Burrows puts it, "The capacity to believe is energised from divine contact and is no longer 'merely human'; it is now theological not just in its object but in its operation."[9] Or again, "There is a 'centre' now which is spirit, and spirit means 'what is God's,' what is being transformed into him, what is of his own being, a share in his divine nature, as we say."[10]

In the light of these ideas, we can appreciate Burrows's identification of mystical grace with "the old, familiar doctrine of sanctifying grace and the divine indwelling."[11] Of this doctrine, the Dominican theologian Jordan Aumann writes, "Through [sanctifying] grace we are introduced into the life of the Trinity, which is the life of God, and God dwells in us and communicates his divine life to us."[12] Clearly, Burrows is referring to the very same intimacy with God in her discussion of the impact of mystical grace. Given it is traditionally understood that sanctifying grace and the divine indwelling are conferred by baptism, (*Catechism of the Catholic Church*, n. 1999) Burrows's teaching on mysticism must, and does, contain a word on this sacrament; we shall return to this later.

When we step back and survey what we have seen so far of Burrows's position on the mystical life, it is apparent that she perceives God's mystical intervention to be necessary both to the process of becoming human and to the attainment of sanctity. To take the first point, we know that for Burrows, to be human is to be in intimate communion with God. As we can see from the above discussion, this communion is only possible when God encounters the human person directly, thereby dislodging the ego's reign and initiating a divine mode of relationship. So Burrows is essentially articulating her own view when she writes, "If we grasp what Teresa is really talking about in infused contemplation, then we see it is the very life-line, our very meaning as human beings. It is God himself bringing man to himself, sharing his own way of being with him."[13] To reaffirm what we discovered in an earlier chapter, implicit in Burrows's conception of mystical grace as "the very stuff of human fulfilment" is the fact that mysticism cannot be the preserve of a spiritual elite.[14] With the call to intimacy with God universally inscribed upon their existence, the mystical way is the inheritance of all men and women.

On the subject of the attainment of sanctity, if mystical grace is, in fact, sanctifying grace, then it follows that, to Burrows, sanctity has everything to do with growth in the mystical life. In *To Believe in Jesus* Burrows observes that "to be holy in the absolute sense means that a human being . . . lives with God, in God's own sphere."[15] Of course, such immersion in the divine life is nothing other than the state toward which Burrows sees God's mystical grace to be working. "Sanctity *is* mystical union," she asserts.[16] "One cannot be holy unless one is a mystic and if we do not become mystics in this life we become such hereafter."[17] In the end, then, for Burrows the fullness of the mystical life, the full realization of the human vocation and holiness, are one and the same reality. As she expresses it, using the language of John of the Cross, "The ascent of Mount Carmel is but the fullness of the Christian life, which is synonymous with the fullness of human being."[18]

Burrows is aware that her thinking on the correlation between the development of the mystical life and growth in holiness and human wholeness runs counter to the thought of many other theologians. "The vast majority of spiritual authors, St. Teresa among them," she explains, "claim that there are two paths to holiness, the mystical way and the ordinary way. This we cannot accept."[19] She goes on to detail: "The notion of the dual carriage-way derives from a misconception. . . . The mystical has been identified with certain experiences. When these are present in a person such a one is a mystic or contemplative; he or she has received the gift of infused contemplation, not essential for holiness but undoubtedly a great help towards it. Inevitably you get overtones of a high road and a low road."[20] So, while Burrows maintains that mystical grace is something objective and universally offered: God's gift of his immediate presence to end the supremacy of the ego and activate our human potential, others hold that it is something subjective and exclusive: a conscious experience of God's presence that at least implies the recipient is favored by a particular intimacy with God.

Now is not the time for us to attend to Burrows's stance on our conscious experience of the mystical life or her thinking on Teresa of Ávila in this regard. Rather, let us listen to two voices from the "subjective" approach to mysticism in order to further our exploration of Burrows's understanding of the essence of the second stage. In his book *From St. John of the Cross to Us*, James Arraj offers a short refutation of Burrows's position on mysticism. Contrary to Burrows, he argues that "someone could reach a high degree of sanctity without infused contemplation," and that "the divine indwelling is not

identical to infused contemplation."[21] For Arraj, "contemplation is a mysterious experience of that indwelling that makes
its way into consciousness."[22]

Arraj's view echoes that of the Jesuit Auguste Françoise
Poulain. Burrows takes issue with Poulain's writings on mysticism in *Interior Castle Explored*. As she reports, Poulain writes
in *The Graces of Interior Prayer*, "If the supernatural states of
prayer were merely means of sanctification, graces of sanctity,
the question of desiring them would present no difficulty. But
they are extraordinary graces, privileges, divine familiarities,
bringing with them marvels of condescension on God's part,
and elevating the soul to heights that are regarded without
exception by ordinary people as sublime."[23] Quite evidently,
within Poulain's perspective, the mystical state ("the supernatural states of prayer"), with its "extraordinary graces," "privileges" and "divine familiarities," is by no means equivalent
to the "graces of sanctity," which are well within the grasp of
"ordinary people."

The response that Burrows makes to Poulain, and that she
would similarly level at Arraj, reveals a fundamental aspect of
her conception of the nature of mysticism. In the face of Poulain's separation of the mystical life and progress in sanctity
and his exalted regard for the special favors experienced by the
"mystics" she writes,

> Surely the message of the New Testament is that union with
> God, divine intimacy, familiarity, unheard of privilege, is
> what man is for, it is the promise of the Father offered in
> Jesus and for which he died. We are called to be sons in the
> Son, heirs of God because co-heirs with Christ, sharing in
> the divine nature, filled with the fulness of God. If mysti-
> cal union is not one and the same thing with this promise

of the Father totally effected in a human being, redemption completed, then it is something bogus. There can be no higher gift than what the New Testament tells us is the common destiny of man.[24]

So Burrows perceives her doctrine of the mystical life to be precisely the message of the New Testament. In discussing God's gracious self-bestowal that liberates us from subjection to the ego and draws us into sacred intimacy, she is simply describing the new life for all proclaimed by the Gospel. For Burrows, God's mystical grace is the very same reality as what is named "the 'kingdom of God' in the synoptists, 'eternal life' in John, living with the life of Christ in Paul."[25]

It is by thus identifying her teaching on mysticism with the wholly new relationship with God variously heralded by the New Testament that Burrows has the confidence to oppose Poulain, Arraj, and those that line up with them. Burrows finds in the Scriptures no warrant for positing a singular degree of intimacy with God that is registered by the consciousness and enjoyed by the chosen few. She asserts that the God of Jesus, "this Self-squanderer, does not carefully weigh out his gifts, offering 'divine familiarities' to a few, withholding them from others; he is not overflowing generosity to some, miserliness with others."[26] Hence, Burrows is at pains throughout her writings to dismantle such notions of mysticism. Grounded in the authority of the

> God's mystical grace is the very same reality as what is named "the kingdom of God" in the synoptists, "eternal life" in John, living with the life of Christ in Paul.

Gospel, she seeks to convey to all men and women "that there is not a mysterious realm of spiritual reality from which they are debarred. If they wish, they too can be filled with all the fullness of God, 'heights,' says Poulain (and how many with him!), 'regarded by ordinary people as sublime,' and, by inference, not for them."[27]

The Direct Touch of God Mediated by Jesus Crucified

In contemplating Burrows's idea of mysticism as equivalent to the New Testament ideas of being sons in the Son, being heirs of God because coheirs with Christ, living with the life of Christ, and so on, we have had a foretaste of that to which we now turn—the second constituent of Burrows's understanding of the essence of the second stage. It is this: the dawning of the mystical life is about the life of the kenotic Jesus progressively replacing the life of the ego. We have already touched upon this principle in this chapter and the preceding ones; it is central to Burrows's contribution to the Christian spiritual tradition. Here is the proper place to develop it in detail.

We have established that, in Burrows's view, the mystical life is the direct inflow of the very life of God into the human person. This immediate touch of God breaks our innate orientation toward self-sufficiency by drawing the intellect and will to participate in the divine life. Accordingly, growth in the mystical life is coextensive with growth in human wholeness and holiness. For Burrows, this conception of mysticism must be radically informed by the New Testament teaching that Jesus is the sole mediator between God and humanity; she is determined to face up to the full implications of Scripture's insistence "that only Jesus has seen God, that the Father dwells in inaccessible light."[28] The "mystical life, infused contemplation, these things mean absolutely nothing to me," claims Burrows, "unless they mean Jesus and his life in us; Jesus who alone brings God and man together; Jesus our holiness."[29] Elaborating on this assertion she writes, "[The] mystery of God is always met in Jesus and nowhere else. . . . We can only have 'pure God' in Jesus. Only through Jesus does 'pure God' touch us and we touch him."[30]

Burrows holds that it is the humanity of Jesus, more particularly the self-emptying, ultimately crucified humanity of Jesus, that mediates God's mystical grace. Referring to the newness of the mystical life she remarks that the cross "is the only gate by which this wholly new thing can invade. The cross, surrender to death in order to be created anew . . . these awesome thoughts must be present always when we think of mystical union."[31] It is by embracing the contingency and poverty of the human condition with unique trust in the Father's love that Jesus is the immediate presence of God in this world. And this concomitant unreserved embrace of our human dependency and mediation of God's very life reached its culmination on the cross. As Burrows declares, "The act which effected the union of all mankind with God was wrought when Jesus himself had been brought to nothing."[32] A favorite text of Burrows for expressing this idea of the kenotic Jesus as the sole mediator of God's presence is Jesus' pronouncement in the Gospel of John, "I am the way, and the truth, and the life. No one comes to the Father except through me" (Jn 14:6). At one point Burrows observes, "Way, Truth and Life—comprehensive terms. He is simply everything for us. But note, these words are put on the lips not of the risen Lord but of the earthly Jesus when he stood on the brink of his awful passion. The earthly Jesus whom John shows us as troubled, distraught, overflowing with tears. He is the Way precisely as this 'poor' one, experiencing the weight of human emptiness and incompletion. As such he is Truth, as such he is Life."[33]

If the second stage is about being in intimate communion with God, and if such intimacy is only accessible in the Crucified, then it follows that for Burrows, the one at the second stage of the spiritual life is essentially taking on the life of the kenotic Christ. Burrows captures this transformation at the heart of the second stage when she affirms, "Jesus was so given, so surrendered, so emptied out, that he was like a hollow shell in which the roar of the ocean could be heard. . . . We have to be living embodiments of Jesus, as he is of the Father. . . . Each of us has to become Jesus."[34] Another way of expressing Burrows's approach to the living reality of the second phase is to say that the effect of God's mystical grace is to realize within us the crucified Jesus' utter abandonment to the divine life. "Conformity to Jesus," she explains, "this total surrender, is impossible to human effort, a divine gift is needed, an infusion of divine energy, the Spirit of Jesus himself. . . . This is precisely what we mean by mystical, infused contemplation."[35]

So, according to Burrows, just what does it mean for a person to take on the life of the Crucified, the sole mediator of the divine life? How does being conformed by God's mystical grace to the self-emptying Christ translate into lived reality? "To follow Jesus, to have his mind," says Burrows, "means entering into his death, that is, *accepting the essential poverty of our human existence*."[36] Stephen Sundborg elaborates this pivotal aspect of Burrows's thought:

> We become one with Jesus by accepting the human-
> ity he shares with us and that made him one with the
> Father. . . . Jesus' acceptance of humanity was an emptying

of who he was, not clinging to the prerogatives of his divinity, and through this acceptance he became a victim, to the
end that as man he could be completely possessed by God's
love. Our acceptance of humanity is similarly an empty-
ing, not of our divinity, but of self, of "that which gives us
a sense of importance," of "success in the spiritual life," a
"self-emptying" so that we stand "in the truth of our being."
The choice to surrender to Jesus is the choice to accept
our true humanity, not as we try to fill it up with importance, success, riches, but to accept it in its radical nature as
incompleteness, as a capacity for God.[37]

It is clear, then, that Burrows understands the mystical life to
be about allowing Jesus crucified to utter in us his unqualified
"yes" to the Father through our unqualified embrace of the
basic poverty of our particular lived experience. It is by thus
allowing our own expression of fundamental human dependency to be gathered up into his that we share in Jesus' unique
intimacy with the Father. What it means in practice to respond
to God's mystical intervention by embracing our poor humanity will be the subject of the third section of this chapter.

The Varying Degrees of Mystical Life across the Second Stage

A noteworthy implication of what we have now unfolded of
Burrows's mystical doctrine is that the second stage of the
spiritual life is not a uniform reality. Mysticism is about being
conformed to the Crucified, yet, Burrows remarks, "Perfect
transformation into Jesus does not take place all at once. Man
must co-operate with the action of the Holy Spirit who is
now able to operate freely from within, where before he could

only direct the mind and heart from outside."[38] The reality of our mystical life, then, is proportionate to the degree of our assent to be taken into Christ crucified, to be a poverty disposed toward outpoured Love. Another way to say this is that we become a mystic to the extent that we consent to be truly human.

There are three points to be made regarding this idea that the mystical life is lived at varying intensity throughout the second phase of the Christian journey. These points are really a foreshadowing of the third section of this chapter, dealing as they do with our *response* to God's mystical grace. First, Burrows notes that our journey in the mystical life is not something strictly linear; we can vacillate in our resolve to stand empty-handed before the God of love. Fluctuation in the path of mysticism is connoted, for example, by the image of the bridge in *Guidelines for Mystical Prayer*. The bridge—which spans the sea between the first island and the second island[39]—represents an incipient degree of direct communion with God; here "God's action is intermittent and light. It does not preponderate."[40] Burrows claims that while most of those on the bridge are stepping out from the boundaries of the first island into the mystical phase, "a few really do belong to the second island but have fled from it."[41] Evidently, Burrows perceives that it is possible for those who have known a mystical relationship with God beyond the beginnings, who have consented to be drawn into the nakedness of Jesus' self-abandonment, to regather the fortifications of their self-sufficiency and retreat along the spiritual path.

While admitting the reality of inconsistency in our mystical progress, Burrows maintains that there is a juncture along the second stage of the spiritual life after which one's consent to God's direct self-bestowal is virtually irrevocable. This is the second point. It is in her interpretation of Teresa's fifth mansion that Burrows develops this position most explicitly.[42] She presents the fifth mansion as "a dynamic moment of decision, an invitation offered and accepted, understanding that this acceptance is beyond our power and is a direct effect of God's contact."[43] Burrows goes on to explain that with this graced assent to Love, "the work of God in us

> The reality of our mystical life is proportionate to the degree of our assent to be taken into Christ crucified, to be a poverty disposed toward outpoured Love.

now is consistent because we are consistent in our surrender. Hitherto we were not. For a short while, perhaps, we maintained an attitude of surrender and then our resolution waned and we abandoned it, falling again into self-protecting evasions of the loving pressures of God."[44] This definitive plunge into the life of the Crucified is identifiable, Burrows suggests, with the grace bestowed "on the apostles after the resurrection of Jesus, whereby they became disciples in *very fact*."[45]

It is Burrows's view that many are brought to the threshold of committed discipleship yet few actually abandon themselves into Jesus' unwavering "yes."[46] For those who do accept, the course to union with God is well-nigh set. "Though we must theoretically allow for failure (that is a real going back not just shortcomings and falls)," says Burrows, "for all practical purposes this step, of its very nature, is an irrevocable one."[47]

The final point in this look at varying degrees of mystical transformation is that, according to Burrows, *complete* transformation into Jesus crucified does not belong to the second stage. We read earlier that at the culmination of the second stage, "We are in the painful condition of not being wholly in self and yet not belonging wholly to God." That is to say, no matter how resolutely we allow the Spirit to take us into Jesus' self-emptying by embracing the fundamental dependency of our being, we do not become completely dispossessed of self and alive with the life of Christ in the second stage. As we will explore in the next chapter, in Burrows's schema, to know the Crucified as the sole principle of existence is the living reality of the third stage of the spiritual life.

The Sacraments as Embodiments of the Mystical Life

Throughout her writings, Burrows teaches that the sacraments are an embodiment of the essence of the mystical life. "The sacraments are direct encounters with God in Christ," she states. "In them God touches us directly, he himself, unmediated. This is the mystical life in concentrated form, flashing out in all its intolerable brightness for one vitalising minute."[48] Accordingly, Burrows portrays the sacraments as making concretely present the foundational mystical truth that Jesus is our only way into the divine life. She expounds that the sacramental life of the church "constantly, practically affirms that everything is given to us. . . . We cannot make our own way to God but God has come to us in Jesus who himself has become our worship, our perfect offering, our union with the Father, our life, our holiness, our atonement."[49] The sacraments, then, are fundamentally about us uniting the poverty of our being with the radiant emptiness of Jesus crucified and thus being drawn into his personal communion with God. Burrows principally focuses upon baptism, the Eucharist, and reconciliation as she discusses the sacraments as living expressions of the heart of the mystical life.

By Burrows's account, the emergence and development of the mystical life is basically the progressive activation of our baptism. Explaining this thought, she notes, "Baptism is ultimately the sacrament of the Fatherhood of God, by it we become his sons and daughters, which is what humanhood is all about. How is this metamorphosis of becoming a child of God effected? By dying to our purely natural life and being born again into new life, spiritual life, the life of the Risen Christ which is the life of God himself."[50] We can see here that Burrows views baptism as a process: the promise of intimacy with God that baptism contains is realized inasmuch as we live from the truth that we are essentially emptiness for the divine life. Indeed, she claims, "Properly understood, this is what the Christian life is: an ever deeper integration of the reality of baptism, a deeper penetration into the inheritance that is ours, a surrendering of ourselves to the Spirit to be 'conformed to the image' of God's Son."[51]

Now, "dying to our purely natural life and being born again into new life," "surrendering ourselves to the Spirit to be 'conformed to the image' of God's Son"—this is precisely what we have identified to be the work of God's mystical grace. It is obvious, then, that to Burrows, the mystical life is nothing other than the actualization of the loving communion with God toward which we are oriented in baptism. Baptized into the death and resurrection of Jesus in principle, we labor to imitate the Crucified in anticipation of God's mystical coming to immerse us into that living union with the divine that our baptism promises.[52] As Burrows herself puts it, "Our baptism, the privilege of our Christian calling is affirming that . . . mystical union is what life is for, this is what God is calling us to do, this is our vocation. It is not a 'hey presto,' it is done."[53]

In reference to the Eucharist Burrows claims, "Expressed in this sacrament is all that we mean by mystical prayer."[54] Perhaps her most effective exposition of this statement is to be found in *Our Father: Meditations on the Lord's Prayer*. There, expressing herself through prayer, Burrows writes, "We give you, dear Lord, all we have and are under the veil of bread and wine. In themselves, as of themselves, they are ineffective, they can never carry us to the Father. Make them into your own offering, your own flight of love which does get there. Transform us into your immolated self. In Holy Communion we receive back the humble offerings we first presented, not as themselves, but as sacrament of union, of transformation."[55] In other words, in this sacrament the God-oriented dependency that defines our being is taken directly into the Crucified's direct communion with the Father. Thus we can see quite simply that for Burrows the Eucharist is a concentrated expression of the mystical life.

Burrows's account of the sacrament of reconciliation as a manifestation of the essence of the mystical life focuses, naturally, on the forgiveness of sin. Reaffirming in terms of forgiveness the Gospel insight upon which her mystical doctrine is grounded, Burrows insists that "[God] and [God] alone can 'put things right,' can make it possible for the estranged world to find its rightful place in the divine heart. At-one-ment is already achieved. In the Father's eyes we hung on the cross with Jesus."[56] Accordingly, for Burrows reconciliation is about opening out the empty hands of our true selves within Jesus crucified and entering into his perfect atonement to the Father. "Our part," she explains, "is to take our act of sorrow, paltry and inadequate as it is, to that heart which alone has gauged sin, taken its full weight. Our poor sorrow is taken up into, transformed into, the perfect reparation of Jesus."[57] As a privileged moment for allowing the breath of the Crucified to catch our poor humanity up into his living "yes" to the Father, the sacrament of forgiveness is clearly a distillation of the mystical reality.

THE LIVED EXPERIENCE OF THE SECOND STAGE OF THE SPIRITUAL LIFE

We have been discussing Ruth Burrows's understanding of the essence of the second stage of the spiritual journey, that is to say, the essence of the emergence and development of the mystical life. We turn now to Burrows's thought on what we experience of the second stage within the consciousness— the senses, the emotions, and the mind.[58] Her thinking here encompasses our direct as well as indirect experience of God's mystical intervention; the latter category takes in Burrows's teaching on both the matter of "spiritual" experiences and the essential effects of mystical grace.

Direct Conscious Experience of the Mystical Life— An Impossibility

Burrows's position on the prospect of a direct conscious experience of the mystical life proceeds immediately from her approach to the essence of mysticism. We know that, for Burrows, the mystical life is God himself touching the human person. This encounter occurs in Jesus—the only one who has seen God—and is incarnated in our lives as a resolute embrace of our inexorably dependent human condition; "emptiness is a holy void that Divine Love is filling."[59] From this understanding of the nature of mysticism it follows that a direct conscious experience of God's mystical grace in itself is impossible. "An encounter has taken place in the depth of being, in the growing point of spirit," Burrows maintains, "and human consciousness, essentially material, can know nothing of it directly."[60] Fundamentally earthbound, our conscious life simply cannot be aware of "pure" God coming to us, actuating our capacity for the divine life.

The States of "Light Off" and "Light On"

A look at Burrows's categories of "light off" and "light on" will enhance our exploration of her assertion of the impossibility of directly experiencing God's mystical presence. According to Burrows, "In all mystical union there are two different ways of experience . . . 'light off' and 'light on.'"[61] The state of "light off" is precisely the "normal, proper obscurity" of the mystical life that we have so far been considering.[62] Burrows holds that "light off" is the experiential mode of the vast majority of those traveling the mystical path. For them, "Something unspeakably wonderful is happening in the depths of self and the self cannot see it. No light shines on it."[63] It would be mistaken to interpret "light off" as a state bereft of sensible consolation, or as a condition of spiritual dryness; with this category Burrows is simply referring to the hiddenness of the divine presence from our created faculties. Indeed, both "light on" and "light off" mystics are, in Burrows's mind, liable to know the consoling echoes of the hidden mystical grace that we shall discuss shortly.[64]

Burrows contends that while "light off" is the usual mode of experiencing God's mystical intervention, "it is possible for God to switch on a light, so to speak, [so] what is happening is 'seen.'"[65] This is the condition of "light on"; by it, God's direct self-bestowal is somehow illuminated. While she is mainly interested in "light on" as a permanent state, Burrows also acknowledges "it is possible for God to switch on the light occasionally for one normally in the 'light off' state."[66] Burrows is adamant that because "light on" is a matter of perceiving "God himself, this seeing is non-conceptual; it simply cannot be held by the mind, looked at, still less described."[67] Thus, Burrows reasons, "We must say that [the 'light on' experience] is supernatural in the strict sense, that is, that it is of God and not in itself proper to the human experience of God in this life."[68] So while we cannot strictly claim that those who are "light on" have a direct conscious experience of the mystical grace, we can nevertheless hold that, for them, a divinely enabled mode of perception lifts the veil that normally enshrouds God's mystical presence.

In Burrows's view, the experience of "light on" is not only exceptional but also serves a didactic function within the church.[69] "For this to be the usual mode of receiving the mystical embrace is exceedingly rare," she claims. "A 'light on' state . . . may perhaps occur no more than once or twice in an era."[70] Burrows goes on to state that the one thus endowed, understanding "beyond the ken of human kind . . . must enlighten others. This light throws its beams on the ordinary way and enables us to understand it."[71] Hence she believes it is generally the "light on" mystics who are the great teachers of the spiritual life—though she by no means regards this as their exclusive domain.[72] Burrows names Paul as exemplary here.[73] Moreover, in *Guidelines for Mystical Prayer* she writes, "Teresa and John belong to this category of 'light on.' I say this not because of their intense, sublime, emotional states, for these can equally belong to 'light off' but because of their ability to analyse spiritual states. They see what is happening."[74] Rather disconcertingly, she admits in a later work that it is "not certain that John of the Cross was ['light on']."[75] I will have more to say about that point later. Finally, Burrows maintains that she could not have written *Guidelines* without the spiritual insight gained through her friend Claire's "light on" state.[76] Despite all of this, Burrows is well aware "that we don't need this propheticism absolutely, all we need is to follow Jesus in the Gospels and keep his commandments of love."[77]

Burrows observes that when one possessed by the gift of "light on" wants to communicate to others their nonconceptual sight of the mystical embrace, they must translate what they "see" into material that can be handled by the consciousness. "'Light on' has nothing to show for itself, so to speak," she reminds us. "It escapes all categories of human expression. . . . It is this 'externalisation' of the 'light on' revelation which can be written and spoken of, not the revelation itself."[78] Exalted language, Burrows tells us, is a key means by which direct "sight" of God's mystical presence is externalized. She remarks, "Say a 'light on' person wanted to describe as best he could what he saw of God holding the soul . . . then, profoundly moved by what he saw, he might pour out the most extravagant images, all the while knowing that his words were totally inadequate to give any idea of this ineffable, nonconceptual reality."[79]

We are told of more possible ways of externalizing "light on" insight in Burrows's analysis of the sixth mansion of Teresa's *Interior Castle*. Referring to the various sensible consolations that Teresa records there—and "she gives us an apron-full"[80]—Burrows appraises, "Possibly what can be said of nearly all of them: 'influences so delicate and subtle that they proceed from the very depth of the heart' and enkindle fire (c 2); the certain consciousness of the presence of the Spouse (c 2); rapture (c 4); flight of the spirit (c 5); prayer of jubilation (c 6); intellectual visions (c 8); impetuous transports of love (c 11), is that the foundation of them is a profound embrace of divine Love, actually 'seen' by the 'light on' faculty. Now in one way, now in another, Teresa's highly sensitised psyche reacts."[81] Elsewhere, Burrows speaks further about "light on" "sight" being externalized in the form of visions. She explains that in this case, the "light on" mystic "has to search around their storehouse of images and symbols for something with which to fashion a substance and form for what has been seen in a totally non-conceptual way."[82] Overall, I have some concerns about Burrows's presentation of the "light on" mode of experiencing God's mystical presence. However, we need to examine more of her thought on consciousness and the mystical life before I can share my misgivings.

Indirect Conscious Experience of the Mystical Life: Burrows's Position on "Spiritual" Experiences

Our discussion of the externalization of the hidden mystical encounter by "light on" mystics has taken us into territory proper to Burrows's general position on "spiritual" experiences. Burrows asserts that appreciating her position on the various sensible phenomena commonly associated with the spiritual life is of "great importance to a clear understanding of mysticism."[83] We have established that the mystical life is simply imperceptible to human consciousness: finite humanity cannot lay hold of what is in essence divine. The reverse side of this is that, for Burrows, any phenomenon registered by the consciousness cannot be God's mystical grace per se. "Mysticism [has] nothing to do with 'experiences,'" she declares.[84] Expanding on this claim Burrows writes, "My conviction is that anything that can be described, given an account of, simply cannot be the mystical encounter in itself. Why is this so? Because the mystical encounter is precisely a *direct* encounter with God himself."[85] So, to Burrows's mind, there is no intrinsic relationship between God's mystical activity, that is, our secret transformation into the Crucified, and "spiritual" experiences. As we will see—indeed, as we have already seen in the case of the externalization of the "sight" of "light on" mystics—in Burrows's perspective these phenomena are, at most, an echo of God's mystical presence.

Within Burrows's mystical framework, all "spiritual" impressions registered by the consciousness are essentially material; they belong to our creaturely state (we touched upon this point in the previous chapter). Given that what is felt cannot be the hidden God, she concludes that "basically ['spiritual' experiences] are self-induced, not in the sense of self-deception though this is possible, but as rising out of the psyche under certain stimuli."[86] It is Burrows's belief that any estimation of experiences must be grounded in an appreciation of modern psychological insights. While she does not expressly indicate allegiance to a particular school of psychology, it is clear that she accepts the idea that the psyche functions on both the conscious and unconscious levels.[87] Burrows maintains, "If we have paid attention to modern scientific investigations of the psyche . . . then we shall have come to the conclusion that it is a most mysterious, largely unexplored dimension where almost anything might happen. . . . This vast range of experience, often awesome and mysterious, belongs to, is part of our material being. It is not of the 'spirit' in the scriptural, theological sense. It is of 'flesh and blood' as Paul has it that cannot enter the kingdom. It belongs to man as 'animate being,' that which we share with the material creation."[88] Accordingly, Burrows is emphatic that "our knowledge of psychology has made us healthily skeptical of much of what was formerly thought to be supernatural."[89]

Burrows allows that for some people sensible phenomena may be a result of God's mystical presence echoing into the psyche. "In some cases," she observes, "the mystical grace overflows as it were into the psychic powers."[90] For Burrows, whether or not the mystical grace echoes into the psyche basically depends upon temperament. In one work she presents "sensitives" as a broad temperament category.[91] Generally predisposed to psychic stimulation, if a sensitive is in the mystical phase of the spiritual life they are likely, Burrows holds, to know sensible phenomena. Outlining in *Guidelines for Mystical Prayer* this same idea that the psychic rever-

> Burrows is emphatic that our knowledge of psychology has made us healthily skeptical of much of what was formerly thought to be supernatural.

beration of the hidden mystical grace is essentially a function of temperament, Burrows suggests, "We could think of the recipients' psychological make-up . . . as a channel: a deep straight canal, a rocky ravine, a shallow bed—whatever. The over-flow from this grace of union will flow into the channel that is there and take its character from it: phlegmatic, choleric, depressive—reactions will differ widely. What is being revealed is not the grace as such but the psychic 'apparatus' of the person and its reaction to stimuli."[92] Predictably, Burrows is emphatic that "this overflow has little significance compared with the reality of the grace";[93] substantially speaking, the psychic overflow is to the mystical grace as a mirrored image is to the object it reflects.

Given that, by Burrows's account, the various phenomena associated with the spiritual life belong inalienably to the psyche, it follows she is insistent that their occurrence is no criterion of the presence of the mystical grace. "Our psychic powers may echo and tremble at the touch of God," she says, "but we have no proof that what happens on the psychic level emanates from the touch of God in our depths. It could just as easily come from other sources."[94] Expounding this idea, Burrows points out in *Interior Castle Explored*, "Rapture, flight of the spirit, as described by Teresa as phenomena, are not confined to the truly mystical realm. We can hear of them, read of them happening in wholly secular, humanistic, even evil contexts."[95] She goes on to cite an experience described by a contemporary practitioner of yoga that "closely resembles what St. Teresa considered one of her most sublime experiences, the flight of the spirit."[96] And in another place she emphasizes that experiences discussed in the context of Christian mysticism "are of the kind that result from other stimuli: extreme fasting, drugs, aesthetic pleasure and so on. Natural mysticism, as it is called, claims similar phenomena."[97]

Further developing her argument that what is felt is a thoroughly unreliable indicator of God's mystical presence, Burrows observes that "spiritual" experiences can take similar forms at different stages of the Christian journey. As she expresses it, "Someone in the very early beginnings of . . . [the spiritual life] could sincerely identify with experiences St. Teresa describes in her fifth and sixth mansions. The gulf between the two *states* is immeasurable but not necessarily between what is experienced on the emotional and psychic levels."[98] Clearly, it is incontrovertible for Burrows that sensible phenomena do not offer any sort of foothold for assessing the interior life.

Now that we are familiar with the main lines of Burrows's approach to experiences let us develop this position by looking with Burrows at other spiritual writers. This will help us to appreciate her belief that her thought is distinctive within the field of spiritual writing. More specifically, it will give us insight into Burrows's assertion that her position on experiences is "wholly in line with tradition . . . [yet] within that tradition, a bold break is being made, a break with age-long, popular, even 'professional' interpretation of the tradition."[99] As to the substance of this "bold break," Burrows is forthright: "Insisting on [the] distinction between the mystical encounter itself and the possible effect of this in the psychic powers, is to oppose centuries of high esteem for 'the feeling of the presence of God' to single out perhaps the most modest claim to mystical grace."[100] To be sure, we noted Burrows's divergence from other writers on the subject of experiences earlier in this chapter. There, the emphasis was on her understanding of the mystical life as the new life in Christ proclaimed to all by the New Testament. Here, however, the emphasis is squarely on what we know to be the flipside of that insight: her insistence that mysticism essentially has nothing to do with psychic phenomena.

We have no proof that what happens on the psychic level emanates from the touch of God in our depths.

Burrows's Divergence from Other Spiritual Writers

As we have been glimpsing along the way, Burrows develops her stance on sensible phenomena in the mystical life largely in contradistinction to what she perceives to be that of Teresa of

Ávila. Burrows acknowledges from the outset Teresa's frequent insistence "that, in themselves, spiritual 'favours,' no matter how sublime they seem, give no certainty of holiness and it is dangerous to desire them."[101] "Over and over again she will reiterate," says Burrows, "that there are holy people who have never seen a vision or heard a locution, and there are those who have who are far from holy."[102] However, and this is the rub, Burrows contends that "[Teresa] is not wholly convincing because of her practical preoccupation with 'favours.'"[103] She expands upon this assertion in her introduction to a compilation of Teresa's writings: "It must be acknowledged . . . that [Teresa] . . . was enamoured of 'favours' and was too dependent on them, conscious that they had, so she believed, brought her immense benefits. We should not shrink from admitting that this was a weakness on her part."[104]

For Burrows, Teresa's handling (really, her mishandling) of the various psychic phenomena she experienced led to confused notions in her spiritual writings and to perplexity at a personal level. In order to make her case, she identifies four dynamics at work within Teresa. First, there is the reality of God's mystical presence in Teresa's depths. Second, there is Teresa's "light on" endowment; "Teresa, in this mysterious way, 'saw' God present, loving her, embracing her."[105] Third are "the vibrant echoes in her emotional and intellectual life" of the mystical encounter in general and her "light on" perception of it in particular;[106] "Teresa was a marked 'sensitive,'"[107] Burrows observes, and was thus prone to such an abundance of psychic experiences.

Finally, Burrows identifies in Teresa apparently spiritual experiences that, she argues, actually arose purely from Teresa's psychic need. She contends, "[Teresa] does not seem to have been of a contemplative temperament. . . . She was not naturally passive. Her psychic pressures forced her, wholly unconsciously, to manufacture 'experience.' . . . Some of her favours are false on their own evidence; locutions that refer to events that never, in fact, happened. All those relating to Gratian, so obviously from her own subconscious, make a mockery of God's intervention. And surely we must see her relationship with Gratian for what it was, a crying maternal longing to have this lovely youth for her very own. A revelation of frailty."[108] Further establishing the existence of this dynamic within Teresa, Burrows maintains,

> Teresa seems to have an unusually powerful need for security. . . . Unconsciously, this craving for security could have had much to do with [the] occurrence [of experiences] in Teresa's life. Imagine the comfort and reassurance of hearing God calling you, "beloved," or saying, "fear not"! What a sense of specialness, security, it could afford! There is, of course, no question of saying Teresa made them up. To have done so would have been to depart from truth and effectively block God, which clearly Teresa did not. It is simply saying that she was a real, human person with a particular makeup, with good points and weak points.[109]

Of course, Burrows means here that Teresa did not *deliberately* make up experiences. It is the mysterious unconscious that Burrows perceives to be at work here.[110]

As Burrows sees it, Teresa misapprehended the four dynamics at work within her. In a word, she argues that Teresa assumed her "light on" faculty, the psychic repercussions from God's mystical presence and her "sight" of it, and the experiences ultimately derived from her unconscious were all the mystical grace itself. Burrows refers to "Teresa's inability to discern the distinction between the actual mystical grace itself, what she 'saw' of it through her endowment of 'light on,' and her psychic response to both."[111] Making this same point in a slightly different way, Burrows insists that "[Teresa] was continually confusing three things: the mystical grace, her 'light on' experience of it, [and] the psychic response."[112] And, illustrating her contention that Teresa identified as pure God what her own psyche generated, Burrows writes, "Take St. Teresa's understanding of 'locutions.' For her, they simply must come from God or from the devil, there is no possible alternative. True, she allows for the self talking to the self but then, she says, these are not locutions, and it is only the simpleton with an over-vivid imagination who would go in for that sort of thing. It could not have occurred to her that the mysterious unconscious might be the source of them all."[113]

By Burrows's account, it is Teresa's confusing of "spiritual" phenomena with the hidden mystical grace that led to ambiguity, both in her writings and at a personal level. Such confusion means that what is felt becomes an indicator of God's mystical presence. We know that this is insupportable to Burrows: "Never should what we feel be used as a criterion. . . . It is on this point we disagree with St. Teresa."[114] In order to exemplify the opacity that she believes Teresa's blurring of the felt and the mystical brought to her writing, Burrows draws our attention to Teresa's account of the fourth mansion: "At the very outset of this mansion she informs us that the reptiles from the moat cannot do the same harm here as in former mansions. Nevertheless they harass and upset us and force us to struggle. This is a boon, she says. It would be dangerous for us to be in this state of consolation always and she is suspicious of any prolonged absorption in it. Rightly we may object that, if this consolation is the mystical grace it cannot possibly harm us even though it were permanent, and is it possible for the devil to counterfeit a truly mystical grace?"[115] Offering another instance of the ambiguity she sees in Teresa's teaching, Burrows observes that Teresa was convinced it is impossible to cultivate sensible consolation. "She is wrong here," Burrows declares. "What she means is that no matter what we do we can never acquire infused contemplation, this is very true, but it is possible to attain all sorts of psychic awareness if one sets one's mind to it."[116]

As for the lack of clarity that issues at a personal level due to Teresa's mistaking psychic phenomena for the mystical grace, Burrows detects its presence both in Teresa's evaluation of others and in her regard of her own spiritual condition. Burrows maintains that Teresa's misapprehension meant that, in "receiving the confidences of others . . . she was only too ready to accept that the identical psychic state [to her own] argued to the same depth of grace [as operative in her]."[117] Inevitably, Teresa was left "bewildered," says Burrows, when in some instances the people "did not bear the expected fruit."[118] While "it is likely that in some cases the 'experience' was an effect of some mystical grace,"[119] this could never be universally true; feelings are never a reliable indicator of the mystical reality. It is worth noting that Burrows concedes here, "Possibly most of these communications were by letter or by a passing exchange. [Teresa] was not in a position to apply her ultimate criterion as to the reality of the virtues of the one in question."[120]

Teresa's perception of her own spiritual state was unnecessarily angst ridden, Burrows contends, as a result of her failure to distinguish between what she felt and God's secret work within her. The supernatural gift of "light on" gave Teresa an essentially inexpressible certainty of God's immediate presence in her depths: "'Light on' bears its own testimony within it.

It cannot be doubted."[121] Blurring the unseen with the seen, Teresa identified this certain, secret knowledge of her mystical state with the experiences that abounded in her psyche. At the same time, Burrows explains, Teresa sought authoritative confirmation of this (mistaken) belief that her psychic experiences were, in fact, the direct work of God's hand. In Teresa's world at large, it was assumed that such experiences proceeded from either God or the devil. Not surprisingly, then, Burrows observes, "for the measure of assurance afforded, there was meted out to [Teresa] appalling anguish evoked by confessors and others who doubted their authenticity. . . . She longed for the authoritative word, 'this is the work of God.' Often she heard, 'the devil,' 'delusion.'"[122] Thus, as Burrows recounts, Teresa was ultimately left in perplexity: on the one hand, her gift of "light on" gave her unutterable certainty of her mystical state, and on the other, she feared she was under the sway of the devil.[123] Within Burrows's perspective, Teresa's anxiety over her inner state could have been entirely avoided had she not directly identified what she experienced on the surface with her interior reality.

Lest Burrows's treatment of Teresa leave us shell shocked, it is important to acknowledge her vivid appreciation of Teresa's historical context. She points out that, "like the rest of us, [Teresa] . . . was conditioned by the times in which she lived."[124] Hence, it is not to be wondered at that Teresa did not perceive that the supernatural simply cannot be regarded as coextensive with psychic phenomena. "She could not have known this," Burrows insists. "We know it because of our modern knowledge of the workings of the psyche, and, above all, our knowledge of the existence of the unconscious."[125] Additionally, Burrows details that the socioecclesial reality of Teresa's era led to a disproportionate emphasis being placed on "spiritual" experiences. She explains, "In St. Teresa's day only clerics had access to the full Bible and at one point even vernacular translations of it were forbidden to women! Ordinary folk were dependent on priests for their theology, and how staid, how meagre it seems to have been! Where were they to find stimulation? Within their own psychic world."[126] Clearly, Burrows is deeply cognizant of just why it is that Teresa, a woman of the sixteenth century, is misguided regarding the relationship between the mystical life and the realm of sensible experiences.

Throughout her writings, Burrows asserts that Teresa's confusing of psychic phenomena for the mystical grace itself is characteristic of spiritual writers in general. And this means that she perceives herself to be swimming against the tide as she insists on the fundamental distinction between experiences registered by the consciousness and God's mystical presence. Burrows sees Teresa's misunderstanding perpetuated in analyses of Teresa's work. On the whole, she maintains, commentators on Teresa "assume the identity of what Teresa *describes* of her state of prayer, that is, what she *felt* of that state, with the *state itself*; what, in her case, *accompanied* the mystical state with the *reality itself*."[127] Burrows reflects on spiritual writing in a broader sense and her own role as a voice of contradiction in *Letters on Prayer*. Addressing her friend Mark Allen she writes,

> When I have been writing about prayer, I have made a point of addressing myself to those who experience little or no religious emotion in order to encourage them. I do this because it would seem that spiritual writers tend to take it for granted that, sooner or later, consolation will come, and that we must indeed persevere in difficulties which are sure

to be there, but looking forward to the day when the sun will shine. Almost always the implication, even though very subtle, is that consolation is the real thing, real prayer. The writer might deny this and yet, it seems to me, that as often as not the implication is there. This, I believe, has to be firmly refuted.[128]

Evidently, Burrows understands her position on experiences to be more than a corrective to a current of misapprehension; it is also an insight with lively pastoral applications.

As we saw in her analysis of Teresa's writings, Burrows points to theological distortions present in other works on the spiritual life that issue from failure to distinguish between the mystical grace itself and sensible phenomena. She cites, for example, "the disputed question as to whether the call to the mystical life is for all."[129] This issue, she observes, has "absorbed the attention of grave men over the centuries, leading to the formation of different 'schools' of spirituality—one holding one view, another the other. The Carmelite school had to devise a form of prayer called 'active contemplation' to cope with the problem."[130] According to Burrows, this uncertainty would simply dissipate were it appreciated that the Gospel invites *all* into the mystical life, that is, into intimate union with God in Jesus crucified, and that effects of this divine union may or may not echo in the created psyche.[131]

Furthermore, Burrows argues that spiritual writers distort the very meaning of prayer when they attribute mystical significance to psychic phenomena. She reasons that when the sensible is identified with the mystical "the attention and emphasis are on the human partner in the relationship of prayer. The criterion for assessing a state of prayer is taken to be what the human partner either does or feels."[132] But,

Burrows objects, "Is not this an extraordinary thing to do? Surely the very essence of prayer, even in the early stages, is to be there for the God whose very nature is to give. This is superlatively true in the mystical prayer, for this, *par excellence*, is "what God is doing." . . . How can we think that what we feel or don't feel, what we know or don't know is all important. If we have faith, surely we *know* that God gives himself without measure and we won't attempt to gauge the depth of the giving by our totally inadequate plumb lines of sense."[133] As we will see in the final section of this chapter, developing a living knowledge that prayer is primarily about what God, in all his hidden "otherness," does in us is a key component of Burrows's teaching on how we should respond to God's mystical intervention.

> The Gospel invites *all* into the mystical life, that is, into intimate union with God in Jesus Crucified; the effects of this divine union may or may not echo in the created psyche.

Burrows's Position as Continuous with Tradition

Having established Burrows's sense of distinctiveness from other spiritual writers, we can now consider what she means when she asserts that her position on experiences is also "wholly in line with tradition." Of course, Burrows perceives her conviction regarding the distinction between the mystical grace itself and possible sensible repercussions of the grace to be fundamentally rooted in the New Testament. If the mystical life is the very participation in the divine life that Jesus both proclaims and mediates then it can have nothing intrinsic to do with phenomena experienced in the created psyche. In fact, Burrows discerns within the pages of the New Testament itself an emphasis on the essential separation between God's mystical presence and the sensible realm. Referring to the mystical grace she observes,

> There is nothing whatever in the New Testament to suggest that this holy gift, the kingdom, eternal life here and now, hits the headlines, compelling assent. Quite the contrary. Jesus suggests its hidden character, lost as it is in the ordinary texture of life. The seed is growing but the farmer does not see it; it grows silently, hiddenly, attracting no attention. His own life among us was just like that and he was scorned and rejected because it was just like that. He repelled the demands for signs and wonders to prove the presence of divine activity. The sign of the outpouring love of God, to be received by all who wish, is the surrender of Jesus on the cross. This is the most divine, the supreme act of creation, the summit of being, and yet, what struck the senses? The tumultuous wind of Pentecost, shaking the foundations of the world, the tongues of fire are only pictorial images of the hidden activity of God, the promise of the Father which indeed shakes our world to its foundations and fills us with the fire of love.[134]

So, when Burrows claims that her view regarding experiences and the mystical life aligns with tradition, it is first of all the teaching of the New Testament that she has in mind.

In outlining the general lack of support within spiritual writing for her scripturally based position on experiences, Burrows remarks, "No author has helped me save John of the Cross."[135] As Burrows sees it, John shares her insistence on the distinction between God's mystical presence and the possible sensible repercussions of this grace. She presents John as transcending his era in this regard. We have seen that in John's times it was taken for granted that experiences had a supernatural character; it was thus simply a question of discerning case by case whether they were diabolic or divine. Burrows maintains that "John side-steps the question. He does not attempt to discern the origin of 'favours' nor does he want his readers to waste time doing so. Perhaps here is revealed an insight he could scarcely express to himself. Did he not intuitively discern that which we of the post-Freudian age are fully aware of: that our *felt* reactions ("visions, revelations, locutions and spiritual impressions") come from ourselves, and *everything depends on us* as to whether they are 'of God' or 'of the devil.'"[136] What Burrows is highlighting here, if somewhat dramatically, is John's perception of the psychic character of experiences. He realized, Burrows holds, that whatever may stimulate the phenomena, they belong to the psyche and must therefore be treated as any other created means to union with God.

It is noteworthy that, according to Burrows, John, like Burrows herself, develops his position on experiences partly as a counter to the confusion found in Teresa and her interpreters. She explains that while both John and Teresa knew psychic echoes of the mystical grace,[137] John was conscious of differing from Teresa in his analysis of these experiences. "I am not alone in detecting in John's work a deliberate if delicate corrective to mistaken interpretations of Teresa," writes Burrows.[138] "In his systematic exposition of the mystical life in the *Ascent* and *Dark Night*, he hammers home time and time again that infused contemplation of its very nature is hidden, most secret to the one receiving it. He counsels ruthless detachment from 'impressions, images, representations in which spiritual communications are involved' (or might be involved)."[139]

Of course, in Burrows's estimation, it is precisely because he, unlike Teresa, perceived the creaturely status of experiences that John urged such detachment from them.

A Brief Critique of "Light On"

I mentioned earlier that I have some misgivings regarding Burrows's discussion of the "light on" mode of experiencing the mystical life. Let us look at them now. Burrows maintains that "light on" mystics serve a didactic function within the church; they communicate their privileged nonconceptual "sight" of God's mystical activity by translating it into data that can be handled by the consciousness. However, how are we to know if one—and here I particularly have in mind authors who have left us an account of their spiritual journey—is a "light on" mystic or not? Burrows does not offer us any criteria for discerning whether or not a sensible phenomenon is an externalization of an insight from a "light on" mystic. How are we to know if we are being given a privileged revelation about life in union with God or one person's particular reaction to psychic stimulation?

And there are further layers of obscurity after this one. It would appear from Burrows's analysis of Teresa that not all of the psychic phenomena experienced by "light on" mystics are external representations of their unique perception of God's direct presence. Even if we could identify "light on" mystics, how are we to know just when they are functioning as spiritual teachers and when to treat their experiences as purely personal phenomena? Furthermore, Burrows suggests that God may occasionally switch on the light for one normally in the "light off" state. How can we tell whether or not a particular account is a representation of such a privileged moment when the veil was drawn back from the mystical encounter?

It seems clear from Burrows's overall appraisal of spiritual writing that those who themselves depict psychic events are generally untrustworthy evaluators of just what is being offered in the depiction. Speaking in the person of Petra, Burrows asserts, "Anyone who has known a true 'light on,' however fleeting, will clearly distinguish it from its psychic echoes—the lightning and the echoing thunder."[140] But where—except here in the case of Petra's fleeting "light on" experiences—are we shown that principle holding true? Certainly not in the case of Teresa. If, as Burrows maintains, there is widespread blurring of the mystical grace with psychic phenomena then it surely follows that we are not going to have clarity as to when it is a "light on" insight that is being translated into psychic categories; such a distinction is simply lost in the overall collapse of the boundary between what is felt and the divine. Indeed, inadvertently countering the assertion that she makes through Petra, Burrows claims in *Interior Castle Explored* that "light on" mystics "probably . . . are unable to discern the actual kernel of the grace they are receiving from the outward shell which is that of their own . . . making."[141]

Additionally, Burrows does not herself demonstrate how to identify and learn from "light on" mystics. We have noted that while she is convinced in *Guidelines for Mystical Prayer* that John is a "light on" mystic, this conviction has waned by the time she writes *Interior Castle Explored*. The problem is that Burrows does not give us any reason why she would question her initial certainty that John's portrayal of the spiritual life derives from a "light on" state.

Burrows displays remarkable ambivalence about Teresa's "light on" state; this further indicates that she does not demonstrate how to handle the "light on" gift. For example, on the one hand, Burrows urges us to "receive [Teresa's] precious wisdom, make use of that which her 'light on' was given for."[142] And on the other hand, referring to Teresa, Burrows declares, "'Light on' revealed her own soul and what God was doing there. When she tried to use this knowledge universally, she made big mistakes."[143] But surely such universalization is to be expected if "light on" mystics serve a didactic function?

Or again, at times Burrows encourages us to heed Teresa's psychic phenomena as exterior manifestations of her "light on" perception. In such a vein she proclaims,

> What must it be to "see" God loving us? Is it any wonder that Teresa was ravished with joy? It does us good to read her outpourings, even to read of her psychic response provided we understand it, for it is not easy in our everyday lives, in our greyness and dryness, to keep our hearts aloft, to keep the mountain top before our eyes. We can go for encouragement and refreshment to the one who "saw." True, her own mode of expression, her choice of imagery may not appeal to us but at least we perceive the rapture of one who "saw" in a similar way in which the apostles "saw" the risen Lord. We can be inspired and encouraged without in any way desiring a like vision for "blessed are they who have not seen and yet believe." We must be absolutely convinced . . . that exactly the same grace of intimacy is offered to us; we too can be totally transformed in love even in this life. "Sight" such as Teresa had is given only to the few but when as in her case, she shares something of her sense of blinding Reality, we can happily accept the stimulation to our own faith and desire.[144]

Yet at other times Burrows counsels us not to attend too closely to Teresa's experiences lest we "give attention and importance to what is of so personal a nature as to be irrelevant for us, and the more so because . . . she, unlike ourselves, had 'light on' experience."[145] It seems to me that if Burrows herself had a clear method for recognizing and learning from "light on" mystics she would not approach Teresa with such ambivalence.

All of this is not to negate the validity of the category "light on." There is nothing conceptually incoherent or theologically unsound in the idea of a direct, nonconceptual perception of God's mystical presence and its consequent externalization. My contention is purely that Burrows's presentation of "light on" mystics as didactically significant would be considerably more helpful, and more convincing, were we given some guidelines on identifying and making use of utterances that derive from "light on" perception.

Indirect Conscious Experience of the Mystical Life: Essential Effects of God's Mystical Presence

Two key points are now established on the subject of what, in Burrows's view, we consciously experience of God's mystical intervention: first, God's mystical presence cannot be experienced directly; and second, the most that can be said for the various phenomena commonly associated with mysticism is that they may be an indirect experience of the mystical grace. Burrows further maintains that when God encounters a person directly, the fabric of his or her lived experience is inevitably affected. She observes, "Clearly God cannot touch someone without changing them, without effects."[146] For Burrows, these effects can be classed with psychic phenomena echoing from the mystical grace in that they are both indirect conscious experiences of God's immediate presence; the "effects flowing from this happening . . . are consciously experienced," she clarifies, "but not the happening itself."[147]

However, Burrows insists that these two types of experience do not share the same status: the inevitable changes that God's mystical grace effect within a person's life are "essential" and "what count,"[148] whereas the sensations that some experience are "secondary" and "quite unimportant."[149]

Before going into detail about Burrows's conception of the essential effects of God's immediate presence, let us consider the basic texture of these effects. What we are discussing here is the lived impact of God touching the human person directly and thereby breaking the supremacy of the ego as the intellect and will are drawn into divine intimacy. We are looking at the lived impact of Jesus crucified, the mediator of the divine presence, substituting his life for that of the ego.[150] Accordingly, by Burrows's account, our overall conscious experience of being drawn into the mystical life is that "instead of going forward—our own idea of going forward—we seem to be going backwards."[151] Expanding on this point that, by our creaturely standards, progress in the spiritual life does not feel like progress, Burrows writes, "The effect of God drawing close to us always means that what Isaiah said of the suffering servant becomes true for us. In a very deep way we have to sacrifice that which seems to make us man, what we think of as a beautiful spirituality; we have to be changed in a way that *seems* to make us less, not more human. There is nothing here naturally attractive to man; rather, his instinct must be to turn away in revulsion. This, in practice, in hard reality, is what it means to embrace Jesus crucified, and embracing him, embrace he who sent him and whose revelation he is."[152] So as the Crucified graciously takes over in the depths, what basically resounds into our lived experience is a deflation of our self-importance. We taste the reality that to be truly human is to be a dependency disposed to the Infinite, "that nothing in ourselves can charm love from the beloved; the love given to us is dependent on itself alone."[153]

Burrows specifies that the living impact of being taken into the kenosis of Christ is threefold. The three essential effects are, she details, "a painful awareness of sinfulness, lack of satisfaction in meditation (that is, 'aridity'), and growth in goodness."[154] We can say that the first two effects stand for all the felt repercussions of that gradual toppling of the ego wrought by God's mystical action. Burrows also describes the third effect as "a growing willingness to accept on every level, a sense of unimportance, to become as small as a child."[155] It is the divine enablement to sustain

> Our overall conscious experience of being drawn into the mystical life is that instead of of going forward—our own idea of going forward—we seem to be going backwards.

the deflation of the ego. These three effects present in living terms what it means to be at once purified and transformed by God's mystical grace: the grace that unmasks the extent of our self-seeking also holds us in Jesus' self-emptying "yes" to the Father. Or, as Burrows puts it, "the divine gaze of love, even as it imprints its own likeness on us reveals most painfully our own swarthiness."[156]

The three basic effects of the in-breaking of mystical grace are, according to Burrows, experienced ever more penetratingly throughout the second stage of the spiritual life. We determined earlier that our transformation into Jesus crucified is a process that depends upon our cooperation; here we see the lived experience of this gradual transformation. In *Guidelines*

for Mystical Prayer Burrows observes that what we experience
of God's mystical presence across the second island "is basically the same as on the bridge: aridity, and a painful knowledge of self, only now these are more diffuse and deeper."[157]
The intensity of these two effects, however, can only be commensurate with the degree to which we allow the third basic
effect of immersion into the kenotic Christ, the enablement
to withstand the undoing of the ego, to take root in us. Thus
Burrows concludes that one who is truly being taken into the
depths of Christ's surrender to Love will be "consenting to
have no security but God and him unseen, unfelt, resolutely
choosing him and abandoning self, always, all the time."[158] We
shall now make a brief study of Burrows's understanding of
each of these three interrelated effects of the mystical life.

Infused Self-Knowledge

At the second stage of the spiritual life, self-knowledge concerns the limited, false self of whom we become conscious
as, secretly, we encounter God directly. We have seen that for
Burrows, spiritual self-assurance is characteristic of beginners.
For them—inevitably captive as they are to the tyranny of the
ego—the God they follow and the standards he sets are ultimately of their own making. Accordingly, perfection appears
eminently achievable.

Burrows teaches that as God himself touches our inmost
being, the egoistic foundation on which we were building our
castle of sanctity is broken open and thus our conception of
ourselves as spiritually successful, or at least potentially so,
begins to crumble. Developing this impact of God's mystical
action she writes, "When God, all-love, love that in its human
expression sheds its last drop of blood for us, draws close, the
ego can have no part with him, it is the dead opposite of such

self-giving love. The ego is then shown up for what it is in its distortion and ugliness. In its own estimation and in the estimation of other egotisms it had seemed fine enough. Now it is beginning to be unmasked and revealed as it is."[159] Penetrated by the living light of the true God, that light which is darkness to our consciousness, we realize that the Christian identity we had been creating is shot through with selfishness. "We see," Burrows explains, "the hollowness of what we conceived of as our goodness, our truth, our virtues, generosity and achievement. . . . We see in terror and dismay that every road to spiritual success and achievement is blocked."[160] Consequently, "we are forced to come to grips with our secret vices, perverted motivations and general sinfulness."[161]

Bitter though it is, Burrows conceives of the self-knowledge that issues from God's mystical presence as a gift. As she sees it, "we have no holiness, goodness or wisdom of our own. So to be made consciously aware that we are spiritually inadequate, faulty, wretched—that we fail and sin—is a precious grace."[162] Burrows's point here is that this awareness of the poverty of our interior condition is necessary if we are to stand before God, in Jesus, empty handed, a living nothingness for him to fill; this stance is the essence of mystical living. For Burrows everything depends on actually "letting go of the controls, handing them over to [Jesus] and accepting to have no holiness, no achievement of my own, to be before God as nothing. This is to die so that Jesus becomes my all."[163]

Spiritual Aridity

Burrows describes aridity, the second effect of God's mystical presence, as "a state of consciousness that lacks a sense of spiritual well-being. The things of God hold no attraction for us."[164] In order to appreciate the emergence of this state it is necessary to recall first that Burrows depicts the first stage of the spiritual life as a phase in which God relates to us indirectly, through the various forms that are the proper data of the human faculties. "At the beginning," she reminds us, "it was essential to make every possible use of good thoughts, ideas, impressions, to help us to choose to follow Jesus. We needed to live with these, savour them, treasure them."[165] Furthermore, we know that with the in-breaking of mystical grace our inmost being is graciously enabled to receive God as he is in himself; in our depths we begin to participate in the very life of God. Thus whereas initially God fed us mediately, now "he puts the food into our mouths without our knowing it, into that spiritual being which is only now emerging and of which our mind and senses can have no direct knowledge."[166]

In Burrows's portrayal of the spiritual life, aridity ensues when the ground of our relationship with God is shifted from the means proper to the created self to our emerging spiritual center. Explaining this effect of God's mystical grace she states, "The growing spiritual being within is now impatient of the coarse food the mind supplies. Hence a sense of aridity, distaste. Spurned by the inner self, useless, empty, the ordinary channels of communication echo hollowly with every kind of noise and disturbance whilst the choosing self feeds secretly on divine food."[167] In other words, with the onset of the mystical life, the material fitted to our human nature—thoughts, ideas, and so on—no longer mediates God to us; what were formerly springs of water are now but dry ground. We can see from all this that a duality underlies Burrows's perception of the experience of aridity. As she observes, "The mystical coming and knowing which ensues makes all other knowledge seem empty, and yet it is by this we must shape most of our conduct, for this is all we can possess."[168] Thus suspended between two kinds of knowing, the traveler across the second stage of the spiritual journey inevitably experiences some "sense of being torn, divided, false."[169]

Burrows modifies the teachings of John and Teresa as she develops her understanding of aridity. She observes that "Teresa describes states of aridity in her usual high tones."[170] Burrows, however, prefers to treat this effect of the mystical life as an experience that is shaded differently for different people. There is sufficient room within her conception of aridity to allow that "there are those who have never known what is commonly understood as sensible consolations and do not suffer the classic 'come-down.' On the other hand aridity, as commonly understood, seems never to have touched others. The majority perhaps, in varying tonalities, know both consolation and desolation and move from one to another."[171]

Concerning John of the Cross, Burrows notes that in describing how the second stage of the spiritual life is experienced, "John says the soul believes it is abandoned by [God]."[172] After countering that "God has told us emphatically that he never abandons his children,"[173] Burrows claims, "We must simply reject this notion of John's, which does not square with the Gospel and therefore is not authentic."[174] She goes on to express, "I am afraid some people take hold of this idea of abandonment as the culminating spiritual trial and sure sign of great progress: they too think they are abandoned by God and oh, the sheer agony of it! This is nonsense and an insult to God. . . . I live by faith and not by what I feel."[175] What Burrows is ultimately pointing to here is the folly of clinging to a sense of abandonment as a mark of spiritual progress. It is misleading, I think, to accuse John of teaching that God ever abandons anyone; to state that the soul *believes* it is abandoned is not to affirm that this is, in fact, the case. Indeed,

Burrows does not make this criticism of John anywhere else in her corpus.

As with self-knowledge, Burrows considers the aridity that ensues from God's mystical presence to be a divine gift. Basically, she sees it as a prolonged opportunity to consent to being taken into Jesus' pure receptivity to the ecstasy of God's love; as she puts it, in experiencing aridity, "we are being summoned to the espousals of the cross."[176] "The sense of God's absence, of God's not being there," Burrows expounds, "is only telling us that, mercifully, the God that is no God but only our own fabrication, satisfies us no longer. . . . Our sense of loss becomes an invitation to find, or rather lose, ourselves in the real God."[177] What is required of us is resolutely to stand in the truth that we are essentially an emptiness for God to fill. Thus, "We are asked to let prayer disappear, surrender our 'spiritual life,' have no control over it. We have to give full space to the Spirit awaking within us, uttering his secret inarticulate prayer."[178] In the following section we shall consider just how, in Burrows's view, we enact this abandonment to the mystical inflowing in prayer.

Before we turn to Burrows's understanding of the third effect of the mystical life, it will be worthwhile to consider her approach to mystical suffering. "Mystical suffering" refers to the living pain that is our experience of the gradual toppling of the ego. We have already noted that, for Burrows, the dawning of infused self-knowledge and spiritual aridity are painful processes. These effects represent our overall experience of being shifted from the sphere of materiality into the divine sphere. Burrows explains that although this sphere is "ultimately our total beatitude and sole fulfilment, [it] is alien, frightening and painful to our limited corporality."[179] Thus, she says, "What we read of in scripture of the birth pangs of the age to come, what we see of Jesus' own dying, is telling us of what it means for human beings to surrender to the divine invasion of love."[180]

In essence, Burrows insists that "an attempt to assess the reality and depth of divine purgation by the kind and intensity of suffering is erroneous."[181] So, while it is inevitable that we will suffer as we are taken into the Crucified's perfect exposure to Love, Burrows does not want us to construe the nature of our subjective experience as a measure of our inner transformation. This idea is present throughout Burrows's discussion of the effects of God's mystical presence; indeed, we have just seen it in her reference to the varying experiences of spiritual aridity. It is most fully developed however, in her treatment of the culminating phase of the second stage of the spiritual life.

> Burrows does not want us to construe the nature of our subjective experience as a measure of our inner transformation.

For Burrows there is no necessary correlation between the ultimate toppling of the ego and "extreme suffering—using that word in its usual sense, covering the experiences we generally have in mind."[182] She develops this position mindful that, in fact, "both John and Teresa testify to a period of most intense suffering just before a person's entrance into the third island,"[183] as she puts it in *Guidelines*. She elaborates elsewhere that "John seems to imply that the passive night of spirit, understood as the final purgation preceding union, is an experience of intense terrible suffering that he likens to purgatory, if not to hell."[184]

Clearly, there is, for Burrows, a distinction to be made between the mortal wounding of the ego in itself and the lived experience of this death. Using John's terms to convey this distinction she writes, "The essence of the night understood as purgation . . . is the burning away of egotism, the death of the 'old man' and the substitution of the divinely human life, Jesus-life, for the sinful human life. What it *feels like* will vary enormously from person to person."[185] Burrows also produces her own image to establish this point:

> We can use the homely image of laundering. Essentially the purification of washing is the same, but different materials need different treatment. A linen tablecloth will "experience" a most intense form of washing: boiling water, vigorous pummelling in the machine, thorough wringing out and hanging up exposed to wind and sun. An angora jersey is immersed in warm soft-soap water, gently swished, not wrung but patted tenderly and laid out in a protected place to dry. A camel-hair coat will be sent to the dry cleaners for progressive attention; it will know nothing of water or washing machine. Though all three are cleansed, purified, the experience of each differs considerably. We could say the linen is cleansed in a dramatic way with passionate intensity; the wool with slowness and gentleness; the camel-hair with aridity and in a manner hard to associate with washing.[186]

Quite evidently, Burrows's idea is that while the ultimate purification, the death of the ego, is a single reality, the embodiment of the ego's final undoing, or the culminating mystical suffering, takes various forms.

Having established her argument that the final mystical suffering can be experienced in many ways, Burrows proceeds to claim that this suffering is likely to be woven into the fabric of ordinary life. "I could well imagine," she details, "the mortal wounding of the ego . . . taking place, perhaps more effectively, where great suffering, in the ordinary sense, is absent. The real thing is likely to operate in an unobtrusive way, hidden behind what seem purely natural factors."[187] Presenting this idea in terms of her laundering image, Burrows begins, "John's descriptions in the *Dark Night* are more akin to the linen-washing process. Perhaps this was closest to his own experience. Maybe, as 'favours' in his day seem to have been of a dramatic kind, so also was the experience of purgation."[188] She goes on to maintain, "In our day the dark night seems to be more commonly experienced as a 'dry clean,' a long-drawn-out greyness where nothing happens and where it seems inconceivable that anything will happen—ever. Is not this painful to our nature? Sometimes is there not a temptation to escape from this into dramatic sufferings? These at least give us a sense that something is happening, that we *are* suffering. . . . True affliction deprives us of every vestige of self-complacency. It is often low-keyed, miserable, something we are ashamed to call suffering."[189] So without denying that a death truly occurs at the culmination of the second stage of the spiritual life, Burrows maintains that the death throes of the ego, or the birth pangs of the Christ-life, may well be embedded within the commonplace.

Burrows points to temperament and circumstances as "banal," "earthy," "ordinary" factors through which we may suffer the final undoing of the ego.[190] In *Guidelines*, she draws directly on her own lived experience, under the guise of that of Petra, to illustrate what she means. After reminding us of Petra's neurotic, "self-torturing temperament,"[191] Burrows details that her psychic fragility mediated God's final work of purification. She observes,

> It seems inevitable that psychic weaknesses and conflicts
> will be shown up in God's light so that they can be faced

and resolved. God works on the whole person, and it is the whole that is purified and transformed. It is easy to see how natural factors may account for why one person suffers more acutely at this stage than others. It is response to suffering that matters and in Petra's case the helpless, long-drawn-out anguish, no matter what its cause, forced her into God's arms. There was no alternative. When trust was total, her problems fell off like a snake-skin. Neurosis is essentially a clinging to self.[192]

Further, Burrows narrates that Petra also experienced the pain of the final overthrow of the ego through a series of events wherein, "within the space of two years she was called upon to relinquish her last toe-holds on human happiness and security."[193] She makes known to us,

> No one could say that these troubles, of themselves, were worth writing home about. They belong to the common lot. But Petra saw God in them—ah, not in a way that "sublimated" them, no, they were experienced in their earthy bitterness—but she understood that this is how he comes. He asked her to abandon the last shreds of security, shreds that gave her some sort of meaning; asked her to look only to him for meaning and fulfilment. Ah, who can say how desolate she felt. She saw nothing ahead, no joy, nothing, nothing, nothing as far as she could see stretching for ever. And yet she went on telling God he was her all. She felt nothing.[194]

Thus Burrows demonstrates that the culminating mystical suffering need not be abstracted from the texture of the everyday; it may be as immediate and unspectacular as psychological suffering or painful circumstances.

Divine Enablement to Sustain the Undoing of the Ego

Burrows remarks that the "third effect of the mystical grace is seen in the quality of life."[195] Earlier, this effect was described as the divine enablement to sustain the deflation of the ego. All this is to say that what Burrows is discussing here is the infusion into the fabric of our lived experience of the impulse to cooperate with the transformation that God is initiating in our depths. The mystical life is about being taken into the Crucified's abandonment to the God of love. This requires our consent to resolutely stand in the innate poverty of our human condition. The third effect of the mystical life is precisely the strength to make that consent.

Expanding on this impact of God's mystical presence Burrows states, "Mystical prayer . . . has *always* the effect of imparting *wisdom*, that is, a living knowledge of God which is transforming."[196] She also discusses her thinking here in terms of faith: "Faith is a 'knowing' not 'about God' but a knowing God—an obscure, secret knowledge which is the source of one's living."[197] This living knowledge is nothing other than a participation in the mind of Jesus. "It is the wisdom Paul speaks of," Burrows declares, "a communication of the Spirit of God who alone knows the depths of God. It is this Spirit who enlightens Jesus, revealing to him the mind of the Father, and Jesus' mind is ours."[198]

So, according to Burrows's portrayal of the spiritual life, we are able to embrace our fundamental human dependency because we are infused with Jesus' own "knowing," his very way of being. This is the innermost meaning of her understanding of the third effect of the mystical grace. Thus Burrows can say of this aspect of our experience of the mystical life, "It is the wisdom of the crucified One—sheer folly, scandalous!—a wisdom that perceives divine love and love's action where natural wisdom would deride or shrink back in disgust. Divine wisdom gently coaxes us to submit to being purified of self, to being comforted in our helplessness and poverty; it persuades us to surrender control, and to abandon ourselves blindly to love."[199]

Or again, "It is a 'being held' that makes us hold on in darkness and bewilderment, when commonsense, all that we ordinarily mean by experience, draws a blank. Faith holds us within, in our inmost citadel, without rhyme or reason, it seems."[200] We can consent to being an emptiness before the living God because we are upheld by the definitive self-abandoning "yes" of Jesus.

A final word needs to be said concerning the third effect of God's mystical presence. Burrows explores the relationship between this living, mystical knowledge and conceptual knowledge. She is clear that "mystical knowledge is something given, never within our grasp. Mystical knowledge has to do with absolute reality, with the unspeakable mystery of God."[201] In the same vein she asserts of this knowledge, "We cannot hold it, it holds us. . . . Try to examine it, try to clutch it and it flees like the deer."[202] Burrows goes on to unfold the idea that while mystical knowledge is essentially nonconceptual, "The mind tries to give it images."[203] She is quick to clarify, however, that there is an essential difference between the living wisdom itself and its conceptual expression. She maintains, "We may seek to communicate our vision . . . finding images and words, but we can never fully succeed. Images, words, form, become ciphers and that is all."[204] Parenthetically, the externalization of what is "seen" through the gift of "light on"—in which what is essentially divine is translated into human concepts—is a unique instance of what Burrows is discussing here.

In addition, Burrows regards mystical knowledge as a spring that can infuse objective, conceptual knowledge with the living waters of divine wisdom. Developing this idea in *Ascent to Love* she writes, "'Beginners' lack this mystical knowledge, the 'advanced' are imbued with it—more and more it becomes the 'ground' from which their conceptual knowledge springs. Two persons could be dwelling on the same passage of scripture and have basically the same ideas. In the case of the beginner the ideas would be the sum total, whereas 'behind,' around, permeating the ideas of the other would be the obscure, divine 'knowing.'"[205] An attendant point that Burrows mentions here is the necessity of growing in our distinct knowledge in order that mystical knowledge will have content to work on, so to speak. As she puts it, "We have the duty to apply our minds to the forms, facts, words, structures of divine revelation. This means, of course, getting to know Jesus—but always aware that the content can never be grasped by the human mind; the content is pure gift to us, infused into our inmost heart."[206]

It is worth noting that Burrows is certain there can be no fundamental contradiction between conceptualized expressions of divine wisdom and the teaching of the church. She explains that "the true friend of Jesus will only be saying what Jesus is saying and this means what the Church is really saying, hidden as it not infrequently is within a lot of untruth."[207] In other words, expressions of mystical knowledge and church teaching must ultimately be consistent with each other because they derive from the same source.

The Essential Effects as Criteria for Assessing Spiritual Progress?

To conclude this discussion of the three essential effects of the mystical grace, an important question needs to be addressed: given that these effects are inevitably imprinted upon the fabric of our existence as we are taken into the life of the Crucified, does it follow that they can be used to assess whether or not one is in the mystical state? While Burrows is rather elusive on this topic, we can identify the main lines of her thought. At one point she pronounces, "The direct action of God in the human being is wholly secret. It can be known only by its effects and even these are not easily assessed by 'flesh and blood.'"[208] For Burrows, the presence of living knowledge is the most reliable indication that one is in the second stage of the mystical life. "Unless we can witness this growth in living wisdom," she states, "we have no criterion of the presence of the mystical."[209] In Burrows's estimation, the experiences of self-knowledge and spiritual aridity may be effected by factors other than immersion in the kenotic Christ and thus are too often subject to misinterpretation.[210]

Burrows indicates that in the early phases of the second stage it is not possible to self-assess one's spiritual status. In reference to initially being given God's direct touch she observes, "We will be unaware of the fact and we do not need to know of it."[211] And, in describing the phase denoted by the bridge in *Guidelines for Mystical Prayer*, she notes "that in these early stages of the spiritual life we cannot know where we are."[212] Indeed, if one's egoism is only beginning to be dismantled it would seem incongruous to have an awareness of one's progress into the mystical realm; with the ego still in the ascendancy, this knowledge would surely be distorted into complacency. Burrows highlights, however, that others may be able to intuit in a person the nascent presence of the mystical grace. She explains, "Here, for the discerning, is proof of the presence of at least the beginning of the mystical. Below the level of sense and reason, a life is going on, secret from the person himself. . . . There is a 'quality' of life . . . far removed from showiness, the desire to impress others or to be among the advanced."[213]

As for those who have made significant progress in the mystical way, Burrows accepts that they may have a sense of their position on the spiritual journey. She comments in *Guidelines*, "Only later on, perhaps far on the second island, perhaps not until the third, can we know where we are."[214] With regard to the experience of this "knowing," Burrows says that the well advanced "do not know how they know or what they know."[215] Clearly we are in the realm of mystical knowledge here; it is an "unknowing" knowing, ultimately obscure to human judgment. Moreover, Burrows maintains that a "deeply discerning heart" is needed if we are to identify one who is far along in the second stage.[216] "Listen to the person herself," she counsels; "listen beyond what one sees and hears, listen to the heart and you will know she thinks nothing of herself. Not only that, she is accepting her nothingness and making no fuss about it."[217]

> While she engages it to some degree, Burrows would have us remain at a certain distance from the matter of assessing spiritual progress.

In the end, while she engages with it to some degree, Burrows would have us remain at a certain distance from this matter of assessing spiritual progress. "We have to banish from our hearts everything but the naked desire for God alone," she affirms.[218] We have seen that the overall movement of the three essential effects of the mystical grace is into the kenosis of Christ; the impetus is toward self-abandonment, poverty, empty-handedness. If we are to be in accord with the impact of God's grace we must direct our gaze away from ourselves—which includes becoming detached from preoccupation with our spiritual status—and toward the self-giving God.

RESPONDING TO THE MYSTICAL GRACE

By now, Burrows's teaching that the mystical life requires of us an unflinching embrace of our fundamentally dependent human condition is evident. As she observes, "The way of being of the becoming self is that of Jesus. . . . Self is being taken over by, held by, this mysterious life within, increasing in the measure that the loving, transforming action of God meets with a generous response."[219] And we respond to God's mystical action of transforming the ego into the life of Jesus by resolutely accepting the potential for the divine fullness that is contained within the poverty of our particular human existence. "Our total 'obedience' with Jesus to our human lot," says Burrows, "is our surrender to God; it is sharing in the death of Jesus, but a death that is all the time blossoming in divine life."[220] Or, making the same point in a different way, she writes, "Jesus can unite himself to us only if we consent to become like him—without beauty, glory, grandeur."[221] In this third and final section we will explore what it means in practice, according to Burrows, to claim the emptiness of our being and thus to allow Jesus to utter in us his "yes" to the Father.

Responding to God's Mystical Grace as the Work of the Theological Virtues

We have just seen that the third effect of the mystical life is the divine enablement to respond to God's direct self-giving. It is the impetus, Burrows explains to her friend Mark, "to choose to become at the root of your being a little child";[222] it is the impetus to consent to being conformed to Jesus crucified. Now in Burrows's presentation of the mystical life, the choice to cooperate with the infusion of divine strength and respond to the mystical inflowing is the work of the theological virtues. "Faith, hope, love," she maintains, "form one movement of choice and surrender to the mystery that has been revealed in Jesus as purest, self-bestowing love, Father."[223] Accordingly, Burrows claims, "If we want to make progress, to respond fully to the grace we are beginning to receive, then all our intent must be to develop these three virtues."[224]

As Burrows sees it, trust is the innermost meaning of each of the theological virtues. In her brief exposition of Burrows's thought, Elizabeth Ruth Obbard highlights this idea that trust is the essence of our graced surrender to the mystical life when she writes, "Trust is the one thing which allows us to accept ourselves as we are and God as he is."[225] So, for Burrows, developing the theological virtues is essentially a matter of growing in trust. Thus she can conclude, "The whole of the spiritual journey can be seen in terms of trust, growing in trust until one has lost oneself in God."[226]

So what does developing the theological virtues, or growing in trust, mean for Burrows? What are the central dynamics of our consent to stand in the truth of our poor humanity, sharing in Jesus' self-abandonment to the Father? We have seen Burrows discuss faith in terms of the divine enablement to sustain the stripping of the ego. Here, in this context of response, she approaches faith from the other side, so to speak, as our enabled *choice* to surrender to God's transformative self-giving. Burrows details, "Faith is not a thing of the mind, it is not an intellectual certainty or a felt conviction of the heart, it is a sustained decision to take God with utter seriousness as the God of our life."[227] Thus, in Burrows's vision, faith "means renouncing myself as my own base, my own centre, my own end. It means so centring myself on another, so making that other my *raison d'être* that it is, in truth, a death to the ego."[228] It is worth noting that Burrows understands her conception of the work of faith to be comprehensive enough to subsume what we will see her detail as the work of love and hope. "For all practical purposes we do not need to make any distinction," she observes, "and the word faith will cover all, denoting the proper response of the whole person to God."[229]

The defining note of Burrows's understanding of love as response to the mystical inflow is that "for us, to love is to let ourselves be loved."[230] "As human beings," she expands, "we are there only to receive Love. . . . It is in this way that we glorify the pure, totally gratuitous love of God."[231] Clearly, Burrows holds that the principal work of the virtue of love consists in cultivating receptivity to God's self-gift. As to what developing such openness implies she asserts, "To be loved means a naked, defenceless surrender to all God is. It means a glad acceptance of our nothingness, a look fixed only on the God who gives, taking no account of the nothing to whom the gift is made."[232] Of course, sustaining this stark abandonment to the inundation of God's love depends upon actually believing that God is outpoured love. Accordingly, Burrows advises that "every effort must be made to convince ourselves of this love and to deepen our faith in it: God's unfailing, unshakeable love for me, no matter what it feels like, no matter how unlike love it seems."[233] So, in Burrows's conception, the work of love calls for the most radical self-abdication. There is no assertion of sentiment or religious ambition here; rather, there is unremitting consent for God to be God.

Burrows's word on hope comes principally through her presentation of the thought of John of the Cross. John, Burrows highlights, teaches that the memory must be purified by the virtue of hope. As she elaborates upon this idea, Burrows expresses her position on the work of hope in responding to God's mystical presence. She maintains, "If one sees memory as the root of self-identity, then the contemplative action of God will strike it fiercely and the self must correspond with this action of God. We must refuse to recall what we have done for God or how well others think of us; of past 'favours' which seem to validate progress. We must refuse to fall back on anything of ourselves to give us some sense of spiritual achievement when God is despoiling us and inviting us to stand in naked truth. Nothing must be left to us save the unfailing goodness of God."[234] Thus we learn that for Burrows, to cooperate with the divine impetus and develop the virtue of hope is to detach our grasp from the fraudulent securities offered by the ego and choose to stand empty handed before the ecstasy of God's love.

We have been establishing Burrows's idea that if we are to cooperate with God's mystical action, if we are to accept being transformed into the Crucified, we must embrace the truth of our human poverty by developing the theological virtues. It is Burrows's conviction that we *incarnate* this trusting surrender to God by refusing to evade the limitations, contingencies, and fragility of our experience of life. We have seen that the basic effect of God's mystical presence is to immerse us in the sheer vulnerability of the human condition; we are penetrated with the truth of "what it means to be man and there is nothing glorious in this. It is to feel 'no-man,' a worm, a poor misshapen beast."[235] Now it becomes clear that, in Burrows's understanding, if we are to respond to the mystical grace, we must trustfully abandon ourselves to God precisely from within this most unspectacular experience of powerlessness; this is the ground within which we exercise faith, hope, and love. Summarizing this work of cooperating with Love, Burrows observes, "Our task is fundamentally the same as Jesus'. We have to live out our own individual life with its own particular amalgam, in love of God and our neighbour, bearing all things, believing all things, hoping all things, enduring all things. With all our heart we have to embrace this painful condition of dependency even when it presses most sorely, never trying to pretend that it is other than it is, never railing against it but accepting it in humble, trustful obedience to the Father."[236]

Burrows offers us a schema for exploring her insight that we respond to God's mystical presence by standing resolute in trust amidst every revelation of our human frailty when she writes, "Faith lives nakedly exposed to God in the experience of reality, in the experience of ourselves, in the experience of prayer."[237] We shall consider—in reverse order—how Burrows would have us launch out in trust in each of these "places" of powerlessness. Of course, the counsel Burrows presents here in no way abrogates the ascetical practices we saw her commend to beginners. Rather, those ascetical efforts become "ever more penetrating and pure" as we progress in the spiritual life and come actually to share in—and not simply imitate from the outside—the life of the Crucified.[238]

Trust at Work in Prayer

When Burrows discusses abandoning ourselves to the mystical inflowing in prayer, it is times of solitary prayer that she has in mind. To be sure, she claims, "The whole of a truly Christian life is prayer. Prayer is simply laying ourselves open to receive God's gift, and that we can do every moment of the day."[239] Further, we saw her assert earlier that the mystical life is offered to us in a concentrated way in the prayer of the sacraments. However, Burrows maintains that personal prayer is an "indispensable vehicle for . . . mystical union."[240] Indeed, she admits, "without such a period of prayer it is hardly possible for our faith in the sacraments to have the depth that will enable us to receive them fruitfully. Nor is it likely that we shall recognise and respond to God's self-gift in the humdrum of daily life."[241]

Burrows's position on how faith lives nakedly exposed before the living God in solitary prayer comes principally through her counsel regarding how to handle the onset of aridity. We noted previously that Burrows perceives a lack of satisfaction in meditation to follow upon God's mystical coming. As our intellect and will are imperceptibly taken into the divine life, "what is likely to happen is that, at least from time to time, we simply cannot think useful thoughts, nothing helps us and we are in a state of rootless helplessness which is hard to bear because drab and unsatisfying."[242] Burrows's focus here is on what we are to do with the mind when meditation thus "forsakes us" and we are left feeling barren.[243] She is adamant that, even though it is no longer the breadwinner (as it were), we must not attempt to void the mind in prayer. "In one way or another," she declares, "our minds must work all our life long: helpful or tormenting, it is part of our human condition and must be accepted wholeheartedly."[244] Building on this claim Burrows observes, "We have got it into our heads and many books encourage the notion, that it is more advanced and spiritual to give up thought and reflection . . . that it is much more contemplative to remain with blank minds waiting for God to act. . . . [This] is pride, a refusal to be human."[245]

In Burrows's view, the role of the mind in mystical prayer is to sustain our exposure to the God of love, and this demands trust. For her, prayer in the midst of aridity calls for "faith at its purest, refusing to stand on our own perception and casting our whole weight on the Father of Jesus"[246]— "and this always involves an act of the mind adverting to his presence."[247] Again, she counsels, "we must endeavour to stay in prayer, offering ourselves to God, accepting the painful awareness of indigence. . . . What we must do is to keep in mind as best we can that we are with God and that he is the God who loves us. We can count utterly on him. In other words, exercise our faith."[248]

Burrows teaches that the mind may use various methods to help us respond in faith to the unseen, unfelt inundation of God's love. Referring to methods such as "the use of the rosary, litanies of a repetitive nature and even the 'Jesus prayer,'" she observes, "not infrequently, whilst the mind is partially employed in the words, the mysteries indicated, a deeper dimension is exposed to God's loving communication."[249] Burrows cautions here that methods must "not become a screen behind which we hide our spiritual impotence. Their purpose must be to help us to maintain our undefended aloneness before our God."[250] All this is to say that Burrows envisions mystical prayer to be "a sort of non-passive passivity, a quiet reaching out, a longing and, of course, a self-surrender."[251] As God draws close, faith, hope, and love, working through our mental capacity, uphold us in naked receptivity before him.

It is germane to mention here that Burrows also holds we respond to God's mystical presence during our times of prayer by accepting with faith any favors we receive. This is basically an extension of the advice we saw her offer beginners. Burrows insists that any psychic experiences we may have in prayer are not the mystical grace itself, nor even a certain indication of God's mystical presence. Nevertheless, Burrows allows that favors can serve a most positive function in our spiritual journey. "There may . . . be times," she observes, "when we are supported by consolations, when our feelings are in tune with the truth or our minds receive profound intuitions as to the reality of God's presence. These are blessed moments to encourage and strengthen us."[252] What matters to Burrows is that we treat whatever is experienced with faith; thus we stand resolute in the truth that to be fully human is to be comprehended by incomprehensible Mystery. This means we must "refuse to identify [God] with any means to him no matter how sublime and spiritual these may seem."[253] "Faith," maintains Burrows, "allows for no rest or security anywhere, it stands steadfast, alone."[254]

Trust at Work in Our Response to Infused Self-Knowledge

We know Burrows is clear that "to become 'without beauty, without majesty,' is the price of union with Jesus in his death,"[255] and infused self-knowledge provides a privileged revelation of our fundamental destitution. What she holds as crucial is the response we make to our experience of our absolute neediness, this "state where we have no assurance within ourself that all is well with us."[256] We have, Burrows observes, "a fundamental choice: will I let Jesus be my holiness and stand in the blazing truth, or will I insist on having a holiness of my own—to offer him, of course, to be pleasing in his eyes?"[257] She goes on to insist, "The whole essence of the Christian demand is to let God be our God and refuse to be God to ourselves. . . . It consists fundamentally in a total acceptance of the bitter experience of our poverty and an obstinate refusal to evade it; to accept to stand, in very deed not just in pious imagination, stripped before the living God, our leprosy laid bare, crippled in limb, blind, deaf, dumb—a living need."[258] When Burrows refers to faith living nakedly exposed to God's self-gift in the experience of ourselves it is precisely such unwavering acceptance of our fallen human condition that she has in mind.

In Burrows's thought, to accept our interior fragility with radical trust in God is what is meant by Christian humility. "True humility *actually* experiences that of ourselves we can do nothing," she details. "It knows itself as incapable of goodness and relies only on God to keep it safe and supply what it needs at each moment. It has nothing and hopes for all from God. This is the effect of profound grace."[259] As we probe this further, we realize that, for Burrows, to be humble is to allow Jesus to be our holiness, our virtue. Reflecting on this mystery she writes, "Christian humility . . . calls to mind that there is One who always did his Father's will; who offers the Father perfect love and worship. And this One is the Father's gift to us. From the shelter of the Son's heart we go on trying, with him, to do always what pleases the Father; but at the same time never wanting to feel we are becoming holy and good, without spot or wrinkle. Never are we more truly in Christ Jesus than when, deeply conscious of our sinfulness, we peacefully rest in the heart of our Redeemer."[260] So, to respond to the mystical inflowing, to be humble, is to refuse to escape the reality of what it means to be a sinful creature, in full confidence that Jesus is our only sanctification.

Throughout her writings Burrows is emphatic that lack of trust in the face of our sinful humanity—and the converse of this, self-trust—is the chief reason many do not progress in the spiritual life.[261] Her cautions regarding thus resisting God's mystical grace provide a helpful counterpoint to her presentation of Christian humility. Exposing our tendency to spiritual self-possession in *Guidelines for Mystical Prayer*, Burrows remarks,

> When we really get down to it, are not many of our good actions, what others might call our generosity, inspired more by the desire to feel good than by real love of God? The way we worry about spiritual failure, the inability to pray, distractions, ugly thoughts and temptations we can't get rid of . . . it's not because God is defrauded, for he isn't, it's because we are not so beautiful as we would like to be. How difficult it is for us to grasp in a real way, a way we live by, that we must take the risk of relying solely on the goodness of God. Covetous as we are, we want to have our hands full, want to have something of our own, not God's but ours, which we can bestow upon God or at least hold out to him should the worst come to the worst, and thus claim the reward of heaven.[262]

Burrows believes that, just as Jesus was generally rejected by the religious experts in their self-righteousness, the danger of not responding to God's transformative presence through self-sufficiency "is far greater among what we might call professionals—priests, religious, and lay people who are bent on 'living a spiritual life'—than among ordinary lay people who see themselves modestly trying to be good Christians, trying to please God."[263] She explains, "Only too easily we substitute the 'spiritual life' or the 'contemplative life' for God. Without realising it we are intent on a self-culture."[264] Clearly, Burrows is adamant that there can be no *via media* in our response to the God whose love reveals the bitter limitations of our creaturehood. If God is to be God, then, in utter trust, we must throw ourselves overboard.[265]

Trust at Work in Our Engagement with Other People and Circumstances

Burrows's thought on faith living nakedly exposed to God in the experience of reality concerns responding to God's transforming work within us through the way in which we interact with the people and circumstances that constitute our world. What she offers here is a deepening of the advice we saw her give to beginners regarding imitating the self-giving Jesus in their interactions with others. For Burrows, "it is of the essence of our surrender to God that we surrender to our neighbour too; it is largely, almost entirely in surrendering to our neighbour that we surrender to God."[266] Extending this idea she writes, "In surrendering to life as it unfolds no matter what it offers, in exposing ourselves to it—not evading, not fantasizing, not subtly (half consciously if not consciously) foreseeing things we don't want and warding them off, protecting ourselves in trying to control life—we are surrendered to the Father. We must live with intense faith."[267] In Burrows's view, then, we surrender to mystical grace, we consent to be taken into the "yes" of Jesus crucified, by accepting to stand vulnerable before the demands of life, utterly receptive to people and events in all their otherness.

In her book *Living Love*, Burrows considers what is involved in responding to God's mystical action by surrendering to circumstances and to our neighbor. She observes,

> Union with Jesus consists not in sitting in glory but in sharing his cup of shame, opprobrium, dishonour and powerlessness. . . . How can we share this cup in our daily life? By renouncing all power and every desire for it, every manoeuvre to obtain what we want, to prevail over others; by taking an attitude of unimportance and subjection to the

community; by rejecting the right to insist on our rights; by sacrificing the image we have of ourselves and which we sensitively want upheld in our own eyes and that of others; renouncing all desire for status, of being important to others. The cup Jesus wants to share with us is that of selfless love, which is its own reward—he offers no other.[268]

It is worth noting that, thoroughgoing in her exhortation to selfless love as she is, Burrows has little to say throughout her corpus about ever qualifying our surrender to others or to our life circumstances. At one point, however, she does acknowledge, "The needs of the neighbour are limitless; there is always something more to do, someone more to help."[269] Her counsel regarding how to approach an incessantly demanding reality in order to yield to God through it is simple: "All human situations are open to God. Prayer, constant reflection on the Gospel, desire, vigilance—these will reveal how, in the concrete, hour by hour, we find him in them, respond to him in them."[270]

Teresa and Thérèse as Exemplary in Responding to God's Mystical Grace through Trust

In Burrows's estimation, Teresa of Ávila and Thérèse of Lisieux are exemplars of responding to God's mystical grace by embracing with trust the essential dependency of the human condition. We know Burrows has objections to Teresa's handling of the mystical life. We have seen her maintain that Teresa confused the mystical grace itself with the echoes of that grace in her psyche and that this led to ambiguities in her writings and perplexity in her appraisal of herself and others.

However, Burrows insists that beyond any limited theorizing, Teresa actually lived in unalloyed receptivity to God's mystical presence. She remarks, "If only we learn to cast our-selves into God's care all sorts of things can be amiss with us and they do not matter. I am thinking of St. Teresa at this point. She had not a few illusions, as any impartial observer will admit, but ultimately they did her no harm because she handed herself over to God."[271] Developing this point that trust ultimately made Teresa transparent to God, Burrows claims, "Hers was a deeper prayer than she knew and it was by this that she lived. In its abandonment and living union, it is a prayer all of us are called to—a prayer of letting Jesus *be*."[272] By Burrows's account Teresa, somewhat paradoxically, was led to stand before God in empty-handed trust by way of the psy-chic phenomena she experienced. Earlier we noted that Teresa received conflicting assessments regarding the origin of her experiences. In the face of this distressing uncertainty, Burrows details, "There was only one answer, and it is the only human answer to God whatever way he comes; that of utter trust and abandonment. This Teresa gave. One way or another, we must be brought to this total abandonment, this relinquishing of every security save that of the goodness and fidelity of God. It seems a roundabout way in Teresa's case but how marvellously skilful. Thus, he came to her in her phenomena (*hers*, not his), and he came to her in her agony of doubt."[273]

The final point to establish here is that in Burrows's view, Teresa, as an exemplary mystic through her radical, self-emptying trust, is a model of practical charity. "She . . . [puts] the whole weight on love of neighbour," Burrows notes, "because, in practice, this is the way in which we love God. This is where she is so magnificent a guide."[274] Burrows highlights that Teresa's wholehearted commitment to practi-cal charity is "the more impressive . . . simply because she personally *was* enamoured of 'experiences' and thought them important."[275] Thus Burrows's position on Teresa is that it is most valuable for us to approach her as a woman completely emptied out before the living God. She points out, "The Teresa of visions and ecstasies remains on the pedestal, out of reach; an object of delight and admiration but unchallenging."[276] In truth, however, "all that made Teresa a great mystic, a passionate lover of God, is available to each of us if we would take the same path of faithful prayer, humble perseverance and generosity in doing God's will and not our own, and a tireless effort to love others as Jesus has loved us."[277]

> Teresa's wholehearted commitment to practical charity is the more impressive because she personally *was* enamored of "experiences" and thought them important.

As for Thérèse of Lisieux's exemplary response to God's mystical grace, Burrows explains, "There were two 'moments' in Jesus' life that unveiled to her the inmost nature of love and that inspired and shaped her response: his infancy and his passion. In both, the Son of God is defenceless, vulnerable, delivered up to human hands. Here was something that caught at her heart and on which she dwelt incessantly. Love can only be love and nothing else. It must offer itself nakedly and be received in its nakedness."[278] Thérèse grasped that when God's ecstasy of love inundates humanity, the only response can be empty-handed assent, the response made once and for all by the kenotic Christ. Accordingly, she claimed the innate poverty of her humanity as a sharing in Jesus' perfect surrender to Love. Burrows observes that as Thérèse's spiritual life progressed, contrary to the spirit of her milieu, "far from being discouraged by all that she experienced of herself, she began to see that what she called her poverty, her littleness, her nothingness, was in fact her treasure, provided she opened it all out in boundless trust to God."[279] "There was no limit," Burrows elaborates, "to what God could do in Thérèse once she held out her empty hands, abandoning forever any thought of earning or achievement. She opened herself to receive the floodtide of God's love, pent up, waiting for the surrender which would loose the floodgates."[280] Thus, with the indigence of her being utterly opened out into the Crucified as pure capacity for God's life, Thérèse stands before us as a model of what it means to be a mystic, to be human, and to be holy.

The Response to God's Mystical Grace of the "Anonymous Christian"

To complete our exploration of Burrows's conception of our response to the mystical grace, let us note a rather inchoate idea that is present in her work. Burrows suggests that openness to God's mystical action can be found among non-Christians. Receptivity to God's transformative hand demands a trustful embrace of our poor humanity, and for Burrows, "wherever this acceptance of the human lot is found and in the measure that it is present, there is the Lord. An explicit acknowledgment of him is not necessary. In embracing what is truly human Jesus is embraced."[281] She goes on to remark, "I suspect that this is often the case and there can well be more true acceptance of him in people who do not explicitly acknowledge him than in many who do, yet continually evade life and 'what is,' often in his name. These others obey an inner urge which assures them there is meaning somewhere and that what they must do, the demand of their humanity, is to refuse to slump down in self but to surrender to life, bravely confronting it as it is and bowing before that which they cannot overcome."[282] Clearly, consenting to be truly in Christ, consenting to be a poor dependent creature, is what matters for Burrows; such consent may or may not correspond to the name "Christian."

Summary

Ruth Burrows summarizes for us her position on the second stage of the spiritual life when she declares, "I hold the unswerving conviction that the mystical way, properly understood, is identical with genuine Christian discipleship and with what we mean by true faith and a life of faith."[283] The mystical life begins as God himself gratuitously encounters the person who, within the limitations of the ego, has been stretching out to receive him. In Burrows's thinking, this is nothing other than "the coming of the kingdom into the individual heart."[284] No longer is the human spirit subject to the tyranny of the ego. Rather, "a new sort of life is beginning with its own needs and its own operations and these latter are not circumscribed by material limitations."[285] And this new life is precisely the life of Jesus crucified. For Burrows, the mystical grace is about transformation into the kenotic Christ; only in him, the mediator between God and humanity, do we encounter God directly. To put it a different way, the mystical life is the advent of the kingdom of God, and "the kingdom is fully present in Jesus for he has allowed God to be his God, his Abba."[286] Obviously, then, the mystical life, according to Burrows, is in no way reserved to a spiritual elite. Not only is it the life of divine intimacy toward which all Christians are oriented at baptism, but also it is the fulfillment of what it means to be human: a capacity for God himself.

Burrows is convinced that, as a participation in the very life of God, the mystical life can have nothing essentially to do with what is experienced in the psyche; our material being simply cannot possess the infinity of God. She acknowledges, however, that in some temperaments the mystical grace can produce a repercussion within the psychic powers. While Burrows urges us to use such sensible consolation to deepen our Christian commitment she is resolute that "we must always stand in truth and not mistake shadow for substance."[287] What is felt is not God in himself, and not even a reliable indication of his mystical presence. What is certain is that God's hidden presence will issue forth into our conscious life as a revelation of our essential human frailty. As the life of the Crucified replaces the life of the ego we experience the terrifying, glorious truth that humanity has nothing to offer God other than capacity for Love.

Consenting to be held in the reality of our fundamental human emptiness is what, by Burrows's account, it means to respond to God's mystical action. By accepting to be a living need before God we allow Jesus to take us into his perfect self-abandonment to the Father. Such acceptance demands trust. Burrows maintains that the mystical grace enables us to launch out toward God in faith, hope, and love—all dynamics of trust. "It is thus," she explains, "that we cease to be in control by trying to be our own god, our own creator, and we accept, as [Jesus] did, to be human: wholly contingent; with no answer, no fulfilment in ourselves; an emptiness that looks to infinite love for its completion."[288] If God is to be God in us, this self-abandoning trust must be incarnated unremittingly, within every dimension of our human existence. Thus responding unceasingly to God's mystical work in the depths of our being, our participation in the "yes" of Jesus crucified becomes, eventually, complete transformation.

Notes

1. Ruth Burrows, *To Believe in Jesus* (1978; repr., London: Continuum, 2010; Mahwah, N.J.: HiddenSpring, 2010), 91.
2. Ibid.
3. Ruth Burrows, *Interior Castle Explored: St. Teresa's Teaching on the Life of Deep Union with God* (1981; repr., London: Continuum, 2007; Mahwah, N.J.: HiddenSpring, 2007), 42.
4. Ibid., 68.
5. See ibid., 36.
6. Ibid., 99.
7. Ibid., 42.
8. Ibid., 58.
9. Ruth Burrows, *Ascent to Love: The Spiritual Teaching of St. John of the Cross* (London: Darton, Longman and Todd; Denville, N.J.: Dimension, 1992, 1987), 70–71.
10. Burrows, *Interior Castle Explored*, 83.
11. Ruth Burrows, *Guidelines for Mystical Prayer*, foreword by B. C. Butler (1976; repr., London: Continuum, 2007; Denville, N.J.: Dimension, 1980), 9.
12. Jordan Aumann, *Spiritual Theology* (1980; repr., London: Continuum, 2006), 77.
13. Burrows, *Interior Castle Explored*, 66.
14. Ibid., 36.
15. Burrows, *To Believe in Jesus*, 90.
16. Burrows, *Interior Castle Explored*, 41.

17. Burrows, *Guidelines for Mystical Prayer*, 10.

18. Burrows, *Ascent to Love*, 1.

19. Burrows, *Guidelines for Mystical Prayer*, 10.

20. Ibid., 10–11.

21. James Arraj, *From St. John of the Cross to Us: The Story of a 400 Year Long Misunderstanding and What It Means for the Future of Christian Mysticism* (Chiloquin, OR: Inner Growth Books, 1999), 215.

22. Ibid.

23. Cited in Burrows, *Interior Castle Explored*, 40.

24. Ibid., 41.

25. Ibid., 43.

26. Ibid., 42.

27. Ibid., 44.

28. Burrows, *Ascent to Love*, 74.

29. Burrows, *Guidelines for Mystical Prayer*, 1.

30. Burrows, *Interior Castle Explored*, 73.

31. Ibid., 45.

32. Burrows, *Ascent to Love*, 80.

33. Burrows, *Interior Castle Explored*, 109.

34. Ruth Burrows, *Our Father: Meditations on the Lord's Prayer* (London: Darton, Longman and Todd, 1986; Denville, N.J.: Dimension, 1986), 40–41.

35. Burrows, *Interior Castle Explored*, 42.

36. Burrows, *To Believe in Jesus*, 40 (emphasis added).

37. Stephen Sundborg, "Sexual-Affective Integration in Celibacy: A Psycho-Spiritual Study of the Experience of Ruth Burrows in the Light of the Psychology of Rollo May" (STD diss., Pontifical Gregorian University, 1984), 531, 533. The citations within this passage are from Ruth Burrows, *Before the Living God* (1975; repr., London: Burns and Oates, 2008; Mahwah, N.J.: HiddenSpring, 2008), 117.

38. Burrows, *To Believe in Jesus*, 31.

39. See Burrows, *Guidelines for Mystical Prayer*, 14.

40. Ibid., 43.

41. Ibid.

42. Burrows draws directly on her own "conversion" experience in this interpretation of Teresa's fifth mansion. Although she writes anonymously, the veil of anonymity is thin, given her self-disclosure in *Before the Living God*.
43. Burrows, *Interior Castle Explored*, 83.
44. Ibid., 90.
45. Ibid., 84.
46. See ibid., 85.
47. Ibid., 86.
48. Burrows, *Guidelines for Mystical Prayer*, 29.
49. Ruth Burrows, *Living in Mystery*, introduction by Wendy Beckett (London: Sheed and Ward, 1996), 89.
50. Ruth Burrows, *Through Him, With Him, In Him: Meditations on the Liturgical Seasons* (London: Sheed and Ward, 1987; Denville, N.J.: Dimension, 1987), 56.
51. Ruth Burrows, "Amen," in *Essence of Prayer* (London: Burns and Oates, 2006; Mahwah, N.J.: HiddenSpring, 2006), 71.
52. Burrows maintains that "it must be very rare for the reality of baptism to fit the sign. For most of us it is a continuing thing. We must go on trying to implement our baptism, bring it to completion in our lives." Burrows, *To Believe in Jesus*, 31. She notes, however, that St. Paul is exceptional. She explains, "Paul was happy to have no righteousness of his own but only that which comes through Jesus. . . . He died to himself and all that had gone before. He accepted being created anew in Christ Jesus. His baptism was the acting out in rite of what had already happened. He had gone down into the waters of death with Jesus and risen with his life. The inmost reality really matched the sign." Ibid., 26.
53. Burrows, *Interior Castle Explored*, 54.
54. Ruth Burrows, "Some Reflections on Prayer," in *Essence of Prayer*, 9.
55. Burrows, *Our Father*, 48–49.
56. Burrows, "Amen," 73.
57. Burrows, *Our Father*, 52.
58. See Burrows, *Guidelines for Mystical Prayer*, 88.
59. Burrows, "Some Reflections on Prayer," 6.

60. Burrows, *Interior Castle Explored*, 59.

61. Burrows, *Guidelines for Mystical Prayer*, 45.

62. Ibid., 46.

63. Ibid.

64. See ibid., 50.

65. Ibid.

66. Ibid., 47.

67. Ibid.

68. Burrows, *Interior Castle Explored*, 48.

69. Burrows makes brief mention in her work of "another deep reason why God occasionally destines a person to the 'light on' state." She claims that those who are "light on" drink with Jesus "the chalice of his Father's grief, the awesome mystery of God's suffering love, love rejected." Thus "to share Jesus' cup," she explains, "one must 'see.'" Burrows, *Guidelines for Mystical Prayer*, 144–45. This stunning observation requires, I believe, further development. For example, we can surely assume that Burrows is referring here to a "light on" mystic perceiving God's love being rejected by others; yet it is not evident from her discussion of "light on" that the ability to "see" the activity of God in others is inherent to this state.

70. Burrows, *Guidelines for Mystical Prayer*, 46.

71. Ibid.

72. See Burrows, *Interior Castle Explored*, 49.

73. Ruth Burrows, interview by author, Quidenham, UK, October 4, 2009.

74. Burrows, *Guidelines for Mystical Prayer*, 46.

75. Burrows, *Interior Castle Explored*, 49.

76. See Burrows, *Guidelines for Mystical Prayer*, 46–47.

77. Burrows, *Interior Castle Explored*, 49.

78. Ibid., 95.

79. Burrows, *Guidelines for Mystical Prayer*, 49.

80. Ibid., 97.

81. Burrows, *Interior Castle Explored*, 99.

82. Burrows, *Guidelines for Mystical Prayer*, 143.

83. Burrows, *Interior Castle Explored*, 52.

84. Burrows, *Guidelines for Mystical Prayer*, 3.

85. Burrows, *Interior Castle Explored*, 37–38.

86. Burrows, *Guidelines for Mystical Prayer*, 50.

87. It is important to note that Burrows can be imprecise in her use of psychological terminology. In particular, she sometimes interchanges "subconscious" for "unconscious." Exemplifying this, Stephen Sundborg notes that in *To Believe in Jesus*, Burrows writes, "Lots of things have been pushed down there [i.e., the 'subconscious'] because the facing of them would hurt too much." Burrows, *To Believe in Jesus*, 57. Sundborg goes on to remark, "This is more a description of repression and as such belongs in strict terminology to the unconscious rather than the subconscious." Sundborg, "Sexual-Affective Integration," 262n46.

88. Burrows, *Interior Castle Explored*, 47.

89. Burrows, *Guidelines for Mystical Prayer*, 11.

90. Burrows, *Interior Castle Explored*, 39.

91. See ibid., 46–47.

92. Burrows, *Guidelines for Mystical Prayer*, 50–51.

93. Burrows, *Interior Castle Explored*, 39.

94. Burrows, *To Believe in Jesus*, 28.

95. Burrows, *Interior Castle Explored*, 99.

96. Ibid.

97. Burrows, *Guidelines for Mystical Prayer*, 50.

98. Burrows, *Ascent to Love*, 87–88.

99. Burrows, *Interior Castle Explored*, 36.

100. Ibid., 39–40.

101. Ruth Burrows, introduction, in *The Wisdom of St. Teresa of Ávila* (Oxford, UK: Lion Publishing, 1998), 7–8.

102. Burrows, *Interior Castle Explored*, 94.

103. Burrows, *Guidelines for Mystical Prayer*, 11.

104. Burrows, introduction, in *Wisdom of St. Teresa*, 8.

105. Burrows, *Interior Castle Explored*, 57.

106. Ibid., 92.

107. Burrows, *Interior Castle Explored*, 47.

108. Burrows, *Guidelines for Mystical Prayer*, 98.

109. Burrows, *Interior Castle Explored*, 93.

110. Rowan Williams, whose thought is influenced by that of Burrows, expresses this dimension of Teresa well. With particular reference to the locutions that Teresa experienced he writes, "It seems plain that much of all this is indeed Teresa's own 'work,' though not in any sense she would have recognized. But to say this is not to write off these experiences, or to say Teresa was deceived. She was confident of her mission; and the experience of locutions generally follows the period in which this confidence was being forged in the sense pervading her whole experience of being accepted and authorized by God. These communications are at their most regular in the years when she is most active in the Reform and in the struggles surrounding it. It makes perfect sense to say that her awareness of her own authority in these events was a matter of grace, the gift of a profound serenity in the love of God, while at the same time seeing her locutions as an unconscious crystallizing and projecting of this security. . . . In short, it is possible to grant both that these experiences are the fruit of a life lived in grace and that they are in some degree the creation of her own need, and therefore vulnerable and fallible." Rowan Williams, *Teresa of Ávila* (London: Continuum, 2003), 95.

111. Burrows, *Interior Castle Explored*, 74.

112. Ibid., 50.

113. Burrows, *Guidelines for Mystical Prayer*, 12.

114. Ibid., 52.

115. Burrows, *Interior Castle Explored*, 57. See also Burrows, *Guidelines for Mystical Prayer*, 50–52.

116. Burrows, *Interior Castle Explored*, 67.

117. Ibid., 74.

118. Ibid., 75.

119. Ibid., 74.

120. Ibid.

121. Ibid., 94.

122. Ibid.

123. See Ibid., 94–95.
124. Burrows, introduction, in *Wisdom of St. Teresa*, 7.
125. Burrows, *Interior Castle Explored*, 93–94.
126. Burrows, *Ascent to Love*, 95.
127. Burrows, *Interior Castle Explored*, 37.
128. Mark Allen and Ruth Burrows, *Letters on Prayer: An Exchange on Prayer and Faith* (London: Sheed and Ward, 1999), 74.
129. Burrows, *Interior Castle Explored*, 40.
130. Ibid.
131. See ibid.
132. Ibid.
133. Ibid., 41.
134. Ibid., 45.
135. Ibid., 37.
136. Burrows, *Ascent to Love*, 85.
137. See Burrows, *Guidelines for Mystical Prayer*, 51.
138. Burrows, *Interior Castle Explored*, 52–53.
139. Ibid., 53.
140. Burrows, *Guidelines for Mystical Prayer*, 48.
141. Burrows, *Interior Castle Explored*, 121–22.
142. Ibid., 50.
143. Ibid., 67.
144. Ibid., 78.
145. Ibid., 92.
146. Burrows, *Guidelines for Mystical Prayer*, 50.
147. Ibid., 46.
148. Ibid.
149. Ibid.
150. See Ruth Burrows, "Doctor of the Dark Night," in *Essence of Prayer*, 100.
151. Burrows, *To Believe in Jesus*, 93.
152. Ibid., 24–25.
153. Burrows, *Ascent to Love*, 87.

154. Burrows, *Ascent to Love*, 51.

155. Burrows, *Guidelines for Mystical Prayer*, 34.

156. Burrows, *Ascent to Love*, 50.

157. Burrows, *Guidelines for Mystical Prayer*, 90.

158. Ibid., 91.

159. Burrows, *Ascent to Love*, 58.

160. Burrows, *Guidelines for Mystical Prayer*, 90.

161. Burrows, *Interior Castle Explored*, 72.

162. Ruth Burrows, *Living Love: Meditations on the New Testament* (London: Darton, Longman and Todd, 1985; Denville, N.J.: Dimension, 1985), 22.

163. Ruth Burrows, "Prayer That Is Jesus," in *Essence of Prayer*, 39.

164. Burrows, *Ascent to Love*, 58.

165. Ibid., 74.

166. Burrows, *Interior Castle Explored*, 70.

167. Ibid., 60.

168. Burrows, *Guidelines for Mystical Prayer*, 92.

169. Ibid.

170. Burrows, *Interior Castle Explored*, 98.

171. Burrows, *Ascent to Love*, 54.

172. Burrows, *Guidelines for Mystical Prayer*, 36.

173. Ibid.

174. Ibid., 36–37.

175. Ibid., 37.

176. Burrows, *Interior Castle Explored*, 63.

177. Burrows, *Living in Mystery*, 103.

178. Burrows, *Ascent to Love*, 57.

179. Burrows, *Interior Castle Explored*, 61.

180. Ibid.

181. Burrows, *Ascent to Love*, 109.

182. Burrows, *Guidelines for Mystical Prayer*, 107.

183. Ibid.

184. Burrows, *Ascent to Love*, 107.

185. Ibid., 108.
186. Ibid.
187. Burrows, *Guidelines for Mystical Prayer*, 107.
188. Burrows, *Ascent to Love*, 108.
189. Ibid., 109.
190. Burrows, *Guidelines for Mystical Prayer*, 107.
191. Ibid., 109.
192. Ibid.
193. Ibid., 110.
194. Ibid., 113–14.
195. Ibid., 34.
196. Burrows, *Interior Castle Explored*, 120.
197. Ibid., 64.
198. Burrows, *To Believe in Jesus*, 100.
199. Burrows, "Amen," 80.
200. Burrows, *Interior Castle Explored*, 64.
201. Burrows, *Ascent to Love*, 72.
202. Ibid., 71.
203. Burrows, interview, October 4, 2009. Burrows points to a poem that she composed during a time of retreat as exemplary here; see appendix.
204. Burrows, *Ascent to Love*, 71.
205. Ibid., 55.
206. Allen and Burrows, *Letters on Prayer*, 78.
207. Burrows, *To Believe in Jesus*, 101.
208. Burrows, *Interior Castle Explored*, 118.
209. Ibid., 101.
210. See ibid., 60.
211. Ibid., 68.
212. Burrows, *Guidelines for Mystical Prayer*, 39.
213. Burrows, *Interior Castle Explored*, 64.
214. Burrows, *Guidelines for Mystical Prayer*, 39–40.
215. Burrows, *Interior Castle Explored*, 59.

216. Burrows, *Guidelines for Mystical Prayer*, 105.
217. Ibid.
218. Burrows, *Interior Castle Explored*, 62.
219. Ibid., 71.
220. Burrows, *Living in Mystery*, 72.
221. Ruth Burrow, letter to Stephen Sundborg, July 18, 1979. Cited in Sundborg, "Sexual-Affective Integration," 534–35.
222. Allen and Burrows, *Letters on Prayer*, 50.
223. Burrows, *Ascent to Love*, 72.
224. Ibid., 77.
225. Elizabeth Ruth Obbard, introduction, in *The Watchful Heart: Daily Readings with Ruth Burrows* (London: Darton, Longman and Todd, 1988), xii.
226. Burrows, *Guidelines for Mystical Prayer*, 59.
227. Burrows, *Our Father*, 19.
228. Burrows, *Guidelines for Mystical Prayer*, 59.
229. Burrows, *Ascent to Love*, 77.
230. Burrows, *Guidelines for Mystical Prayer*, 102.
231. Ruth Burrows, "Carmel: A Stark Encounter with the Human Condition," in *Essence of Prayer*, 194.
232. Burrows, *Guidelines for Mystical Prayer*, 83.
233. Ibid., 28.
234. Ibid., 96.
235. Ibid., 90.
236. Burrows, *To Believe in Jesus*, 39–40.
237. Ruth Burrows, "Consecrated Life," in *Essence of Prayer*, 206.
238. Burrows, *Ascent to Love*, 48.
239. Burrows, *Living in Mystery*, 95.
240. Burrows, "Amen," 79.
241. Ibid., 80.
242. Burrows, *Interior Castle Explored*, 69.
243. Ibid.
244. Ibid., 70.
245. Ibid., 107.

246. Allen and Burrows, *Letters on Prayer*, 45.
247. Burrows, *Interior Castle Explored*, 70.
248. Ibid., 69.
249. Allen and Burrows, *Letters on Prayer*, 37.
250. Ibid., 44.
251. Ibid., 66.
252. Burrows, *Living in Mystery*, 98.
253. Burrows, *Ascent to Love*, 73.
254. Ibid., 98.
255. Burrows, *Through Him*, 90.
256. Burrows, *Guidelines for Mystical Prayer*, 60.
257. Ibid., 89.
258. Ibid.
259. Burrows, *Ascent to Love*, 88.
260. Burrows, *Living Love*, 22–23.
261. See Burrows, *Guidelines for Mystical Prayer*, 68.
262. Ibid., 76–77.
263. Burrows, *To Believe in Jesus*, 94.
264. Ibid.
265. See Burrows, *Living in Mystery*, 109.
266. Burrows, *To Believe in Jesus*, 81.
267. Burrows, *Living Love*, 63–64.
268. Ibid., 38.
269. Burrows, *Ascent to Love*, 30.
270. Ibid., 32.
271. Burrows, *Guidelines for Mystical Prayer*, 43.
272. Ibid., 99.
273. Burrows, *Interior Castle Explored*, 94.
274. Ibid., 87.
275. Ibid.
276. Burrows, introduction, in *Wisdom of St. Teresa*, 9.
277. Ibid.
278. Ruth Burrows, "St. Thérèse of Lisieux and the Holy Child," in *Essence of Prayer*, 107–8.

279. Ruth Burrows, "Thoughts on the Doctorate of St. Thérèse," in *Essence of Prayer*, 122.

280. Burrows, *Guidelines for Mystical Prayer*, 68.

281. Burrows, *To Believe in Jesus*, 44–45.

282. Ibid., 45.

283. Burrows, "Consecrated Life," 198.

284. Burrows, *Interior Castle Explored*, 4.

285. Ibid., 58.

286. Burrows, *Our Father*, 36.

287. Burrows, *Guidelines for Mystical Prayer*, 53.

288. Burrows, "Consecrated Life," 207.

CHAPTER 5

The Third Stage of the Spiritual Life according to Ruth Burrows

Transformed into the "Yes" of Jesus Crucified

Ruth Burrows declares that those at the third stage of the spiritual life "are identified with Jesus. He surrenders to the Father in them and each of their lives is sealed with his."[1] If the first phase of the spiritual journey is about preparing to be taken into Jesus' definitive abandonment to divine love, and the second about our primordial egocentricity actually being progressively replaced by the life of the Crucified, then the third stage is about perfect transformation into Jesus. For Burrows, this complete union with the kenotic Christ, this transformation into perfect receptivity to the Father's ecstasy of love, is at once the culmination of what it means to be a human, a Christian, and a mystic. As she puts it in *Ascent to Love*, "There is only *one* fulfilment to be achieved either in this world or the next, that which we call mystical marriage or transforming union."[2]

In this chapter we will explore Burrows's exposition of, respectively, the essential features of the third stage of the spiritual life, the lived experience of those at this spiritual summit and the effect wrought by such Christians upon the church and the world. It will become evident that, as with her treatment of the spiritual journey to this point, Burrows's presentation of the final stage is thoroughly Christocentric. Referring directly to her approach to the third stage, and implicitly to her understanding of the spiritual pilgrimage as a whole, Burrows comments, "[It is] back to the Gospel, back to Jesus, isn't it, all the time. Not what others have said, or what our psyche would like, or what our expectations are, but the truth of our blessed Lord."[3] In Burrows's hands, no aspect of life at the mystical summit can escape the measure of the Gospel.

THE ESSENCE OF THE THIRD STAGE
OF THE SPIRITUAL LIFE

Our exploration of Burrows's teaching on the essence of the third stage of the spiritual life begins with an image that has also been instructive for the previous two chapters wherein Burrows compares the Christian life to being endowed with a wing structure. While in the beginning, "no matter how much we try, we cannot get off the ground, that is, away from self," there comes a time when the divine life itself penetrates the wings so we are no longer wholly captive to earth's (egocentricity's) pull.[4] At this second stage, however, "we are still within the influence of the earth, pulled back by gravity even though we are moving towards God."[5] Continuing her image, Burrows goes on to explain, "If we are faithful there will come a moment when God will stoop down, catch hold of us and sweep us up to himself, taking us right away from earth (self), so definitively that its power over us is lost for ever; there is no return. Henceforth we live with and in God. His powers, not our own, control all our activities. No effort of ours can achieve it. It is he himself who must snatch us away from ourselves."[6] Evidently, to speak of the essence of the third stage of the spiritual life is to speak of two extremes at once—indeed, these extremes are two sides of the one reality: the one at the summit is completely devoid of ego and utterly penetrated by divine love. All along we have observed that the measure of our self-emptying is the measure of our immersion in the life of God. Here the process is complete.

We know that Jesus' role as absolute mediator is central to Burrows's mystical doctrine: only in the crucified, glorified Christ can humanity stand empty handed before the living

God, utterly receptive to his love. Accordingly, by Burrows's account, those at the third stage know perfect communion with Jesus. Commenting in *Ascent to Love* on the interpenetration of dispossession of self and possession by God at the culmination of the spiritual life, Burrows writes, "The dark night has burnt away all egotism from the heart, leaving it a pure receptivity for God. . . . Total receptivity means total selflessness and this means that God is truly all in this heart. There is no ego on the summit of the mountain, only the honour and glory of God."[7] She proceeds to maintain, "Does not the figure of Jesus inevitably rise before the eyes of our mind? Have we not described precisely what the Gospels reveal of Jesus, the Father's beloved?"[8] Burrows offers further insight into the stunning transformation that belongs to the third stage when she details, "Hitherto, God's union with us was temporary and partial, now it is permanent, total. Only now can we really speak of an indwelling. In essence it is a state of rapture, that is, the self taken out of the self and that abidingly. There is no counterpart in nature. It can be understood only in the incarnation. It derives from this and, as someone dared to suggest, can be called an extension of it. A person in this state is totally possessed by Jesus, identified with him in his surrender to his Father. Thus, through her, Jesus is on earth in an incomparable way. His kingdom has come in her."[9] Through those at the third stage, the One who holds humanity and divinity in consummate unity dwells among us.

So, the essential quality of the one in the final stage of the journey is that they have become Jesus. In Burrows's words, in this person, "what Jesus was proclaiming, what Paul, John and others have tried to express of man's ultimate destiny of being with Christ in God, one spirit with him who is Spirit, has become, even in this life, a living reality."[10] For the rest of this section we shall contemplate the mystery of this transformed state, allowing each of its various facets to come into view.

The Realization of the Third Stage of the Spiritual Life

Burrows makes it clear above that, as with the shift from captivity to egocentrism to the beginning of the mystical journey, arrival at the spiritual summit is wholly dependent on the divine initiative: "No effort of ours can achieve it. It is he himself who must snatch us away from ourselves." Thus, reflecting in *Guidelines for Mystical Prayer* on the movement from the second island to the third, Burrows remarks, "How a person passes from the one to the other we do not know. This is the result of a divine intervention in the most absolute sense, it is shrouded in mystery."[11]

Yet Burrows in no way presents one's being brought into the third stage as a matter of divine caprice. Rather, she understands it to be God's response to the uttermost degree of human surrender. The one traveling across the second stage has been trying to allow Jesus crucified to utter his "yes" to the Father's love within her through accepting ever more profoundly the fundamental poverty of her humanity. "It is the total acceptance of this total dependency," Burrows explains, "together with total trust that God will act, which allows God, with a mighty sweep to carry her off as his prey."[12] Obviously, there is no contravention of human freedom here. Burrows notes that "consent has been given all along the way, an unconditional consent 'do with me what you will.' God can therefore act with total respect for his creature's freedom."[13]

To Be Wholly Dispossessed of Self

Let us now consider what is contained in Burrows's idea of sharing in Jesus' utter selflessness. In depicting the transformation effected in those at the summit Burrows writes, "The self has dissolved around its burning centre, Christ, whose centre is the Father."[14] Earlier in the final chapter of *Guidelines*, we find Burrows detailing just what such "dissolution" of self implies: "On the former island, even when surrender was complete as far as lay within our power, it was still 'I' surrendering to God, 'I' choosing God. But here there is no 'I' in that sense. In some mysterious way, God has replaced the self, the 'I.' De Caussade makes a fine and telling distinction. 'There is a time,' he says, 'when the soul lives in God' (the second island) 'and a time when God lives in the soul' (third island)."[15] Of course, in this discussion of the "I" or "self," Burrows has in mind the ego as the center and initiator of our lives. So those at the third stage of the spiritual life find that, completely immersed as they are in the life of the Crucified, the ego has died and God has become the center and initiator of their existence; God has taken over, has become the ego, the self, the "I."

Throughout her discussion of the third stage of the spiritual journey, Burrows insists that the extinction of the ego coincides with the full realization of human personhood. As we first saw when we discussed her anthropology, the great paradox for Burrows is that the ones who have been completely taken over by God are the ones who are fully possessed of their true identity, truly "who [they] . . . are in God's eternal plan."[16] Burrows perhaps articulates this idea most clearly when, after explaining that God is the living center of those at the summit, she states, "To avoid any notion of pantheism or loss of identity, we must return to the principle that the individuality, the distinction, the otherness of the creature is established in direct proportion to its nearness to the creator. The more surrendered to and possessed by God, the more immersed in God, the more the self is self."[17] Another instance of Burrows's treatment of this theme can be found in her analysis of Teresa's seventh mansion. There she proclaims, "It is only when God has been able to love us in fulness that

> The more surrendered to and possessed by God, the more immersed in God, the more the self is self.

we are wholly *there*. Only that in us which is divine is real. Only when we are God-filled are we truly human."[18] Burrows thus concludes that the seventh mansion—that state wherein Teresa envisions God to be all in all—"is nothing but the full growth of the creature."[19]

Burrows highlights that Jesus not only mediates but also exemplifies the coincidence of utter dispossession of self and fullness of personal identity. She points out that "Jesus expressly declares that he has nothing of himself: the works he does are not his but his Father's; the judgments he makes are dictated by the Father; the whole initiative of his life derives from the Father. He exists as a sort of emptiness through which the Father speaks and acts. At the same time, paradoxically, he exists as a highly individual man firm in decision, act and judgment. There is nothing cipher-like in his personality."[20] The Father, not an "I" or ego, is the operational center of Jesus' being, yet Jesus is fully possessed of himself, fully established in his unique identity. Similarly, living wholly by the life of the Crucified, knowing, in him, the Father to be the breath of their existence, those at the summit of the spiritual journey are most "themselves."

To Be Wholly Possessed by God

We have been considering the mystery of transformation into Jesus with regard to self-dispossession. We will now reverse the line of enquiry and look at the kernel of the third stage in terms of being wholly possessed by God. Burrows claims that at the third stage of the spiritual life, "we have become [God] and he has become us."[21] With our foregoing discussion of living without an "I," we have an idea of what Burrows means by "God has become us." But what is contained in her assertion that those at the summit "have become God"?

In Burrows's understanding of the mystical life, complete transformation into the Crucified means "the deification of the human person, becoming God, being equal as it were to God."[22] She elucidates just what she has in mind here in the introduction to *Our Father: Meditations on the Lord's Prayer*. Burrows is discussing the possibility of friendship with God, noting, "Friend implies equality of status."[23] She concludes,

> Friends of God? Can it be? Yes, but there is only one way: to become "son"; to accept the friendship and companionship of Jesus so as to learn sonship from him, share in his sonship. In practice this means being utterly unimportant to ourselves, becoming selfless, empty, nothing but an echo—like Enoch disappearing. This is the paradox: the one who has consented to be nothing but an emptiness for the Father's love, becomes—and only now, in this context of nothingness, dare we breathe the word—somehow "equal" to God, raised up to be his friend, his beloved. "The Father and I are one," says Jesus. Lost in his *kenosis* it can perhaps be said of us.[24]

Allowing Jesus to embrace completely in them the painful dependency of the human condition, allowing him to express perfectly in them his surrender to the inundation of Love, those at the third stage are absorbed into the divine life. Accepting fully the nothingness of humanity, they come to participate fully in the "all" of divinity.

Burrows teaches that if those at the culmination of the spiritual pilgrimage have become God by participation, then, for them, all acts of the intellect and will are inevitably animated by the divine breath. This is what she has in mind when she states that, at the end of the spiritual journey, "being is identified with its activities."[25] In expounding the significance of this idea, Burrows observes of the one at the summit, "She is all love. All her activities are love, all her strength and energies are concentrated in love. Love is most truly her sole occupation whatever else she is doing. . . . She is never after her own will, her own gratification, nor is she merely following her own inclinations. She is never engaged in anything that is in the slightest degree alien to him. Her mind is occupied in considering what he wants of her, what will most serve him; her will is in desiring him alone."[26] Evidently, as Burrows sees it, there is no alloy in the virtue of the one at the third stage; she partakes wholly in the divine simplicity.

Associated Aspects of Self-Dispossession and God-Possession

The three elements of Burrows's thought on the essence of the third stage that remains to be discussed are basically associated with the interpenetrating dynamics of self-dispossession and deification.

The State of Sinlessness

First, Burrows maintains that those at the summit necessarily live free from sin. "It is generally accepted," she remarks, "that those in the state of transforming union are confirmed in grace, that they cannot sin."[27] We are familiar with Burrows's idea that sin is, at root, the choice to remain in our innate egocentricity. For the one who has traveled far along the mystical path, the graced thrust away from egocentricity and into receptivity to Love is constitutive of their being. Burrows understands the transformation that God effects to bring one to the summit to culminate the moral trajectory that has long defined them. She explains, "The time comes when he can take her completely, hold her so deeply and constantly within himself that she can go out no more. How could she sin? God cannot fail himself. If by an impossibility she could break out of this blessed prison, then of course she would sin, but she cannot; her own structure, built of endless surrenders, and in God's safe keeping makes this impossible."[28] So receptive to divine love as to be identifiable with it, the one at the third stage fundamentally can have nothing to do with the egocentrism of sin.

Burrows does not consider the sinlessness of those on the summit as tantamount to perfection. She acknowledges that while "the roots of sin are cut . . . some droopy little bits of green are still there—feelings of jealousy, annoyance, contrariness."[29] In Burrows's estimation, these vestiges of our bondage to egocentricity "are absolutely harmless, mere feelings, rather like those that remain when a limb has been amputated."[30] And she notes that, because God's mystical grace has wrought in the one at the third stage the definitive triumph over the ego, "she does not have to struggle against these feelings."[31] Still, Burrows perceives the tokens of past egocentrism known by those at the summit as opportunities for yielding ever more profoundly to God's relentless love. They reveal that "there is still work to be done, but it is not a question of striving, for struggle is over, but rather deeper and deeper surrender, letting God do everything . . . totally sure that he will do so."[32]

We can see from this discussion of the sinlessness that is intrinsic to the third stage of the spiritual life that, to Burrows, there can be neither regress nor progress on the summit, only ever greater depth of surrender. If persons share fully in Jesus' trusting abandonment to God's love, if they have become divine by participation, there can be no return to self-sufficiency, nor any "further on" to reach. Such individuals can, however, always consent that their finite humanity be more and more profoundly penetrated by God's infinity.

> The tokens of past egocentrism known by those at the summit are opportunities for yielding ever more profoundly to God's relentless love.

"Death" before Death

The second point to consider here is that, according to Burrows, if there is total extinction of the ego and absorption into the life of God, then "death is truly overcome . . . death is dead."[33] She asserts that it can be said of the one at the heights of the Christian life, "she 'died' and therefore could never see death, physical death had completely changed its nature for her."[34] What Burrows means here is that those who have arrived at the third stage of the spiritual life do not await physical death as a threshold into complete union with God; that threshold has already been crossed in this life. Utterly emptied of self and living with the life of God himself, the one at the dwelling on the summit has "'died' before she died."[35]

Parenthetically, it must be noted that Burrows in no way suggests that those who have died before they died experience the "unalloyed bliss" of heaven here on earth.[36] As with every aspect of her thought, Jesus is her measure here. She details,

> During his life on earth [Jesus] was always with his Father, in closest union with him, but because of his mortality the full, blissful effect of that union could not be experienced. . . . He had to pass through death in order that God's closeness should transform his whole being, filling it with God's own bliss. So it is with us. We have to live with Jesus in the darkness, held close to his Father's heart, we have to consent to pass with him through the dissolution of death so as to receive ourselves again new-minted, freed for ever from every element of corruption, every particle of our being infused with the radiance and joy of God.[37]

While a person at the third stage of the spiritual life already shares in the full extent of Jesus' intimacy with the Father, he or she must journey with him to the other side of mortality before the full effect of that union can be experienced.

Perfect Participation in the Sacraments

The third and final characteristic of the state of transforming union for us to consider here is that, by Burrows's account, there is direct continuity between the objective reality of the sacraments and the inner life of the person. We have established previously that Burrows sees the sacraments as embodying the essence of the mystical life: the sacraments are Jesus trustfully exposing the full dependency of the human condition before the ecstasy of God's love. Because the one at the climax of the Christian life has been taken right into the radiant emptiness of Jesus, he or she participates perfectly in the sacramental life of the church. To express this insight in Burrows's own words, "Now the sacraments come into their own. That which formerly could be received only partially, now meets with no obstacle. The unutterably 'alien' and 'other,' God himself, meets in the soul a life 'other' to its depths. The sacramental encounter is continuous. Two abysses meet and know one another. Every reception of the sacraments means a deeper surrender and possession by God and always it is in the Church and for the Church."[38] Of course, included here is the idea that the one at the summit knows the full flowering of baptism. "Baptism only becomes total when faith is total," Burrows claims.[39] And, in the state of mystical union, the self-abandonment of faith is complete.

THE LIVED EXPERIENCE OF THE THIRD STAGE OF THE SPIRITUAL LIFE

The various dimensions of the essence of the third stage—complete transformation into Jesus crucified—have now been considered. Our next task is to examine what Burrows has to say about how this definitive transformation resonates within our conscious experience. To be clear, what is under scrutiny here is Burrows's thought on how the state of mystical union is experienced within the created human faculties; we are looking at the lived experience of utter conformity with the Crucified. She maintains throughout, her clarion insistence on the impossibility of a direct conscious experience of the culminating mystical grace itself. "Anything that you can actually describe of the experience can't be *it*,"[40] Burrows says of the final transformation, ever adamant that finite humanity can be grasped by, but cannot itself grasp, the divine.

Burrows's defining word on the lived experience of the third stage of the spiritual life is that this experience is necessarily a thoroughly individual one. In other words, she contends that what the state of transforming union "is *like* must have as many variations as there are persons who attain this state."[41] Earlier, we observed that, in Burrows's view, being wholly possessed by God means knowing the fulfillment of one's unique identity; for those at the summit, the capacity for Love that defines their personal existence is now finally realized. As Burrows notes in *Guidelines for Mystical Prayer*, "This individualisation at its highest peak means that there is no pattern of living on the third island. On the former islands there were patterns; to some extent one could generalise, but here hardly at all. Each inhabitant of this island is a world, a universe of her own."[42]

Given that we are dealing with something so individualized, it is difficult to find a starting point for our analysis of the experiential dimension of the third stage. Burrows herself indicates a way forward when, after establishing that the experience of life at the summit is inherently particular, she remarks, "We can only listen to what each tries to tell us of her experience and see where other testimony agrees."[43] Taking her writings as a whole, Burrows presents five more or less developed individual accounts of the experience of living the Christian life to the full. In addition to conveying what Teresa of Ávila, John of the Cross, and Thérèse of Lisieux communicate about their particular experiences of the state of mystical union, Burrows offers her own testimony and that of an intimate friend (principally in *Guidelines*, under the guises of "Petra" and "Claire" respectively). Within these widely varying accounts, we can discern several common elements of how living solely with the life of Jesus crucified impacts the consciousness; taken together, they give us some impression of how life is experienced at the summit. These common elements will occupy our attention for the first part of this section. We will then consider Burrows's depiction of two extremes of the lived experience of mystical union: "Vast emptiness and longing for [God] or . . . fulness and possession."[44]

Certitude About Being in the State of Mystical Union

The first of Burrows's shared features of the lived experience of the summit is certitude about being in the state of mystical union. What she portrays here is an undeniable mystical knowing echoing within the consciousness that God's loving purposes have been ultimately fulfilled.[45] Exploring in *Guidelines* this experience of certitude Burrows writes, "Must a person know she is in this state? Could she be there and not know it? It would seem that we must affirm that knowledge of it is essential. On the bridge, on the second island, we cannot really know where we are, but it is hard to think that when the work is accomplished, when there is perfect union, we would not know it in some way."[46] We saw in the preceding chapter that Burrows does admit elsewhere the possibility of those at the second stage having some secret knowledge of their progress. Be that as it may, our interest here is her insistence, derived from both observation and theory, that certitude of God's definitive transformative action marks the lived experience of the third stage of the spiritual life.

Burrows details that the way in which her five mystics experience certitude that God has taken over completely depends upon whether they experience the mystical life in the "light on" (Teresa, John,[47] and Claire) or "light off" (Thérèse and Petra) mode. "The basic difference," she observes, "is that the one sees it from God's side, sees God at work, the other sees it from the human, sees the consequent emptiness."[48] In keeping with Burrows's real interest, we shall focus more on the "light off" experience of certainty than the "light on." As she explains in *Guidelines*, "The first state ['light on'] is rare; it is the second that is normal and that is why I must say more about it. Those rare souls in the 'light on' state will not need this book, it is those in the 'light off' category that need help, very little in this state, but some nevertheless."[49]

So, we begin with only a brief word on the certainty known by those in the "light on" state. Burrows has it directly from her own testimony that Claire is convinced she is living by the life of God alone.[50] Additionally, Burrows claims, "No one could doubt that St. Teresa was quite certain where she was. Even if her writing on the seventh mansion were not proof enough, we have her affirmation in a letter (Nov. 1581). Likewise, St. John of the Cross's *Spiritual Canticle* from chapter xx and his *Living Flame* witness to his own personal experience."[51] Of course, as indicated above, the certainty of the "light on" mystics derives precisely from their singular non-conceptual insight into the divine reality. Each of these three "sees that she [or he] is held in God's embrace; the whole being knows it and responds, surrendering to his love."[52]

We know that, according to Burrows, those who are "light on" translate their ineffable vision of God's mystical presence into a conceptual framework. Such articulation of what is seen in secret can serve to encourage those who are making the Christian pilgrimage with the "light off." So how do Burrows's "light on" mystics express what is divinely revealed to them of their perfect intimacy with God? "Teresa expresses it in terms of a vision of the Trinity dwelling within her, and similarly John," notes Burrows.[53] Claire's externalization of her "sight" of her transformed being takes a somewhat different form. She relates the following metaphor: "Jesus has always been my music, but the music was all I noticed. I wasn't aware, before, that it was in some way 'I' who played, or 'I' who was the organ. But after he brought me to the third island, I found the difference. He was now all. The music played of itself— there was *only* the music. I was now living what had seemed my life before, but only seemed because I only looked at him and didn't advert to myself. Now myself has become him."[54]

Burrows's most developed exposition of the experience of certainty in the "light off" state comes through her presentation of her own experience of life on the summit. Speaking of herself in relation to Claire, Burrows observes, "Both Claire and Petra are certain that they are in a state of transforming union. The one 'sees,' 'feels,' 'tastes,' the other simply 'knows.'"[55] As we have noted, it is a mystical knowing that is under discussion here; it is a certitude that possesses, yet cannot be possessed. In a poem in which she describes God's taking full possession of her interior being Burrows writes, "Yet I knew (though it felt as if I did not know) / that he was there with me / waiting . . . / He has come into his garden."[56]

Burrows elaborates that her "knowing," her certitude, derives from a living awareness of that absolute loss of egocentricity that is necessarily concomitant with complete transformation into the Crucified. In other words, Burrows is certain of her spiritual state because she is starkly aware of living the emptiness of selflessness. She recounts that awareness of the irrevocable loss of her ego entered her consciousness through what she describes as a "light on" moment "of a negative nature":[57]

I was in the garden, and for a moment I seemed to be looking within and I saw or realised in a mysterious way that *I*
was not there. There was no "I." I can't say more than that.
I had gone. It wasn't that I saw or felt God, but it was as if I
were in a vast and lonely plain far removed from everything.
For a few weeks I lived to some extent outside myself, by
which I mean only a very small part of me seemed in contact with what was going on around me. I had similar experiences of this estrangement in earlier days but they were
extremely bitter. This was bewildering joy. I felt physically
and nervously exhausted but I managed to carry on, and I
do not think anyone saw anything was different with me.[58]

Evidently, in this stunning moment of illumination, "It was
not God she saw, she saw emptiness, saw that self had gone."[59]

Burrows's living awareness of her complete self-abandonment lost its initial luminosity—"that ['light on'] experience
has never been recaptured in so vivid a way"[60]—and assumed
the tones of the everyday. Describing her friend's daily reality,
Claire writes to Burrows, "Your experience is of *what you are*,
that is, an emptiness God has filled. But you are never shown
the fulness, God, the sole reason for your being emptied—all
you see is the creature side."[61] And this enduring stark experience of humanity in all its vulnerability, this apparently God-
less experience of "Godfulness," is imbued with the secret
assurance that God has taken over definitively. Burrows relates
that "though there is no seeing or feeling of God and his love
and that he is pleased with me, there is a profound certainty. I
can only think that it is God's affirmation of himself because it
does not come from me."[62]

Certitude within barrenness endures as Burrows's lived
experience of the summit. Some twenty years after publishing

Guidelines, she writes in *Living in Mystery*, "It seems to me that what I understand to be my 'I' has been thrown up helpless on the banks of the tidal river flowing deep within. Is the river estuary or sea? Thought can raise a skeptical eyebrow, emotion remain coldly unresponsive, and all the 'I' can do is trust. 'Acts' of trust seem emasculated, no more than the chirping of a tired bird. All energy, all attention are absorbed into the waters flowing there without the 'I,' with a momentum all their own and this, I know, is my real life, a life that is not 'mine.'"[63] Abiding in the wasteland of selflessness, Burrows knows that her inner being, her true self, is utterly immersed in the hidden God.[64]

In presenting her experience of knowing from the "creature side" that she has been completely filled with the divine life, Burrows discusses her need for external confirmation of this knowing. She recounts yearning to receive from Claire confirmation of the truth of her initial illuminated perception of her total freedom from egocentricity, and her joy at receiving it unprompted; "this confirmation was precious to me," Burrows says.[65] In the same vein, Burrows refers to seeking encouragement from Claire when the obscurity consequent upon her union with God becomes too bewildering. As she expresses it, "When her state becomes just a little too donkey-like [Petra] turns to Claire for a word of assurance, and it always comes, a word fragrant with truth: 'Yes, everything in your soul is *really* what he wants. He has searched the world, has searched history, to find souls who will accept to be nothing, who will let him be God. Jesus so fills your soul that all self-delight has died.'"[66]

On the other hand, for all her recourse to Claire's privileged insight into the workings of Love, she is ultimately independent from it; Burrows's own certainty has the final word.

She writes to Claire, "If you were to tell me that I was mistaken, that God had not 'taken over,' I would want to believe you because I feel you speak from God and I want to hear all he wants to tell me, but it would be impossible."[67]

Drawing together both her need for and her ultimate independence from Claire's confirmation of her own mystical knowing Burrows concludes, "There, clearly, is the certitude. It seems that it comes from within, but yet needs or has needed outside affirmation. By God's providence it came through Claire whose experience is of 'light on.' Earlier I made the point that this charism is given for others. Here we have an instance of it. Claire is able to 'see' God in Petra in a way Petra cannot see herself."[68] Living the transforming union from underneath, so to speak, Burrows is enabled by Claire's "light on" perception to claim confidently the undeniable certainty of God's intimate presence permeating her darkness.

Burrows's treatment of St. Thérèse's experience of knowing within the "light off" mode that she was in the state of mystical union is rather less developed than that of her own. She establishes her position on Thérèse's spiritual state and Thérèse's mystical knowledge thereof when she declares, "[Thérèse] knew little or nothing of the 'favours,' the 'delights' of which the Spanish mystics write, but who can doubt that she received 'all God has to give,' and was a true mystic who, within the last two years of her short life, attained and lived the state of transforming union or spiritual marriage? Her tormenting doubts, darkness and trials of faith notwithstanding, she was mysteriously aware that this was so."[69] Burrows has more to say about Thérèse's awareness of her mystical state in *Guidelines*. There, she maintains, "Thérèse was [certain] of her state in spite of the darkness. There is a constant certitude though nothing is seen and nothing is felt. God alone is, filling the horizon and all else. She does not see God: what she does see is herself. Not God enfolding her, not what he is doing, but rather the effect of this in herself. The essence of this state is that God has taken over, despoiled her of her powers, replaced the ego, and the effect in the psychic, conscious life is one of despoliation, emptiness."[70]

What is the basis of Burrows's assertion that Thérèse, within her "light off" state, was certain she was dwelling at the heights of the mystical life? How does she know Thérèse was possessed of such certitude? Burrows does not substantiate this position within her writings. The most we are given is Thérèse's confident declaration from within the darkness that enshrouded her final months that God had accomplished in her everything about which St. John of the Cross wrote.[71] When questioned about her evidence for Thérèse's certitude, Burrows reflects,

> The essence of this state is that God has taken over, despoiled her of her powers, replaced the ego; the effect in the psychic, conscious life is one of despoliation, emptiness.

If you read her letters, you see these great passions and convictions about childhood and her way all came together in the last [two years, perhaps eighteen months]. I think she was feeling her way [until then], but you see a surety in her way, and confidence, and, I don't know, wisdom. Obviously I wouldn't say just when, but I would say that it is in the last, almost, two years of her life. [Up until that point] she could suffer from scruples and anxieties and worries. . . . This

great sense of mission that came upon her, just towards the
end. . . . Her letters are so mature, so much more grown
up than they were earlier on.[72]

Thus, in Burrows's view, Thérèse evinces her certitude that
God's kingdom has come in her through her confident proclamation of her spiritual doctrine. For Thérèse to assert the way
of spiritual childhood, the primacy of receptivity, with such
startling authority, it must mean that she is convinced that her
own embraced and surrendered nothingness has been utterly
consumed by God's love.

Profound Contentment and Security

The second existential quality that Burrows presents as common
to those dwelling on the summit of the Christian life is an experience of profound contentment and security, even in the midst
of affliction. She observes, "Profound happiness is the vibrant
note of all who tell us of their experience, happiness in suffering,
happiness in 'unhappiness.'"[73] As that observation indicates,
Burrows is clear that this experience of security and contentment
is something deeper than emotion. Rather, she discusses it as an
essential effect of living wholly in union with Jesus. "Only those
who really allow God to make Christ Jesus their wisdom and
their holiness can know unshakeable security," Burrows explains.
"Relying on nothing whatsoever within themselves or anything
created, they can never be let down. They are free."[74] With their
fundamental dependency and fragility utterly absorbed in Jesus'
surrender to the Father's love, those at the summit know the joyful liberty of the children of God.

The experience of unassailable security and contentment
appears in Burrows's portrayal of the lived experience of the

third stage of John, Thérèse, Teresa, and "Petra." Admittedly, it appears only fleetingly in her treatment of both John and Thérèse and, in both cases, chiefly in the context of her polemic against what she perceives to be John's misleading emphasis on the experience of exaltation at the summit (to which we will turn later). With consternation over his apparent grandiloquence, Burrows notes, "John would say that soul-suffering is no longer possible [at the summit] and Our Lady's sufferings were a special dispensation."[75] She goes on, however, to allow "John's statement that the transformed soul does not suffer" to signify that, because Jesus lives through the humanity of the one at the third stage, any suffering that is endured is ultimately shot through with freedom.[76] Burrows reinforces this reading of John by citing Thérèse's insistence: "I have reached the stage when I can no longer suffer because all suffering has become sweet to me."[77] Expounding this passage, Burrows writes, "Joy and transport were certainly in [Thérèse's] depths but in a way that still left her a prey to physical and mental agony."[78]

Burrows's discussion of Teresa's experience of deep contentment and assurance is more accessible. She observes of Teresa's depiction of life in the seventh mansion, "An outstanding feature of this state is its security. Teresa hardly knows herself, she who all her life-long has been plagued with insecurity, torn with anxiety."[79] We know from the previous chapter that, in Burrows's estimation, Teresa knew great angst throughout her spiritual pilgrimage due to misapprehension of the psychic phenomena she experienced; here at the summit, this angst is no more. Burrows notes that the joyful security permeating Teresa's lived experience of transforming union issues from her certainty of her spiritual state. "She tells that she cannot really suffer any more because she is no longer lonely, she is enjoying continually divine companionship."[80]

While Teresa's conviction of what God has done in her means that she knows unshakeable peace, she is still subject to the tribulations of human existence. Burrows recounts that the transformed Teresa "tell[s] us that she suffers very much, and, indeed, we have external witness for the fact. The years following the mystical marriage were for her fraught with difficulties of all kinds. Her letters bear witness to them and the testimony of eye-witnesses."[81] Yet, "she suffers but she doesn't suffer. A sort of 'deadness' takes over."[82] So completely is Teresa's ego abandoned to the living God that it is impossible for the suffering she experiences to have any fundamental impact upon her.

What is distinctive, and even audacious, about Burrows's analysis of Teresa's experience here is that she intuits in her writings a hesitance fully to claim the security and peace she enjoys. "It is as if she can hardly accept her present security," Burrows claims, "and looks around anxiously for snags. . . . In her heart Teresa knows she is utterly safe and can never be separated from God, that she is at home forever. . . . But she dare not say so, even to herself."[83] Burrows attributes Teresa's malaise to the fact that with the dawning of invincible joyful freedom, "some of her most cherished notions of what a fervent spiritual life is all about are overturned."[84] She goes on to specify, "Over and over again Teresa has expressed to us her conviction that great sufferings are a prerequisite for great love; the measure of our love is the measure of the suffering we can bear. She must keep on assuring herself that she is ready to suffer. At the same time she sees that it is not suffering that is important at all!"[85] The portrait of Teresa with which Burrows leaves us, then, is marked by paradox, and even poignancy:

"She is perfectly happy and contented but she can't wholly adjust her preconceived ideas to cope with it."[86]

As we saw with her handling of the experience of certitude, Burrows's most extensive account of the experience of invulnerable security and contentment is found in her depiction of her own lived experience of transforming union. For Burrows, as for Teresa, the peace that pervades her existence is a direct effect of knowing indubitably that she has been taken to the mystical summit. Using the voice of Petra, she describes her experience in this way:

> Looking back I see that nearly all my life and with growing intensity I have suffered from profound anxiety. The anxiety was rooted in my relation to God. Not that I feared his "wrath" or anything like that, it was just a fear of existence, fear of the Other; anxiety as to how I stood to him; only he mattered, was I loving him? Time, terrible time was passing away . . . was I near to God? Briefly, I lacked God and as life means nothing but him and time's only worth was in bearing me to him, time was ambiguous and threatening, threatening on all levels. When God suddenly, unexpectedly, carried me to the third island, this anxiety was extinguished. I possess him.[87]

In her autobiography Burrows revealed to us this angst gripping her existence due to her not knowing if she was in any way close to the living God: "Here was existential fear, the fear of existence itself. Here was threatened, meaningless existence."[88] While Burrows's commitment to Jesus' way of empty-handed trust assured her that fear was not the ultimate word over her existence, it did not alleviate it. But when certainty of her utter intimacy with God echoed into her consciousness, this angst was transformed into boundless security. Accordingly, Burrows can now declare of herself, "Always she is aware of deep contentment. She knows she possesses God and having him has all things else. The tearing, the anxiety, the sense of terrible 'absence' are no more."[89]

We need to probe a little deeper here. Burrows's basic conscious experience in the state of mystical union—as it has been throughout her life—is of the absolute contingency of humanity and the hiddenness of God; of course, before the summit, this was the cause of the existential fear we were just discussing. In the state of union, this enduring experience of ultimate limitation is itself borne with radical freedom of spirit. Again presenting her own experience under the guise of that of Petra, Burrows relates,

> Asked if there were any differences between her present trials and those she experienced earlier, she was emphatic that there is all the difference in the world, though in fact they are made of the same stuff. If one gave the name of "suffering" to what went before, then one must find another name for this. Formerly she suffered "without God," in a sense—she was not united to him, she was distanced from him—but now, if she stops to reflect, she sees that she is always conscious of possession yet without being conscious of it! She knows God is always with her.[90]

Clearly, the mystical knowledge that she has been taken completely into the divine life changes everything for Burrows. Not only is her existential anxiety transformed into peace but also, more fundamentally, the sting is removed from her ongoing experience of total fragility. We will return to Burrows's enduring experience of humanity's essential fragility a little later in this chapter.

Complete Freedom in Relating with Created Realities

The third and final common element of the lived experience of mystical union is utter freedom in relating with created realities, including one's own creaturehood. What Burrows discusses here is, to borrow a phrase from Rowan Williams, "A re-conversion to creatures."[91] In chapter 3 we saw Burrows cautioning beginners that their engagement with the things of creation is likely to emerge from, and reinforce, the demands of the ego. She wants those starting out on the spiritual journey to know that "if our hearts belonged wholly to God we could be completely free and happy in the use of everything God has given us, but until we are we have to watch jealously lest craving for our own pleasure blunts our earnestness in seeking God."[92] In what Burrows describes of how John, Teresa, Claire, and she herself experience life on the summit, we see the realization of what she anticipated in her discussion of the base: with the victory over egocentricity won, they are able to embrace the good things of creation with perfect liberty.

Burrows presents us with John's living knowledge of enjoying created things in freedom inasmuch as his spiritual doctrine emerges from his personal experience. In examining John's ascetical counsel, she notes, "It leads towards the fulness of life, bringing freedom of spirit, insight, tranquillity."[93] In the third book of his *Ascent of Mount Carmel*, for example, John emphasizes that "the pure of heart enjoy a hundredfold even in this life, finding joy in all that is, be it human or divine. Creation is restored to its true form and becomes an unsullied mirror of the face of God."[94] All of this is to indicate that John guides those scaling the mount in the ways of loosening their grip on created things in the living certainty that this will culminate in the freedom to enjoy them in their fullness.

As for Teresa, her joyful embrace of created reality is evident in what Burrows shows us of the way in which she realized the various potentialities of her personality. We know that the full realization of personal identity belongs to the essence of the state of mystical union; here we see this property actuated. Burrows observes that "Teresa's will was identified with that of our Lord and so everything she was, both her many gifts and her weaknesses, were brought into the orbit of her love and dedication. . . . Teresa was not afraid of humanness. No gift that God, through circumstances, asked her to develop was left to wither."[95] Exemplifying Teresa's glad acceptance of the various dimensions of her personality—and noting that such flourishing of humanness is not generally associated with holiness—Burrows writes,

> We would not readily acclaim as holy one who was a shrewd businesswoman who took over the management of her brother's financial affairs because she knew more about such things than he did; or a woman who was well aware of her captivating charm and never thought of dimming the headlights but allowed them full play, to the delight of all who approached her—more than that, who consciously employed this charm to gain her own ends. Nor do we readily associate with sanctity one who admitted unashamedly to feeling hurt when her love was not returned, annoyed and angry at times.[96]

Having lost herself in surrender to God, Teresa found the natural capacities that were uniquely hers fully alive within her.

The work of Stephen Sundborg enables us to appreciate something of Burrows's own experience of relating to the created realm in complete liberty of spirit in the state of transforming union. Sundborg has sought out Burrows's word on how she has experienced her womanhood, her sexual-affective self, since being brought to the summit. He details, "Her sexual-affective integration included both a moment of internal, essential surrender to God and a long period of making this surrender an external, lived reality in the concreteness of her life. . . . The [full] concretization of this integration was simultaneous with and continued after her entrance into this state [transforming union]."[97] In other words, Burrows had already embraced her sexual-affective capacities and yielded them to God before arriving at the mystical heights; she refers in her autobiography to "offering myself specifically as a woman, my body, sexual powers and emotions as well as my spirit, to the actions of the Holy Ghost."[98] It is only with the grace of transforming union, however, that she truly experiences her womanhood as wholly given over to the living God.

> John of the Cross guides those scaling the mount in the ways of loosening their grip on created things in the certainty that this will culminate in the freedom to enjoy them in their fullness.

So, just what is Burrows's experience of transformed womanhood? Sundborg presents Burrows as living out the fullness of her sexual-affective selfhood in joyful freedom. Her experience is that "'everything' in her womanhood is now 'taken up, used, meaningful' and that . . . God's plans in creating her as a woman and calling her to a life of consecrated celibacy have 'come to fruition.'"[99] She is convinced that "'she has not lost anything at all of the natural woman' she is; rather 'all that was there' has been brought by God 'to flower.'"[100] Presenting Burrows's account of living fulfilled in her womanhood, Sundborg begins by noting that, earlier in her life, "through the experience of intimate love and its inability to satisfy her desires, [Burrows] realized that her sexuality in its profoundest reality was a need for God's fulfilling love."[101] With the grace of mystical union, she experiences this fundamental neediness as completely taken into Jesus' perfect surrender to God's love and thus the potential of her womanhood realized. Sundborg observes, "[Burrows'] sexuality . . . is realized in its potential in such a way that its forces positively contribute to and enrich the way she loves God and others in her celibate life."[102] With her sexual-affective capacities penetrated by divine love, all her relations are free from egocentricity and oriented to the good of the other.

The complete freedom and contentment Burrows experiences in living as the woman God created her to be is exemplified in her intimate friendship with a man Sundborg names "John." Previously, Burrows struggled with "possessive desires" toward John and had to make "many painful sacrifices" in her relationship with him.[103] Since entering the state of transforming union, however, she has been able to enjoy this intimate, celibate, male-female relationship without reserve. Sundborg's presentation of Burrows's experience is worth citing at length. He writes,

> Because the "mysterious agony" due to her doubts about how she stood to God has been "extinguished" in her

transforming union by knowing she belongs wholly to God, she says that in the relationship with John she is "no longer the suffering creature longing for solace and feeling let down because the loved one couldn't heal me." The removal of this anxiety allows her to accept the relationship for what it is, gives her "real rest" in his love, and makes her "certain" and "unshakeable" about their being "the one and only for the other." . . . Her relationship with John shows that this freedom to love comes from belonging wholly to God. Ruth was always trying to belong more completely to God but only in the state of transforming union does she know that she belongs wholly to God. This assurance affects her way of living her womanhood by making her completely free and happy in the sexual-affective dimensions of her love-union with John. She has faced her own fears of her emotions and sexuality, surrendered them to God so that she belongs to God and is transformed by him even in these dimensions, and comes to experience a complete freedom and happiness in living them out in the intimate love of John.[104]

The conjunction between being in the state of mystical union and experiencing total freedom in relating with the created realm could not be clearer: utterly convinced that she is all God's, Burrows can give herself wholeheartedly to the celibate intimacy she shares with John.[105]

The "freedom about her womanhood and even a glorying in being a woman" manifest in Burrows's lived experience of the summit are also evident in Burrows's portrayal of Claire.[106] Burrows recounts that since reaching the mystical heights, "[Claire] feels . . . that all her potential is realised. She is as God meant her to be."[107] She does not offer any further testimony from Claire in this regard. Throughout *Guidelines for Mystical Prayer*, however, Burrows describes Claire as the "most womanly of women"[108] and as "one who [has] understood and integrated the height, length, breadth and depth of the mystery of sexuality,"[109] and refers to her "feminine intuitiveness, richness and delicacy."[110] Clearly, being taken wholly into the life of the crucified and risen Jesus has freed Claire to embrace the full capacity of her femininity.

Two Extremes of the Lived Experience of Mystical Union

We have now established the principal common elements that Burrows discerns across individual accounts of the lived experience of the mystical summit. To conclude this section we will consider Burrows's presentation of two very diverse ways in which the state of transforming union is consciously experienced. In doing so, I will tentatively raise a question mark over a claim she makes about these extremes: it "makes no difference" whether life at the summit "is experienced as a vast emptiness and longing for [God] or as fulness and possession."[111]

"Fullness" at the Summit

Burrows addresses the possibility of experiencing the mystical union with rapturous emotion principally in her analysis of the writings of John of the Cross and, more specifically, in the context of articulating her concern that "there is in John a disturbing contradiction."[112] We have observed previously that Burrows finds in John firm support for her position on the sensible phenomena commonly associated with the mystical life. Like her, John maintains a necessary distinction between God's mystical presence and the possible repercussions of this grace within the realm of our created humanity.

Now, setting forth the contradiction she discerns in John's work, Burrows writes,

> For me his authentic teaching is summed up succinctly in his drawing of the mount and expounded principally in the *Ascent of Mount Carmel* and the *Dark Night*. It is to be found too in his letters, maxims and counsels, and a careful reading reveals it underlying the *Spiritual Canticle* and the *Living Flame*. However it is in these two latter works that we find the inconsistency. Look at the drawing of the mount. . . . See the road straight as the drive of an arrow to the summit, a summit lost in mystery. It is a way of Nothing, "*and on the mountain nothing.*" How powerful the silence! Now read the *Canticle* and the *Living Flame* with their flamboyant descriptions of what the perfect or near-perfect actually experience. These works seem to belie the truth of John's fundamental teaching. He would have us detached from spiritual riches certainly, but he seems to be saying here, "detach yourselves from crude consolations so that one day you can enjoy something immensely superior even in this life."[113]

So, as Burrows sees it, in *The Spiritual Canticle* and *The Living Flame of Love*, John so emphasizes the experience of glorious euphoria at the summit that he distorts the clarity of his mystical doctrine. Contrary to the overall scheme of his thought, he conveys the impression that exalted sensible phenomena are *intrinsic* to the state of transforming union rather than a possible side effect in some people.

Contemplating the source of this strange inconsistency in John, Burrows relates, "I don't understand it altogether; whether it is part poetic, or whether, probably he did have times of enormous spiritual exaltation—I would wholly accept that—but I don't think that one can absolutely identify that as essential."[114] Elsewhere she remarks, "John . . . gives reign to his poetic genius in eloquent descriptions of what [the state of transforming union] is *like* for the bride . . . especially when there is an overwhelming awareness of that union."[115] In Burrows's mind, then, John's own rapturous experience of the mystical marriage and his great ability to express all that resounded in his psyche account for the distortion in his portrayal of the summit. Depictions of grandeur end up assuming the ascendancy in *The Spiritual Canticle* and *The Living Flame*, even though John is well aware that "the experience [of the transforming union itself] must, of its very nature, elude all precision of thought, all description."[116]

Burrows observes that John's seeming identification of the ineffable reality of the mystical marriage with sublime sensible phenomena results in elements of his treatment of life on the summit being in discord with the Gospel. "Take for example," Burrows asserts, "[John's] description of the death of the perfect which purports to be attended by marvellous sweetness and consolation far surpassing all they have experienced during the course of their life. They die in 'delicious ecstasy.' Well, we have only to turn to Jesus in the Gospel of Mark and the Epistle to the Hebrews to see that this cannot be true at its face value."[117] Burrows goes on to point out, "Elsewhere John claims that the perfect no longer experience natural emotions."[118] To this contention she responds, "Need we comment? What of Jesus himself weeping over Jerusalem and at the tomb of Lazarus? Moved with compassion before a disconsolate widow carrying her dead son to the grave? Showing anger and frustration and shuddering dread."[119] In a word, then, Burrows has no objection to the possibility of the one in the state of mystical union enjoying a rich banquet of sublime emotions. She insists, however, that it is utterly misleading to suggest a necessary correlation between such exalted phenomena and one's actual union with the crucified, glorified Lord.

"Emptiness" at the Summit

Burrows herself embodies the other extreme way in which life at the mystical summit can be consciously experienced. She is possessed by a mystical certitude—it is an unknowing knowing—that she is all God's, and from this certitude issues invulnerable peace and security. Yet, at the heights of the Christian life, Burrows is fundamentally conscious of "vast emptiness," lowliness, destitution. She allows us a glimpse of what the state of mystical union is like for her in the following passage:

> A sense of inner fragility and faintness, which taps, knocks at the wall of my body too. I seem unable to face up to any pressure. I feel faced with an immense "trial" utterly beyond myself, and yet when I look, where is the trial? What have I to suffer compared with so many people? I have good health, am surrounded with love, have everything I need, and yet life itself seems more than I can bear—the unutterable loneliness and emptiness, the mystery and obscurity. . . . I feel overwhelmed with everything: with the beauty of the world, with its terrible pain, with its evil and ugliness, the devilish brutality of man to man—with the Word of God so mighty and so obscure. I could weep my eyes out with—I don't know what! Oh, how fragile I am, without achievement; no human victory, no human beauty.[120]

She goes on to add, quoting a letter to Claire from "Petra," "'Unimportance,' yes, Claire, I feel that is the best word to express a vital point. 'Littleness,' 'helplessness,' 'poverty' can be run to death and lose their life. 'Non-importance' carries with it a dreadful awareness of one's basic insecurity and meaningless-ness. It's not only a question of being non-important in one's community, business and so on, it is on the cosmic level also."[121]

Earlier, in the context of our discussion of Burrows's certi-tude about her spiritual state, we noted that her sense of dwell-ing at the mystical heights in profound lowliness is an enduring one. To reinforce this, and to add further depth to our under-standing of Burrows's lived experience, it is worth turning to another source. In her book *Sister Wendy on Prayer*, Wendy Beckett offers valuable insight into the nature of Burrows's con-scious experience. Referring to Burrows, Beckett relates,

> The holiest person I know has never had the slightest inte-rior intimation that God exists. All she gets back from her prayer is doubt and darkness. She experiences a terrible fear that her life with God is all imagination, that there is no God, that living as a nun is a mockery. With this agonising sense of her own personal weakness and her own absolute absence of felt certainty, she chooses. She chooses to believe. She chooses to act in accordance with that belief, which means in practice a life of heroic charity. This woman—and others like her, because she is not alone in this heroism—is giving God the real sacrifice of faith. This woman chooses to love God and to serve Him and to believe in Him, even if she gets nothing back.[122]

Quite clearly, united with God in the most profound intimacy, Burrows is exposed to the extremes of human frailty in the most absolute way.

Burrows's interpretation of the way in which she experi-ences life at the summit is all-important. She realizes that her experience contrasts entirely with what key figures before her have said the state of transforming union is like. She observes that that "initial 'light on' experience . . . of a negative nature" in which she became stunningly conscious that she stands before God as a living emptiness "seems a far cry from Teresa's vision of the glorious Christ celebrating his nuptials with her."[123] And after recounting her vivid awareness of her absolute fragility and inherent unimportance, Burrows remarks, "How different this lowly admission from the ideas usually formed of the state of transforming union and which mystical writers seem to affirm. For both Teresa and John the state is one of surpassing glory and delight. . . . Everything is in terms of grandeur, glory, heroism, far removed from the common experience."[124]

However, and this is the vital point, Burrows understands her experience of the third stage of the spiritual life to be wholly at one with the pattern of the Gospel. "Even should the witness of [John and Teresa] really be against what Petra claims," she declares, "we need not worry. We look to Jesus. Here is one wholly possessed by God and what do we see? Where is the 'sublime,' the 'heroic' in this precious life?"[125] We can say, then, that Burrows perceives an immediacy, a transparency, between her hidden intimacy with God and what she experiences at the conscious level: in her depths she shares in Jesus' perfect receptivity to God's love, and on the surface she knows nothing but his concomitant immersion in our destitute humanity.

Developing this idea of the Christological significance of her lived experience of the summit, Burrows writes,

> Petra has a profound grasp that her stark, human experience is mystical, that it is, in fact, Jesus living it in her. "Son of God though he was, he learned obedience through what

he suffered." Was not this school of suffering precisely the experience of what it means to be a man and to die, to be born dying? No one has ever plumbed the depths of human littleness and wretchedness as he did; no one ever tasted the bitter draught of human poverty as he. His very sinlessness heightened the awareness of this poverty. Yet Jesus never evaded it, he lived it out fully to the inevitable end, death.[126]

Moreover, Claire expounds the true meaning of Burrows's experience when she says to her friend in a letter, "To know the full smallness, the incompleteness of being human, to open wholly to the suffering and frustration and endless pettiness of living: it is Jesus who knows that, who is living it in you and living it in radiant happiness."[127]

To conclude this exploration of the extreme ways in which life at the mystical summit is consciously experienced, allow me to express my slight discomfort with Burrows's assertion that one's mode of experience "makes no difference." My question is this: despite her contention that the shape of the mystic's experience is incidental, does Burrows actually implicitly suggest that there is something normative about her own way of experiencing the transforming union?

At one point in her portrayal of her lived experience Burrows maintains, "Of course, my temperament has a lot to do with this, others wouldn't react so strongly or be in such a degree conscious of the 'tears of things.' But my heart tells me the Lord is in it; this lowly way is his way."[128] So does Burrows's temperament expose her to the "pure" way of living the mystical union, the way of Jesus himself? Are all other forms of life on the summit—lives in which the truth of human fragility is not so palpable, lives in which great consolation is even felt—simply mitigated versions of this unalloyed lowliness, shaped by the degree to which one's temperament exposes them to humanity's contingency or disposes them to psychic resonances of the mystical grace?

There is something strange, however, about postulating that, among people in the state of transforming union, one's conscious experience could be more surely Jesus' own experience than another's. These people, Burrows tells us, are identified with the Crucified; the ego defeated, nothing within them stands apart from Jesus' definitive self-abandoning "yes" to the Father's outpoured love. And it would be, of course, radically unfaithful to Burrows's spiritual doctrine to ascribe any kind of comparative intrinsic value to what is experienced on the surface; throughout her writings she cannot emphasize enough "the relative unimportance of what is felt."[129] In view of these considerations, it is perhaps best to leave my question unanswered. While it is tempting to claim that there is something more than incidental about the way in which Burrows experiences the mystical union, to do so would require us to relativize the experiences of others, and this does not sit well with the thrust of her mystical thought.

THE EFFECT OF THOSE AT THE THIRD STAGE OF THE SPIRITUAL LIFE

In this final section of the chapter, we will explore Burrows's understanding of the effect that those at the third stage of the spiritual life have upon the world. She indicates throughout her writings two principal ways in which the ones at the summit exercise a transforming influence. First, they are bearers of a profound living knowledge of the divine life. And second, through them, the kingdom of God is established more fully in the world.

Bearers of Living Knowledge of the Divine Life

The idea that those dwelling at the heights of the Christian life bear a living knowledge of God is essentially familiar to us. We saw in the previous chapter that the same can be said of those traveling along the second stage of the spiritual life. What Burrows attributes to those at the summit, however, is a living knowledge of the divine life that is unprecedented in its breadth and depth, indeed, a knowledge that has reached a certain perfection. In *Ascent to Love*, she explains that one's mystical knowing "will . . . be in proportion to the depth and fulness of" one's union with God.[130] And as we know, living only with the life of the Crucified, those at the third stage are in perfect union with God. Accordingly, while the following presentation of the ones at the summit as bearers of knowledge of God will largely repeat previously established ideas, we must remember that what Burrows has in mind now is a wholly deeper level of intimacy than before.

So, by Burrows's account, those who have become one with God in the mystical marriage are imbued with an intimate knowledge of the divine life. Describing the inner life of the bride, she writes, "God assumes full care of her, holds her in his arms, feeds her with all good things and takes her into his deepest secrets."[131] Elsewhere she makes the same point in a perhaps less esoteric way when she observes, "Holiness implies a deep knowledge of God. It is union with God, a union of love, and love always means knowledge. Scripture over and over again testifies to this profound knowledge of God in those who are close to him."[132] Given that Burrows is referring to familiarity with God himself, it follows that the knowing that permeates those at the summit cannot be captured by human categories. As she puts it, "The knowledge itself is beyond conceptualisation; it is not of things, even holy things, but of God himself. It is one thing with union."[133]

Burrows maintains that although the loving knowledge of God that imbues the perfect is essentially ineffable, it can echo out into human expression. "It is as with a vast, deep lake, clasped and hidden in the bosom of a mountain," she details. "No one would know of its presence save the mountain which holds it were it not for the streams breaking through the mountain-side and cascading down into the valleys."[134] The "light on" mystics' externalization of their inexpressible "sight" of their consummate union with God is a particular case of what Burrows is generally discussing here; this process is precisely concerned with translating inexpressible intimacy with God into material that can be handled by the consciousness.

According to Burrows, a certain confidence animates the expressed living knowledge of God offered by those in the state of transforming union. "There is a certainty in this knowledge," she claims. "The person knows he knows and can speak with authority."[135] This assurance is surely connected with the certitude of their spiritual state characteristic of those at the summit. She points to St. Paul's assertion that "he is not subject to judgment by his fellow-men because they have not received such communication and simply cannot stand on the same platform with him."[136] Moreover, Burrows has this to say about the writings of St. Teresa:

> They ring with authenticity. Here is a woman who surely *knows*. She isn't merely speculating, deducing; she isn't relying on what others have said. Here is one with a well

of living knowledge within her and it is from this she is drawing all the time. Her complete certainty is over-whelming. . . . For her it has happened; the kingdom of God has come in her in its overpowering, transforming truth. . . . Teresa is aware that she has a living knowledge known to few and that she is called to communicate this knowledge to others: a wholly new dimension of human existence which can never be known theoretically, but only by moving into it and living there.[137]

There are two further exemplars to mention. We saw earlier that Burrows perceives remarkable confidence in the way in which St. Thérèse articulates her living knowledge of the spiritual life. Finally, Burrows's own writings exemplify the point she is making here: her Christocentric mystical doctrine crackles with an authority derived from her own deep knowledge of the living God.

Bearers of the Kingdom of God

Burrows's idea that those at the summit are furthermore effective in realizing the reign of God on earth is an important aspect of her thought on the third stage of the spiritual life.[138] However, her point is a simple one and thus can be discussed succinctly. In the conclusion to *Interior Castle Explored*, Burrows declares, "The mystical marriage is not a state of psychic bliss, not a comprehensible fulfilment. It is utterly remote from such paltriness; it has nothing to do with self-states. It is to be with Jesus a total 'for-Godness' which must mean being totally for others; it is an ecstasy of devotedness with no concern for self; it is to be Fire on earth, purifying, enkindling others at a depth far below what we can discern. It . . . is those who are totally hidden and lost in God, living only with the life of Christ who are Fire on earth."[139] We know that the ones at the heights of the Christian life have become fully human: they have allowed Jesus to take the utter fragility and dependency of their humanity wholly into his trusting "yes" to the Father, and thus the potential for God's love that defines their existence has been realized. What Burrows is specifying in the above passage is that becoming fully human, being transformed into the Crucified, necessarily entails becoming a channel through which God's ecstasy of love can inundate the fabric of humanity. In short, as Burrows sees it, "a person wholly possessed by God is the presence of Jesus on earth, opening the world to divine love."[140]

In Burrows's view, this mission of being an "entry point" for Love is the primary purpose of the enclosed Carmelite life. Briefly exploring her thought here will prove a worthwhile digression. Burrows expounds her understanding of the Carmelite vocation in her essay "Carmel: A Stark Encounter with the Human Condition." Her starting point is the familiar idea that "basic to human experience is the awareness of limitation, even of helplessness, and of how little control we have over our life."[141] She then proceeds to maintain, "Living myself within the enclosure of Carmel, accepting its discipline and trying to understand its living spirit . . . has left me with the conviction that Carmel offers an extraordinarily effective means for experiencing the reality of our humanity. . . . So convinced am I of this that I am ready to define Carmel as an intense experience of human existence and its innate poverty, containing within it a summons of faith not to evade but to enter through it into a total trust, a leap of the self into divine love which is the essence of union with God."[142] We know that what Burrows is essentially claiming here is that the enclosed

Carmelite life provides ideal conditions for being transformed into the kenotic Christ.

And now we come to our point. For Burrows, the Carmelite's intense experience of the indigence of the human condition and her graced surrender of this neediness to the God of love constitutes her principal contribution to the church and the world. "Carmelites have no external apostolate," she explains. "It is our faith-informed conviction that a life wholly given to God is the most effective apostolate. . . . Nothing must be allowed to take from us or even to mitigate our poverty, our helplessness, our 'nothingness.' This is not a lovely spiritual ideal, but an experienced reality that can be loved and must be loved only because it opens ourselves and the world to the purifying, transforming, beatifying love of God."[143] Thus Burrows demonstrates that the end of the enclosed Carmelite vocation is nothing other than that of the basic Christian vocation, indeed of the human vocation: to give our nothingness to God with such trustful abandon that through our being possessed by God, God comes closer to all.

Summary

For Ruth Burrows, the transformation that belongs to the third stage of the spiritual life is what St. Paul meant by his reference to "what no eye has seen, nor ear heard, nor the human heart conceived, what God has prepared for those who love him" (1 Cor 2:9).[144] It is perfect transformation into Jesus crucified, the One utterly emptied of self and completely yielded to the relentless fire of God's love. This is the mystical marriage, the fulfillment toward which all human beings are oriented; this is the life in union with God, the coming of the kingdom, of which the Gospel speaks.

The one at the summit, Burrows tells us, has so allowed Jesus to take the sheer vulnerability of her humanity into his kenosis that she now lives without an "I"; our self-expending God, not the ego, has become the living center of her being. Paradoxically, this does not imply the extinction of personhood but rather its full realization. Burrows teaches that it is only when we are completely dispossessed of self that we truly become ourselves; this is a reality that Jesus not only mediates but also models. The reverse side of this absolute loss of ego-centricity is that the one at the heights of the Christian life is deified; he or she has become God by participation. In Burrows's presentation of the mystical life, those who have consented to be transformed into Jesus' "yes" to Love become Love: all the acts of the intellect and will are taken up with the divine life.

Throughout her portrayal of the state of transforming union, Burrows maintains her familiar insistence that the union itself, wholly divine as it is, is necessarily imperceptible to human consciousness. Additionally, she holds that the lived experience of the mystical union, that is, what it is like on the conscious level, will inevitably be unique to each person given the full flowering of individuality that belongs to this stage; one may experience it as perfect rapture, another as sheer fragility. However, within this chapter we have seen Burrows identify three common elements across several individual accounts of the lived experience of the transforming union: certitude about one's spiritual state, profound contentment and security, and complete freedom in relating with created realities. Together, these elements offer us some impression of what life is like at the culmination of the Christian pilgrimage.

Finally, Burrows's exposition of the third stage of the spiritual life makes it eminently clear that perfect transformation into the crucified and risen Jesus has an inherently communal significance. One does not dwell on the mystical summit in glorious isolation, alone with the Alone; rather, being all God's, the one at the summit is intrinsically bound to all others. Burrows portrays those in the state of mystical union as bearers of a living knowledge of the divine life; through their consummate intimacy with him, they reveal in a singular way what the living God is like. Furthermore, according to Burrows, to live only with the life of the kenotic Christ is to participate in his mission of establishing the kingdom of God on earth. The mystic stands empty handed before the flood tide of divine love not in isolation but in solidarity with all humanity.

Notes

1. Ruth Burrows, *Guidelines for Mystical Prayer*, foreword by B. C. Butler (1976; repr., London: Continuum, 2007; Denville, N.J.: Dimension, 1980), 132.

2. Ruth Burrows, *Ascent to Love: The Spiritual Teaching of St. John of the Cross* (London: Darton, Longman and Todd; Denville, N.J.: Dimension, 1992, 1987), 1.

3. Ruth Burrows, interview by author, Quidenham, UK, October 2, 2009.

4. Ruth Burrows, *To Believe in Jesus* (1978; repr., London: Continuum, 2010; Mahwah, N.J.: HiddenSpring, 2010), 91.

5. Ibid.

6. Ibid.

7. Burrows, *Ascent to Love*, 114, 115.

8. Ibid., 116.
9. Burrows, *Guidelines for Mystical Prayer*, 118.
10. Ruth Burrows, *Interior Castle Explored: St. Teresa's Teaching on the Life of Deep Union with God* (1981; repr., London: Continuum, 2007; Mahwah, N.J.: HiddenSpring, 2007), 1.
11. Burrows, *Guidelines for Mystical Prayer*, 14.
12. Burrows, *Interior Castle Explored*, 109.
13. Burrows, *Guidelines for Mystical Prayer*, 117.
14. Ibid., 149.
15. Ibid., 118–19.
16. Ruth Burrows, "Amen: The Human Response to God," in *Essence of Prayer* (London: Burns and Oates, 2006; Mahwah, N.J.: HiddenSpring, 2006), 82.
17. Burrows, *Guidelines for Mystical Prayer*, 119. Obviously Burrows is using "self" here to refer not to the ego but to that true identity that emerges as egocentricity is unfurled into Jesus' surrender to the Father.
18. Burrows, *Interior Castle Explored*, 112.
19. Ibid.
20. Ibid., 115.
21. Ibid., 113.
22. Burrows, *Ascent to Love*, 116.
23. Ruth Burrows, *Our Father: Meditations on the Lord's Prayer* (London: Darton, Longman and Todd, 1986; Denville, N.J.: Dimension, 1986), 14.
24. Ibid., 22.
25. Burrows, *Guidelines for Mystical Prayer*, 118.
26. Burrows, *Ascent to Love*, 115.
27. Burrows, *Guidelines for Mystical Prayer*, 146.
28. Ibid., 146–47.
29. Ibid., 147.
30. Ibid.
31. Ibid.
32. Ibid.
33. Burrows, *To Believe in Jesus*, 106.

34. Ruth Burrows, *The Watchful Heart: Daily Readings with Ruth Burrows*, introduced and edited by Elizabeth Ruth Obbard (London: Darton, Longman and Todd, 1988), 59.

35. Burrows, *To Believe in Jesus*, 106.

36. Burrows, *Guidelines for Mystical Prayer*, 138.

37. Burrows, *To Believe in Jesus*, 110.

38. Burrows, *Guidelines for Mystical Prayer*, 132.

39. Ruth Burrows, *Through Him, With Him, In Him: Meditations on the Liturgical Seasons* (London: Sheed and Ward, 1987; Denville, N.J.: Dimension, 1987), 57.

40. Burrows, interview, October 2, 2009.

41. Burrows, *Ascent to Love*, 114.

42. Burrows, *Guidelines for Mystical Prayer*, 119.

43. Ibid.

44. Burrows, *Ascent to Love*, 114.

45. One does not have to listen too hard to hear a protest registered here: "Surely certitude is not a reliable indicator that one is at the mystical summit. Certitude of one's spiritual state need not correspond with reality." This objection is, of course, entirely valid. Such concerns, however, must be set aside in this context. Burrows does not propose to give us a set of criteria for discerning whether or not one is in the state of transforming union. Rather, she simply identifies several elements that are common to the lived experience of particular individuals who, in her estimation, are indisputably in the third stage of the spiritual life.

46. Burrows, *Guidelines for Mystical Prayer*, 119.

47. To be sure, as we noted in the previous chapter, Burrows is not consistent in her affirmation that John experiences the mystical life in the "light on" mode. However, her discussion of certitude is principally found in *Guidelines*, and in this work she treats John as a "light on" mystic. Thus we will follow that classification here.

48. Burrows, *Guidelines for Mystical Prayer*, 125.

49. Ibid.

50. See ibid., 49.

51. Ibid., 119.

52. Ibid., 47.

53. Ibid., 120. In *Interior Castle Explored*, Burrows expands upon Teresa's use of trinitarian imagery to express that which she has seen in secret and from which she has derived such certainty of her spiritual state: "Characteristically, Teresa expresses to herself and us what the seventh mansion is in terms of visions. . . . She is certain now that she is 'endowed with life by God'; that it is by his own life that she lives. . . . This is, she understands, the fulfilment of what Jesus promised, 'that he and the Father and the Holy Spirit will come to dwell with the soul which loves him and keeps his commandments.' Through her mysterious 'light on' faculty she sees the truth of this threefold relationship within herself. . . . Unconsciously her psyche produces a mental image in conformity with her ready-made concept of 'Trinity.'" Burrows, *Interior Castle Explored*, 110–11.

54. Burrows, *Guidelines for Mystical Prayer*, 120.

55. Ibid., 49.

56. Burrows, *To Believe in Jesus*, 102.

57. Burrows, *Guidelines for Mystical Prayer*, 125.

58. Ibid., 121.

59. Ibid., 125.

60. Ibid.

61. Ibid., 122.

62. Ibid., 124.

63. Ruth Burrows, *Living in Mystery*, introduction by Wendy Beckett (London: Sheed and Ward, 1996), 12.

64. Moreover, many years after publishing *Living in Mystery*, Burrows refers in an interview both to the sustained nothingness of her lived experience and to being possessed by certainty of her union with God. Ruth Burrows, interview by author, Quidenham, UK, February 19, 2016.

65. Burrows, *Guidelines for Mystical Prayer*, 122.

66. Ibid., 137.

67. Ibid., 123.

68. Ibid., 124.

69. Ruth Burrows, *Carmel: Interpreting a Great Tradition*, foreword by Peter Smith, preface by Roger Spencer (London: Sheed and Ward, 2000; Starrucca, Pa.: Dimension, 2000), 104–5.

70. Burrows, *Guidelines for Mystical Prayer*, 47. It must not go unmentioned that this passage reads remarkably like a self-description: surely Burrows is here presenting her own experience of living the mystical union from the emptiness of the human side. In her autobiography, Burrows relates, "I saw my own self reflected in [Thérèse], and her growth and insight became my insight." Ruth Burrows, *Before the Living God* (1975; repr., London: Burns and Oates, 2008; Mahwah, N.J.: HiddenSpring, 2008), 3. Here we see this affinity directly exemplified.

71. See Burrows, *Guidelines for Mystical Prayer*, 120.

72. Ruth Burrows, interview by author, Quidenham, UK, October 4, 2009.

73. Burrows, *Guidelines for Mystical Prayer*, 133.

74. Burrows, *Living in Mystery*, 111.

75. Burrows, *Guidelines for Mystical Prayer*, 129.

76. Ibid., 133.

77. Ibid.

78. Burrows, *Ascent to Love*, 5.

79. Burrows, *Interior Castle Explored*, 113.

80. Ibid., 114.

81. Ibid.

82. Ibid.

83. Ibid., 113.

84. Ibid., 113–14.

85. Ibid., 114.

86. Ibid., 113.

87. Burrows, *Guidelines for Mystical Prayer*, 137–38.

88. Burrows, *Before the Living God*, 110.

89. Burrows, *Guidelines for Mystical Prayer*, 139.

90. Ibid., 132–33.

91. Rowan Williams, *The Wound of Knowledge: Christian Spirituality from the New Testament to St. John of the Cross*, 2nd rev. ed. (London: Darton, Longman and Todd, 1990; Cambridge, Mass.: Cowley, 1991), 179.

92. Burrows, *To Believe in Jesus*, 73.

93. Burrows, *Ascent to Love*, 47.

94. Ibid. Burrows details that she is citing here *Ascent*, bk 3:25. She is, in fact, citing bk 3:26.

95. Ruth Burrows, "The Way to Perfection," in *Essence of Prayer*, 92, 93.

96. Ibid., 92.

97. Stephen Sundborg, "Sexual-Affective Integration in Celibacy: A Psycho-Spiritual Study of the Experience of Ruth Burrows in the Light of the Psychology of Rollo May" (STD diss., Pontifical Gregorian University, 1984), 950. In the preceding chapter we observed that Burrows refers in *Guidelines* to a series of painful events that helped mediate the final overthrow of her ego. She actually details four situations in which she was called to surrender the threads of security to which she was clinging and to stand before God in empty-handed trust. See Burrows, *Guidelines for Mystical Prayer*, 110–14. Sundborg highlights that "three of these four surrenders concerned the sexual-affective dimension of her life: total selflessness in regard to loving [her intimate friend] John, accepting the fact that as much as John loved her he could not understand her spiritual way, and facing the operation which seemed to strike at the roots of her womanhood. The fourth surrender had to do with relinquishing her position of authority as prioress." "Sexual-Affective Integration," 951n313.

98. Burrows, *Before the Living God*, 112.

99. Sundborg, "Sexual-Affective Integration," 953. Sundborg is citing here a letter from Burrows dated January 19, 1981.

100. Ibid., 956. The citations here are from Burrows, *Guidelines for Mystical Prayer*, 31.

101. Ibid., 955.

102. Ibid., 954.

103. Ibid., 950.

104. Ibid., 959–60. Again, Sundborg is citing the letter from Burrows dated January 19, 1981.

105. Burrows has more to say about celibate friendships of great intimacy in her unpublished article "A Surpassing Gift of Grace" (Quidenham, UK, 1972).

106. Sundborg, "Sexual-Affective Integration," 960.

107. Burrows, *Guidelines for Mystical Prayer*, 138.

108. Ibid., 110.

109. Ibid., 113.

110. Ibid., 145.

111. Burrows, *Ascent to Love*, 114.

112. Ibid., 3.

113. Ibid.

114. Burrows, interview, October 2, 2009.

115. Burrows, *Ascent to Love*, 114.

116. Ibid.

117. Ibid., 3. Burrows details that she is citing here *Living Flame*, st. 1, v. 6. She is fond of pointing out that Thérèse of Lisieux also recognized that this aspect of John's discussion of the perfect does not align with the Gospel. See, for example, Burrows, *Guidelines for Mystical Prayer*, 132, and Burrows, *Ascent to Love*, 5.

118. Burrows, *Ascent to Love*, 3. She is citing here *Canticle*, st. 21.

119. Ibid., 4.

120. Burrows, *Guidelines for Mystical Prayer*, 126–27.

121. Ibid., 128.

122. Wendy Beckett, *Sister Wendy on Prayer* (London: Continuum, 2006; New York: Harmony, 2006), 83–84. That Beckett is, in fact, referring to Burrows here is confirmed by a letter from her to the author, January 27, 2012.

123. Burrows, *Guidelines for Mystical Prayer*, 125.

124. Ibid., 129.

125. Ibid.

126. Ibid., 133.

127. Ibid., 123.

128. Ibid., 127.

129. Ibid., 49.

130. Burrows, *Ascent to Love*, 91–92.

131. Ibid., 116.

132. Burrows, *To Believe in Jesus*, 100.

133. Ibid.

134. Ibid.

135. Ibid.

136. Ibid., 100–101.

137. Burrows, *Interior Castle Explored*, 1.

138. While Burrows explicitly speaks of efficacy in bringing about the kingdom of God as belonging to those at the third stage, she does not thereby exclude others from participating in this work. In fact, within her writings she implies that one opens the world to God's love to the extent that they have been taken into the life of the Crucified. She remarks in one place, for example, "The more a person is possessed by God, living Jesus' life, the more she herself transmits life." Burrows, *Carmel*, 121.

139. Burrows, *Interior Castle Explored*, 117–18.

140. Ruth Burrows, "Rule of Carmel for Quidenham" (Quidenham, UK, 1993), 3.

141. Ruth Burrows, "Carmel: A Stark Encounter with the Human Condition," in *Essence of Prayer*, 183.

142. Ibid., 185–86.

143. Ibid., 193, 195.

144. See Burrows, *Interior Castle Explored*, 1–2, 116.

CONCLUSION

Ruth Burrows, as has been said of St. Thérèse of Lisieux, "witnesses to a kind of truth that is known only through complete immersion in particularity, yet which blossoms into a communion accessible to all without exception."[1] Burrows's spiritual doctrine—like that of Thérèse, and indeed Teresa of Ávila and John of the Cross—resounds with the unique and compelling authority of her lived experience yet is nothing other than the Gospel. Throughout this book, we have explored Burrows's living spiritual doctrine by examining her wholly Christocentric understanding of the mystical life. So, where have we journeyed throughout these chapters? And is there any way in which Ruth Burrows's Gospel mysticism could possibly be extended?

The unflinching commitment to the person of Jesus that informs Burrows's writings derives from her graced response to the "tortured sensitivity" of her temperament.[2] This was the main finding of chapter 1. By nature, Burrows is peculiarly exposed to the absolute contingency of the human condition: the sheer vulnerability of being human and the fundamental chasm between God and humanity are always unveiled to her. The grace of her conversion, which contained her call to

---

1. Mary Frohlich, "Thérèse of Lisieux: 'Doctor for the Third Millennium?'" *New Theology Review* 12, no. 2 (May 1999): 36.

2. Ruth Burrows, *Before the Living God* (1975; repr., London: Burns and Oates, 2008; Mahwah, N.J.: HiddenSpring, 2008), 5.

257

Carmel, directed Burrows's threatened, suffering self irrevocably toward intimacy with the divine.

In her early years as a Carmelite nun Burrows felt herself to be a living contradiction. Her conversion had set her on the pathway to union with God, yet she could find in Carmel no stepping-stone toward him. In fact, what she encountered—books lauding "spiritual" phenomena and methods of prayer that seemed to keep her somehow "outside" the living God—only increased Burrows's innate sense of estrangement from the One who was now the consuming desire of her life.

Gradually, Burrows came to perceive her vulnerable, needy humanity as the very ground for, rather than an obstacle to, that intimacy with God that defines her existence. She experienced herself as enabled to entrust her raw, yearning emptiness to God as pure capacity for Love. Initially, Burrows considered this surrender a provisional state to be adopted until God granted her a spiritual way that was more humanly satisfying. In time, however, and mainly due to the witness of Thérèse of Lisieux, she resolutely embraced the way of empty-handed trust as the only authentic spiritual path.

As she progressed in her life in Carmel, Burrows discovered that her graced surrender of her nothingness to God is essentially a participation in Jesus' perfect self-abandonment to the Father's love. In seeking to know the real human Jesus and how it is possible to be in union with him, Burrows grasped that Jesus, especially in his passion, knew all the utter destitution and bitter vulnerability of being human. She understood that he can live within her inasmuch as she consents to be fully human, to be an emptiness before the living God. Thus Burrows realized that through her commitment to trust in God from the heart of her poverty, she was already immersed in the life of the kenotic Christ, sharing his communion with the

Father. Accordingly, she grew to perceive her life as an embodiment of Jesus' proclamation that he alone mediates the relationship of love between God and humanity.

Burrows's literary output arises from the way in which she has come to understand her life. As she sees it, her way is, essentially, the only way: as contingent, fallen creatures, we can only come to God in the naked trust of the crucified Jesus. So her singularly fragile temperament, under the influence of grace generously responded to, has yielded universally relevant insights. Burrows's lived Christocentric spirituality of trust is precisely the message that she conveys not only in her autobiography but also throughout all her writings. Her various works, then—including her interpretations of the spiritual doctrines of Teresa and John—flow from, and are imbued with, her living knowledge of the divine life.

With chapter 2, we shifted from considering Burrows's life as such and began the task of making a systematic analysis of her thought by exploring her conception of the mystical life. Our particular task in this chapter was to lay the foundations of her mystical doctrine by setting forth her understanding of human nature and her understanding of the divine nature.

According to Burrows, to be human is to be fundamentally oriented toward union with God; the divine call to relationship is constitutive of human existence. For her, the inexorable helplessness that belongs to the human condition is the reverse side of this fact that we are essentially potential for the divine life. For the human spirit to be consistently thwarted by life's fragilities and limits is to be consistently reminded that we are capacity for God himself.

Given that Burrows conceives of the human person as intrinsically inclined toward the living God, it follows that, as she sees it, there is a basic dynamism to human nature. We become human inasmuch as we surrender to God's call to communion. By Burrows's account, the process of becoming human is essentially a matter of faith, or trust, triumphing over the ego. The ego is our innate drive to be in control of our own fulfillment, whereas faith is the movement into the infinite, the acceptance of the invitation to be fulfilled by God himself. Burrows regards the struggle for Godfulness to usurp selfishness as enacted within the fabric of daily life, taking in both our relationship with God and our relationships with others.

Burrows considers this everyday unfurling of egocentricity into surrender through which we become human to be effected by a collaboration between human effort and divine grace. She teaches that, aided by God's basic, sustaining presence, we must labor to the extent of our ability to reverse our primordial self-seeking. The actual overthrow of the ego, however, can only be achieved through the direct intervention of God. This intervention is precisely what Burrows names "mystical grace."

Burrows is adamant that her view of human nature is a mere concept apart from the life of Jesus crucified. Only in Jesus, she asserts, do we see the invitation to divine intimacy that constitutes humanity accepted unreservedly. Burrows perceives Jesus' perfect self-abandonment to the Father as reaching its culmination on the cross. So, in his utter receptivity to Love, the Crucified realizes definitively what it means to be human. To become human, then, is to progressively enter into the life of the kenotic Christ: the only One who is fully human must mediate the gradual realization of our own call to transcendence. Thus, for Burrows, our efforts at selflessness and God's mystical intervention have everything to do with the crucified Jesus.

In Burrows's view, Jesus crucified reveals not only the essence of humanity but also the essence of divinity. The starting point of Burrows's theology is that the inner life of God is utterly inaccessible to created humanity. Thus, our knowledge of God is dependent upon God's self-revelation. Burrows maintains that, while God made himself known in some measure to the people of Israel, the veil across the divine nature is drawn back in the person of Jesus. Her idea here is that it is in being fully human that Jesus shows us what it means for God to be God. In his utter openness to Love, the Crucified reveals that God *is* a relentless ecstasy of passionate love. Humanity is what it is—an emptiness for God to fill—precisely because of who God is—Love longing to inundate his creation.

In chapters 3, 4, and 5, we developed the ideas contained in chapter 2 by looking at Burrows's presentation of the spiritual life as a progressive immersion into Jesus' self-emptying "yes" to the God of love; such immersion into the kenotic Christ is the substance of God's mystical intervention. Burrows understands transformation into the Crucified to be a threefold process. Chapter 3 was concerned with the first stage of the spiritual life—the "pre-mystical" stage. At this phase of the Christian pilgrimage, according to Burrows, while we may have made some degree of commitment to follow Jesus, we do not yet actually participate in his life.

In Burrows's perspective, there is in beginners some shift away from absolute self-centeredness, some nascent actualization of that capacity for God that defines humanity. However, she sees those at the first stage as basically subject to the reign of the ego; what characterizes beginners is that they live wholly from the created self. Accordingly, in the beginning, God can only relate to us indirectly, through the finite capacity of our human faculties. Furthermore, Burrows understands beginners to be spiritually self-confident. Living from the ego, they experience themselves as completely in control of their spiritual progress; the demands of the Gospel appear eminently achievable. Burrows highlights the paradox in this disposition of spiritual self-satisfaction: it is only when the Crucified takes over from the ego that we can truly live the life of selfless receptivity to God's love that he proclaims.

The real significance of the first stage, Burrows holds, is that it is the preparatory ground for the dawning of God's mystical grace, the advent of our transformation into Jesus crucified. For this reason, she counsels beginners to imitate generously the self-surrender of Jesus; in so doing, we can anticipate, though not elicit, God's mystical action. Burrows presents such imitation as requiring mental labor, or meditation, and moral effort, or asceticism. Meditation involves coming to know the way of Jesus principally through praying with and studying the New Testament. For Burrows, meditation not only reveals Jesus' kenotic heart but also provides the motivation to imitate him: allured by the God of love Jesus makes known, we come to want relationship with him more than ego gratification. With her ascetical counsel, Burrows indicates how we can transform the ego's quest to orchestrate our fulfillment into the openness to Love we witness in Jesus. Her advice includes both the "unselfing" we initiate ourselves and that called forth in our interactions with others.

In chapter 4, we penetrated to the heart of Burrows's thinking as we reached the second stage of the spiritual journey, which encompasses the beginning and development of the mystical life. Here is the dawning realization of the transformation that was anticipated in the previous stage. Burrows understands God's mystical intervention to effect an entirely new mode of relationship between God and the human person. Now God in his goodness touches the person directly, releasing them from captivity to created realities and enabling them to receive his very life.

Since we can only know intimacy with the living God in Jesus crucified, it follows that, in Burrows's understanding, the in-breaking of God's mystical grace is nothing other than the life of the kenotic Christ replacing the self-sufficiency of the ego. The mystical life is Jesus effecting within us the communion with God he proclaims in the Gospel; it is Jesus being the way, the truth, and the life in us and for us. So, as Burrows sees it, it is entirely fallacious to conceive of mysticism as a privileged intimacy with God, reserved for a favored elite. "There can be no higher gift than what the New Testament tells us is the common destiny of man," she declares.[3]

Burrows is adamant that, as communion with the living God in Jesus crucified, there can be no direct conscious experience of the mystical life: finite humanity simply cannot lay hold of what is essentially divine. Thus, she claims that the normal, proper way of experiencing the mystical life is in obscurity, or what she calls the "light off" mode; for those in the mystical state, there is generally no direct awareness of the transformation that is being realized in their depths. In rare instances, however, the mystical life is experienced in the "light on" mode. "Light on" mystics, Burrows explains, are able to perceive God's living presence within them. Given that it is impossible for humanity in itself to grasp divinity as it is in itself, Burrows understands those in the "light on" state to be endowed with a supernatural mode of perception that somehow allows a nonconceptual awareness of God.

In Burrows's thought, the various phenomena commonly associated with the spiritual life are, at most, indirect conscious

---

3. Ruth Burrows, *Interior Castle Explored: St. Teresa's Teaching on the Life of Deep Union with God* (1981; repr., London: Continuum, 2007; Mahwah, N.J.: HiddenSpring, 2007), 41.

experiences of God's mystical activity. While maintaining that whatever we experience at the conscious level, however "spiritual" it may seem, cannot be the mystical grace, cannot be God in himself, Burrows accepts that such experiences may be an echo of that hidden divine presence. She suggests that whether or not one's secret transformation into the Crucified thus resounds into the psyche basically depends upon temperament. In any case, though, Burrows is clear that we can have no guarantee that what happens within the consciousness emanates from God's mystical presence; what is essentially material simply cannot be a reliable indicator of what is essentially spiritual. Burrows contends that all too frequently, spiritual writers have blurred the fundamental distinction between the mystical grace itself and what is felt; she points to the work of Teresa of Ávila and commentators on Teresa as exemplary in this regard.

Of prime importance to Burrows is the inevitable deflation of self-importance that imbues our lived experience as the life of the Crucified replaces the life of the ego. As Jesus draws us into his relationship with the Father, we experience the truth, terrifying to the ego yet ultimately glorious, that humanity has nothing to offer God but receptivity to Love. Burrows teaches that we become aware of our basic empty-handedness before the living God as we realize that our attempts to construct a holy, virtuous life are shot through with selfishness and as we find ourselves no longer able to achieve sensible satisfaction in prayer. Furthermore, she refers in this context to being infused with the divine enablement to sustain this collapse of the ego.

For Burrows, we cooperate with God's mystical activity by unflinchingly embracing the truth of our nakedness before him. "Jesus can unite himself to us only if we consent to become like him—without beauty, glory, grandeur," she writes.[4] Thus to remain before God as a living nothingness, teaches Burrows, is the work of the theological virtues and is basically a matter of trust. She speaks of incarnating this trust, this consent for Jesus to express his self-emptying "yes" to Love within us, in three principal ways. First, by using the mind to sustain receptivity to God's love in prayer. Second, by refusing to evade the bitter reality of our sinfulness, confident that, while we must exert ourselves in the pursuit of virtue, Jesus alone is the holy one. And third, by maintaining a generous vulnerability before the demands of life, accepting people and circumstances in all their otherness.

In the final chapter, we arrived at the third stage of the spiritual life. In Burrows's view, this state is at once the fulfillment of what it means to be a human being, a Christian, and a mystic. Here is complete transformation into Jesus crucified. The ones at the summit have responded to God's mystical grace with such generosity, have so consented to stand before the living God in empty-handed trust, that now Jesus has taken them entirely into his own life. As Burrows puts it, "Holiness means that a human being has so affirmed, stood by, embraced his essential meaning of being a capacity for God, an emptiness for him to fill, that God can indeed fill him with the fullness of himself."[5] Burrows understands the ones at the third stage to be fully possessed of their personal identity; it is capacity for the God of love that defines a person's unique existence, and now that capacity is utterly fulfilled.

---

4. Ruth Burrows, letter to Stephen Sundborg, July 18, 1979. Cited in Stephen Sundborg, "Sexual-Affective Integration in Celibacy: A Psycho-Spiritual Study of the Experience of Ruth Burrows in the Light of the Psychology of Rollo May" (STD diss., Pontifical Gregorian University, 1984), 534–35.

5. Ruth Burrows, *To Believe in Jesus* (1978; repr., London: Continuum, 2010; Mahwah, N.J.: HiddenSpring, 2010), 40.

There is no doubt for Burrows that the fullness of the mystical life, this complete immersion in the eternal communion of love between the Father and the Son, cannot be grasped by the created human consciousness. In addition, Burrows believes that, because this stage marks the full blossoming of individuality, the living reality of the mystical union is necessarily unique to each person. She illustrates this point by observing that John of the Cross seemed to experience perfect conformity to Jesus as unmitigated rapture, while her own experience is of unmitigated fragility. This insight notwithstanding, Burrows identifies three elements that are common to several individual accounts of the lived experience of the third stage of the spiritual life; together, these elements create some impression of what the culmination of the mystical journey is like at the conscious level. Burrows refers to an ineffable certitude that one is at the mystical summit, an experience of unassailable contentment and security, and utter freedom in relating with created realities, including one's own creaturehood.

In her portrayal of the final stage of the spiritual journey, Burrows is clear that the one at the heights of the Christian life is intrinsically bound to all people; to be absorbed into the life of God is to be unremittingly outwardly oriented. She specifies that those who have been taken wholly into the Crucified bear a living knowledge of the divine life; through their intimate union with him, they are able to reveal in a singular way what God himself is like. Additionally, Burrows conceives of those at the summit as utterly given to Jesus' mission of establishing the kingdom of God on earth. Alive with the life of the kenotic Christ, such a one is the very presence of the living fire of God's love in the midst of humanity.

GOSPEL MYSTICISM AT AN ECCLESIAL LEVEL?

Now that we have surveyed the course we have pursued, is it possible to identify potential future directions for Burrows's Gospel mysticism? Throughout this work, we have followed Burrows in considering the mystical life in terms of the individual. We have regarded gradual transformation into the Crucified, from its anticipation to its culmination, as a process that is undergone at a personal level. Is it possible, though, to apply Burrows's lived mystical doctrine to the church as an institution? To be sure, as Burrows herself acknowledges, "We cannot speak in a detached way of the Church. We ourselves are the Church and bear responsibility for her."[6] However, is there scope both to accept this truth and to speak of growth in the mystical life in a corporate sense?

What might it mean to think of the institutional church in the light of Burrows's presentation of the mystical life? Burrows offers us a line of approach here when she remarks, "Many people have come into the Catholic Church or have gladly stayed in her because she represented security in this insecure world, with her incontrovertible authority. Now that this authority is being questioned they are upset and resentful. They have to ask themselves if they are not more concerned with feeling safe than with loving God."[7] It is surely indisputable that the authority of the church—in the sense of both the truth claims it asserts and the legitimacy of it even making such claims—is often significantly challenged in the contemporary world. How does the church, as an institution, respond

---

6. Ruth Burrows, *Guidelines for Mystical Prayer*, foreword by B. C. Butler (1976; repr., London: Continuum, 2007; Denville, N.J.: Dimension, 1980), 72.

7. Burrows, *To Believe in Jesus*, 95–96.

to being thus reduced? We not infrequently witness the church retreating into a ghetto-like stance, protecting itself from the challenges without by asserting its divine otherness. Is this perhaps a recourse to control, such as is characteristic of the first stage of the spiritual life? Could it be that the church is being invited instead to embrace its experience of vulnerability and thus be transformed ever more completely into the crucified, risen Jesus? How could such an embrace be incarnated? These matters, I suggest, are ripe for further consideration.

A Final Word

Albert Herbert's stunning painting *Moses on the Mountain of God* represents the essence of this book.[8] In his work, Herbert depicts Moses as having ascended a mostly precipitous mountain in order to encounter the living God. Moses and his arduous, determined climb can be taken to represent both Burrows's own life and the spiritual pathway she sets forth throughout her writings.

It is humanly impossible for Moses to have made the ascent to union that we can see he has, in fact, made. Burrows knows from within the sheer, terrifying chasm between contingent humanity and the infinite God. Moses stands before his unseen God in empty-handed vulnerability. It is a courageous embrace of raw poverty that has enabled Burrows to scale the mountain of God. It is only by consenting with unremitting trust to be a dependent, fragile creature that she knows union with the living God, the God who is ever other to her, yet the sole meaning of her existence. Such ascent by way of

---

8. Albert Herbert, *Moses on the Mountain of God*, 1991, England and Co. Gallery, London.

descent is the way along which she leads others; it is the way so abhorrent to egocentricity but the only possible way if we are to become fully human.

And how is it that nothingness is the way to Everything? We see the answer in Moses's outstretched arms. To consent to live with naked trust is to live with the life of Jesus crucified. Ruth Burrows has allowed herself to be transformed into Jesus' ecstatic "yes" to the God of ecstatic love. She urges us to let Jesus effect the same transformation in us, so that Love may be all in all.

APPENDIX

Abba
by Ruth Burrows

It's a safe little space the paved garden
foursquare, encompassed
with ramparts of yew, ageold, resistant.

Upward I look
a scotch pine, way beyond, tosses its head
and laughs to the sky
a clump of primrose
smiles at my feet

    and I stand on the edge of the world.

O being, my being, His gift to me
are you mine, frail whisp of gossamer
precarious, suspended
hovering over the abyss?
I reach out my hand to clutch you
it closes on emptiness

    dizzy I stand on the edge of the world.

Being that is no being
in so far as you are mine
to have, to hold, to offer,

you are meaningless to me
unless to be for Him
only for Him
offering Him and Him and Him again,
ephemeral, mysterious nothing
in your fleeting in your floating
over the Abyss.

It is echoing and answering
the fathomless Abyss.
It is thundering and thundering
into all that is
the world in cracking, it is crumbling

   (though the pine is still laughing
   and primrose a smile)

There's a tumult of sound
that's a whispered caress
and I hear . . .

   I cannot tell you what I hear

save
      'thou
          beloved'

Whisp of nothingness He names you
being that is no being
standing on the edge of the world.

A secure space the paved garden
with its ramparts of yew.

BIBLIOGRAPHY

PRIMARY CARMELITE SOURCES

St. John of the Cross

The Collected Works of St. John of the Cross. Translated by Kieran Kavanaugh and Otilio Rodriguez. Revisions and introductions by Kieran Kavanaugh. Rev. ed. Washington, D.C.: ICS Publications, 1991.

St. Teresa of Ávila

The Collected Letters of St. Teresa of Ávila. Vol. 1: *1546–1577.* Translated, with an introduction, by Kieran Kavanaugh. Washington, D.C.: ICS Publications, 2001.

The Collected Letters of St. Teresa of Ávila. Vol. 2: *1578–1582.* Translated by Kieran Kavanaugh. Washington, D.C.: ICS Publications, 2007.

The Collected Works of St. Teresa of Ávila. Vol. 1. Translated by Kieran Kavanaugh and Otilio Rodriguez. 2nd rev. ed. Washington, D.C.: ICS Publications, 1987.

The Collected Works of St. Teresa of Ávila. Vol. 2. Translated by Kieran Kavanaugh and Otilio Rodriguez. Washington, D.C.: ICS Publications, 1980.

The Collected Works of St. Teresa of Ávila. Vol. 3. Translated by Kieran Kavanaugh and Otilio Rodriguez. Washington, D.C.: ICS Publications, 1985.

St. Thérèse of Lisieux

General Correspondence. Vol. 1: 1877–1890. Translated by John Clarke. Washington, D.C.: ICS Publications, 1982.

General Correspondence. Vol. 2: 1890–1897. Translated by John Clarke. Washington, D.C.: ICS Publications, 1988.

The Plays of St. Therese of Lisieux. Translated by Susan Conroy and David J. Dwyer. Washington, D.C.: ICS Publications, 2008.

The Poetry of St. Thérèse of Lisieux. Translated by Donald Kinney. Washington, D.C.: ICS Publications, 1996.

The Prayers of St. Thérèse of Lisieux. Translated by Aletheia Kane. Washington, D.C.: ICS Publications, 1997.

Story of a Soul: The Autobiography of St. Thérèse of Lisieux. Translated by John Clarke. 3rd ed. Washington, D.C.: ICS Publications, 1996.

St. Thérèse of Lisieux: Her Last Conversations. Translated by John Clarke. Washington, D.C.: ICS Publications, 1977.

WORKS BY RUTH BURROWS

Books

* [These titles are particularly recommended to readers who are new to the work of Ruth Burrows.]

Ascent to Love: The Spiritual Teaching of St. John of the Cross. London: Darton, Longman and Todd, 1987. Denville, N.J.: Dimension, 1992.

**Before the Living God.* 1975. Reprint, with introduction by Rowan Williams, London: Continuum, 2008. Mahwah, N.J.: Hidden-Spring, 2008.

Carmel: Interpreting a Great Tradition. Foreword by Peter Smith. Preface by Roger Spencer. London: Sheed and Ward, 2000. Starrucca, Pa.: Dimension, 2000.

Essence of Prayer. Foreword by Wendy Beckett. London: Burns and Oates, 2006. Mahwah, N.J.: HiddenSpring, 2006.

Guidelines for Mystical Prayer. Foreword by B. C. Butler. 1976. Reprint, London: Continuum, 2007. Denville, N.J.: Dimension, 1980.

Interior Castle Explored: St. Teresa's Teaching on the Life of Deep Union with God. 1981. Reprint, London: Continuum, 2007. Mahwah, N.J.: HiddenSpring, 2007.

Letters on Prayer: An Exchange on Prayer and Faith. With Mark Allen. London: Sheed and Ward, 1999.

Living in Mystery. Introduction by Wendy Beckett. London: Sheed and Ward, 1996.

Living Love: Meditations on the New Testament. London: Darton, Longman and Todd, 1985. Denville, N.J.: Dimension, 1985.

Love Unknown: Archbishop of Canterbury's Lent Book 2012. Foreword by Rowan Williams. London: Continuum, 2011.

Our Father: Meditations on the Lord's Prayer. London: Darton, Longman and Todd, 1986. Denville, N.J.: Dimension, 1986.

Through Him, With Him, In Him: Meditations on the Liturgical Seasons. London: Sheed and Ward, 1987. Denville, N.J.: Dimension, 1987.

To Believe in Jesus. 1978. Reprint, London: Continuum, 2010. Mahwah, N.J.: HiddenSpring, 2010.

The Watchful Heart: Daily Readings with Ruth Burrows. Introduced and edited by Elizabeth Ruth Obbard. London: Darton, Longman and Todd, 1988.

Articles and Other Short Writings

"Alone with Him Alone." *Mount Carmel* 47, no. 2 (Autumn 1999): 3–6.

"Amen: The Human Response to God." *Way* 43, no. 2 (April 2004): 78–90.

"Carmel: A Dream of the Spirit." *Mount Carmel* 34, no. 1 (Spring 1986): 47–50.

"Carmel: A Stark Encounter with the Human Condition." *The Way Supplement* 89 (Summer 1997): 97–105.

"Christian Prayer." *Mount Carmel* 38, no. 3 (Autumn 1990): 117–21.

"Come Lord Jesus." *Mount Carmel* 33, no. 3 (Autumn 1985): 166–70.

"The Crucifixion." *The Tablet*, March 12, 2005, 7.

"The Desert and the City." Review of *The Wilderness of God*, by Andrew Louth. *The Tablet*, September 28, 1991, 1180–81.

"Elizabeth of the Trinity." *Bible Alive* (August 1999): 9–16.

Foreword. In *Holy Daring: The Fearless Trust of Saint Thérèse of Lisieux*, by John Udris. Herefordshire, UK: Gracewing, 1997.

Foreword. In *Lamps of Fire: Daily Readings with St. John of the Cross*. Introduced and edited by Elizabeth Ruth Obbard. London: Darton, Longman and Todd, 1985.

Foreword. In *Living Water: Daily Readings with St. Teresa of Ávila*. Introduced and edited by Mary Eland. London: Darton, Longman and Todd, 1985.

Foreword. In *Search for Nothing*, by Richard P. Hardy. London: Darton, Longman and Todd, 1987.

"Fully Human, Fully Alive." *Bible Alive* (January 2011): 4–9.

"The Gift of Understanding." *Mount Carmel* 33, no. 2 (Summer 1985): 83–86.

"Growth in Prayer." *Way* 23, no. 4 (October 1983): 255–63.

"I Felt a Complete Failure, but I Hung On to God Even So." Interview by Bess Twiston Davies. *Times* (London), January 20, 2012, 88–89.

"If You Knew the Gift of God." *Priests and People* 11, no. 3 (March 1997): 87–90.

"Initial Prayer within the Carmelite Tradition." *Mount Carmel* 48, no. 3 (October–December 2000): 14–18.

Introduction. In *The Wisdom of St. Teresa of Ávila*. Oxford, UK: Lion Publishing, 1998.

"I Was Naked and You Gave Me Clothing." *The Tablet*, August 28, 2010, 10.

"Kindling the Fire of Prayer." Review of *Prayers for this Life*, edited by Christopher Howse. *The Tablet*, July 23, 2005, 22.

"Lose Yourself: Getting Past 'Me' to 'Thee.'" *America*, December 23, 2013, 19–20.

"Mary and the Apostles Pray for the Coming of the Holy Spirit." In *Journeying with Jesus: Personal Reflections on the Stations of the Cross and Resurrection*, edited by Lucy Russell, 109–12. Mowbray Lent Book 2013. London: Bloomsbury, 2012.

"Prayer in an Easter Community." *Priests and People* 17, no. 4 (April 2003): 138–42.

"Prayer in the Trinity." *Priests and People* 13, no. 4 (April 1999): 129–32.

"Prayer Is God's Work." Interview by Amy Frykholm. *Christian Century*, April 4, 2012, 10–11.

Review of *St. John of the Cross: Life and Thought of a Christian Mystic*, by Alain Cugno. *Mount Carmel* 31, no. 1 (Spring 1983): 51–55 (as "Sr. Rachel").

Reviews of *Listening to Silence: An Anthology of Carthusian Writings*, edited by Robin Bruce Lockhart, and *Interior Prayer: They Speak by Silences* and *Where Silence Is Praise*, by a Carthusian. *Priests and People* 13, no. 3 (March 1999): 123–24.

"Signed with the Cross." *The Tablet*, December 14, 1991, 1541–42.

"Smile though Your Heart Is Aching." *The Tablet*, April 19, 2014, 10–11.

"Some Reflections on Prayer." *Mount Carmel* 43, no. 1 (April–June 1995): 6–12.

"Soul on Fire." Review of *The Impact of God*, by Iain Matthew. *The Tablet*, September 23, 1995, 1208.

"St. Thérèse of Lisieux and the Holy Child." *Priests and People* 15, no. 2 (December 2001): 448–51.

"Surrender Gratefully to Love." *The Tablet*, June 10, 2006, 12–13.

"Sustained Passion." *Mount Carmel* 30, no. 3 (Autumn 1982): 135–48.

"The Way to Perfection." *The Tablet*, October 16, 1982, 1032–33.

"Where I Can Best Give Myself Wholly to God." Interview by Sam Hailes. Eden, May 16, 2012. Accessed August 16, 2016. *https://www.eden.co.uk*

Other Works

Arraj, James. *From St. John of the Cross to Us: The Story of a 400 Year Long Misunderstanding and What It Means for the Future of Christian Mysticism*. Chiloquin, Ore.; Inner Growth Books, 1999.

Aumann, Jordan. *Spiritual Theology*. 1980. Reprint, London: Continuum, 2006.

Beckett, Wendy. *Sister Wendy on Prayer*. London: Continuum, 2006. New York: Harmony, 2006.

Frohlich, Mary. "Thérèse of Lisieux: 'Doctor for the Third Millennium?'" *New Theology Review* 12, no. 2 (May 1999): 27–38.

Obbard, Elizabeth Ruth. Review of *Carmel: Interpreting a Great Tradition*, by Ruth Burrows. *Bulletin, Our Lady of the Assumption: British Province of Carmelites* 31, no. 8 (Winter 2001): 11.

Rahner, Karl. "The Concept of Mystery in Catholic Theology." In *Theological Investigations*, translated by Kevin Smyth. Vol. 4. London: Darton, Longman and Todd, 1974.

Sundborg, Stephen. "Sexual-Affective Integration in Celibacy: A Psycho-Spiritual Study of the Experience of Ruth Burrows in the Light of the Psychology of Rollo May." STD diss., Pontifical Gregorian University, 1984.

Williams, Rowan. *Teresa of Ávila*. London: Continuum, 2003.

———. *The Wound of Knowledge: Christian Spirituality from the New Testament to St. John of the Cross*. 2nd rev. ed. London: Darton, Longman and Todd, 1990. Cambridge, Mass.: Cowley, 1991.

ACKNOWLEDGMENTS

Cover art

Albert Herbert (1925–2008), The Mountain, 1991 (oil on canvas). Private Collection, England & Co. Gallery, London/ Bridgeman Images. Used with permission.

Cover art text by Wendy Beckett

Taken from *The Gaze of Love* by Sister Wendy Beckett. Copyright © 1993 by Sister Wendy Beckett. Use by permission of Zondervan. www.zondervan.com

Brief excerpts from pp. 13, 16 from *The Gaze of Love,* by Sister Wendy Beckett. Copyright © 1993 by Sister Wendy Beckett. Reprinted by permission of HarperCollins Publishers.

Before the Living God

© Ruth Burrows, 1975, 2008, *Before the Living God*, Burns & Oates. Used by © Ruth Burrows, 1996, *Living in Mystery*, Sheed & Ward. Used by permission of Bloomsbury Publishing Plc.

Excerpts from *Before the Living God* by Ruth Burrows, copyright © 1975, 2008 by Ruth Burrows. Hiddenspring, an imprint of Paulist Press, Inc., New York/Mahwah, N.J. Reprinted by permission of Paulist Press, Inc. *www.paulist press.com*

Carmel: Interpreting a Great Tradition

© Ruth Burrows, 2000, *Carmel: Interpreting a Great Tradition*, Sheed & Ward. Used by permission of Bloomsbury Publishing Plc.

Essence of Prayer

© Ruth Burrows, 2006, *Essence of Prayer*, Burns & Oates. Used by permission of Bloomsbury Publishing Plc.

Excerpts from *Essence of Prayer* by Ruth Burrows, copyright © 2006 by Ruth Burrows. Hiddenspring, an imprint of Paulist Press, Inc., New York/Mahwah, N.J. Reprinted by permission of Paulist Press, Inc.

Guidelines for Mystical Prayer

© Ruth Burrows, 1976, 2007, *Guidelines for Mystical Prayer*, Sheed & Ward. Used by permission of Bloomsbury Publishing Plc.

Interior Castle Explored: St. Teresa's Teaching on the Life of Deep Union with God

© Ruth Burrows, 1981, 2007, *Interior Castle Explored: St. Teresa's Teaching on the Life of Deep Union with God*, Sheed & Ward. Used by permission of Bloomsbury Publishing Plc.

Letters on Prayer: An Exchange on Prayer and Faith

© Mark Allen and Ruth Burrows, 1999, *Letters on Prayer: An Exchange on Prayer and Faith*, Sheed &Ward. Used by permission of Bloomsbury Publishing Plc.

Living in Mystery

© Ruth Burrows, 1996, *Living in Mystery*, Sheed &Ward. Used by permission of Bloomsbury Publishing Plc.

Love Unknown

© Ruth Burrows, 2011, *Love Unknown*, Continuum. Used by permission of Bloomsbury Publishing Plc.

Through Him, With Him, In Him: Meditations on the Liturgical Seasons

© Ruth Burrows, 1987, *Through Him, With Him, In Him: Meditations on the Liturgical Seasons*, Sheed & Ward. Used by permission of Bloomsbury Publishing Plc.

To Believe in Jesus

© Ruth Burrows, 1978, 2010, *To Believe in Jesus*, Sheed & Ward. Used by permission of Bloomsbury Publishing Plc.

ABOUT THIS BOOK

The Gospel Mysticism of Ruth Burrows
Going To God with Empty Hands

An English nun and spiritual writer and an Australian laywoman forge a deep friendship while exploring the mystery and richness of the journey to God.

Ruth Burrows (Sister Rachel Gregory, O.C.D.) and author Michelle Jones in a 2016 photo taken in the chapel of Quidenham Carmel.

This book is the fruit of Australian theologian and author Michelle Jones's long-time interest in the spirituality of Ruth Burrows—the pen name for the British Discalced Carmelite, Sister Rachel Gregory, of the Carmelite Monastery in Quidenham in Norfolk, England—and of the personal friendship between the two women that has grown over the years.

Written with Burrows's full permission, the book is more than a long-distance academic pursuit. It is the result of hours of personal interviews between Jones and Burrows conducted at the Carmel of Quidenham, as well as the author's access to many of Burrows's previously unpublished manuscripts, notes, and personal correspondence.

After reviewing Jones's final manuscript, Burrows gave it her seal of approval: "I have no doubt whatsoever," she wrote, "that you have faithfully and discerningly represented my spiritual insights." This is the pivotal work you now have in your hand.

SISTER RACHEL GREGORY—RUTH BURROWS—has been a Discalced Carmelite nun for over seventy-five years. In 1975, at the prompting of a friend and mentor, she published her autobiography and first book, *Before the Living God.* Twelve additional books and numerous articles followed. As Ruth Burrows's writings grew in popularity over the years, she became a respected spiritual author throughout the English-speaking world; many of her books have never been out of print, or have been re-released as new editions.

While written within her Roman Catholic and Carmelite tradition, Burrows's works span Christianity's ecumenical richness, counting readers in many faith communities and beyond. Because of the deep insights revealed in her spiritual message, Burrows was personally commissioned by then-Archbishop Rowan Williams to write the annual Archbishop of Canterbury's Lent Book for 2012. The result was the popular *Love Unknown.* With its publication, Ruth Burrows became only the third Roman Catholic in modern history to have been officially invited to write for the members of the Anglican Communion.

Within her enclosed Carmelite community, Sister Rachel is not so much an acclaimed author as a beloved and "very ordinary" sister. She still writes, and is a voracious reader. And most of the time she can be found quietly behind the scenes, helping with the dishes and laundry or working in the flower garden while living out her vocation to contemplative prayer and silence.

MICHELLE JONES is a consecrated woman affiliated with the Carmelite Monastery of Quidenham (UK). She lives a contemplative life in the foothills of the Porongurup Range, an ancient mountain range in the Great Southern region of Western Australia. Michelle shares her life of prayer with several hundred kangaroos and kookaburras, and the odd bandicoot and echidna. She is in denial about the snakes and spiders who also call the area home.

From her home in Porongurup, Michelle works as a lecturer in Theology for BBI (Broken Bay Institute) - The Australian Institute of Theological Education, and for the Carmelite Institute of Britain and Ireland. She is passionate about discovering the living flame of love within the theological tradition and helping others to encounter that love. Michelle's areas of interest include Spirituality, Christology, and Trinitarian Theology. She has a Doctorate in Theology and a Licentiate in Theology from the Pontifical University of St. Thomas Aquinas (the Angelicum) in Rome, and a Master of Theology from the University of Notre Dame, Australia.

Michelle enjoys rambling in the beautiful bushlands that surround her and sampling the wines the region has to offer (though generally not at the same time). She also plays the oboe, and is a member of the Albany City Wind Ensemble.

Patricia Lynn Morrison
Editorial Director
ICS Publications

INDEX

Note: Page numbers followed by the letter "n" and a number indicate notes.

About Us

ICS Publications, based in Washington, D.C., is the publishing house of the Institute of Carmelite Studies (ICS) and a ministry of the Discalced Carmelite Friars of the Washington Province (U.S.A.). The Institute of Carmelite Studies promotes research and publication in the field of Carmelite spirituality, especially about Carmelite saints and related topics. Its members are friars of the Washington Province.

The Discalced Carmelites are a worldwide Roman Catholic religious order comprised of friars, nuns, and laity—men and women who are heirs to the teaching and way of life of Teresa of Avila and John of the Cross, dedicated to contemplation and to ministry in the church and the world.

Information about their way of life is available through local diocesan vocation offices, or from the Discalced Carmelite Friars vocation directors at the following addresses:

Washington Province:
1525 Carmel Road, Hubertus, WI 53033

California-Arizona Province:
P.O. Box 3420, San Jose, CA 95156

Oklahoma Province:
5151 Marylake Drive, Little Rock, AR 72206

Visit our websites at:

www.icspublications.org and *http://ocdfriarsvocation.org*